Wine
A Tasting
Course

Wine
A Tasting Course

MARNIE OLD

DK

BUILDING WINE SKILLS

NAVIGATING WINE BY STYLE

CONTENTS

MASTERING WINE VARIABLES

DISCOVERING WINE GRAPES AND REGIONS

CONTENTS

Foreword

I WISH THAT THIS BOOK HAD EXISTED when I first became interested in wine and wanted to know more, because it's a brilliant introduction to the world of wine. It would have been so useful! There are already dozens of "learn about wine" books on the market, but *Wine: A Tasting Course* is different. It's fresh and unique in its approach, and it's probably the first such book that has really engaged me.

Wine is a complicated topic, and to many people, this is part of its appeal. Each wine region has its own personality, each of the 1,400 grape varieties grown commercially has different characteristics, and grape growers and winemakers impart their own imprints on the bottles they produce. This keeps wine professionals like me in a state of constant learning and means that it's almost impossible to grow bored with wine as long as you maintain a curious and open mind. But the complexity that gives wine its great intellectual appeal also makes it a daunting topic for those starting out on their journey. This is why Marnie Old's book is so welcome, because it manages the difficult task of making this fascinating topic accessible without dumbing it down or stripping away its interest.

Above all, I love the way that this book is so visual. The infographic approach is beautifully delivered and presents information in a hugely palatable way – one that I don't think I have ever seen before in a book format. It really sets this book apart. One of Marnie's strengths is that she is able to keep the educational content firmly grounded in the practical reality of what the wine actually tastes like, and each topic is explained really clearly. It isn't learning for learning's sake; it's focused on empowering the reader to select, buy, store, serve, and enjoy wine in a very practical way. All through the text there are also pointers about which wines to try in order to understand what's being talked about.

This focus on tasting wine is so important, because we lack a good vocabulary for tastes and smells. It is incredibly hard to communicate the experience of flavour through the written word. This is why Marnie's visual presentation of the flavours of different wines, in a sort of "flavour space", is so revolutionary. And Marnie really does know her stuff. I came to wine from a rather technical background, as a scientist, so I've taken a great interest in wine science. Where Marnie touches on some of the tricky and controversial areas of wine science – and there are more than a few – she gets it spot on. As a sommelier and wine educator, Marnie understands how complicated it can be to learn about her subject, and this real-world experience has resulted in what I reckon is a much-needed and immensely useful introduction to wine.

Jamie Goode

Dr Jamie Goode

Introduction

If you enjoy wine but find it confusing, this is the book for you.

You don't need to memorize reams of data to feel confident shopping for wine or deciding what to drink in restaurants. All you need to learn are a few powerful ideas, a handful of concepts that help explain wine's dramatic variations of style. Once you know *why* wines taste the way they do and *how* to zero in on the styles that suit your tastes, you'll feel more in control when buying.

Wine can seem terribly complex and impenetrable to beginners, but it becomes much less frustrating when we step back and look at the big picture. Most wine books miss the forest for the trees, providing oodles of wine details but little in the way of practical wine skills. *Wine: A Tasting Course* is different. This visual guide explains how wine works, sharing useful concepts that can help anyone navigate the wine world without feeling insecure or ill informed.

Instead of zooming in on a thicket of wine labels, *Wine: A Tasting Course* combines colourful images and infographics to quickly convey the kind of practical generalizations wine professionals use to make educated guesses about how any given wine will taste. Instead of presenting wine as a wholly foreign topic, *Wine: A Tasting Course* uses what you already know to help you solve the wine puzzle. If you can picture how peaches change in flavour as they ripen, then you can easily grasp why wines from cooler regions taste mild and acidic and those from warmer places taste bolder and more dessert-like.

This is not to say that the traditional wine book is obsolete. No agricultural product is as diverse and rarified as wine, and no commercial product can rival its arcane system of nomenclature. There will always be a need to "look things up", as well as for thick reference tomes. But *Wine: A Tasting Course* takes a refreshingly different path. Instead of focusing on what sets each individual wine apart – grapes and regions, vintages and vintners – it explains what all wines have in common and suggests sensible ways to sort them into groups based on how they taste, not where they were made.

Wine has an unfortunate reputation for snobbery and pretentiousness, but the top wine professionals are almost never snobs. We love "serious" wines, of course, but recognize the need for "un-serious" wines, too. The true wine experts are those who have moved past wine knowledge towards wine enlightenment. With the confidence to make educated guesses based on a few central truths, wine insiders can relax and savour what's in the glass regardless of its origins. This book aims to provide a similar degree of comfort and ease with wine for all drinkers, to share expert-level ideas that can take the stiffness out of wine and put the fun back in. By teaching you how to trust your own senses, *Wine: A Tasting Course* will set you on your own path to *v*inlightenment and *v*independence.

Bottoms up!

USING THIS BOOK

Wine: A Tasting Course is a different kind of wine book, sharing professional-level insights in refreshingly direct terms. It assumes no prior wine knowledge, favours everyday language over wine-trade jargon, and provides guided comparative tastings to reinforce key concepts. What you'll find here are simplified versions of the useful generalizations and practical skills used by sommeliers and winemakers the world over. Since this book's goal is to smooth the path to wine comprehension and to provide the reader with information of real-world relevance, some of wine's complexities must be downplayed to serve the larger objective. This is done not to mislead but because, in every subject, we must learn to walk before we can run.

Within this book, consider the chapters as individual lessons – and if possible, taste along with the pages labelled "The Tasting". Take your time, and have fun with those sections.

- The Tastings are self-guided samplings of two to four wines, designed to be executed at home. If you're pulling more than one cork, why not make it a social gathering? Consider starting your own wine-tasting group with four to ten wine-loving friends. If this isn't practical and you need to taste with only one or two people, don't fret about waste; for a helpful tip on preserving opened wines to drink later, see Freezing Wine, p.62.
- For maximum global relevance, the wine recommendations given are broad and rely on widely distributed styles, but some may be hard to locate in your area. Luckily, many wines share similar characteristics. Explain the situation to your wine retailer and ask them to recommend a reasonable substitute.
- If home tasting isn't feasible, consider your local wine bar. Many of these tastings might be feasible with wines served by the glass.
- Of the wines available in the categories specified here, 80 per cent or more should fit their sensory descriptions well enough to get across the point of each lesson. However, not all wines taste exactly alike. There are always a few that defy even the sommelier's expectations, and that's okay. Simply treat any exceptions you encounter as delicious digressions, and try again.

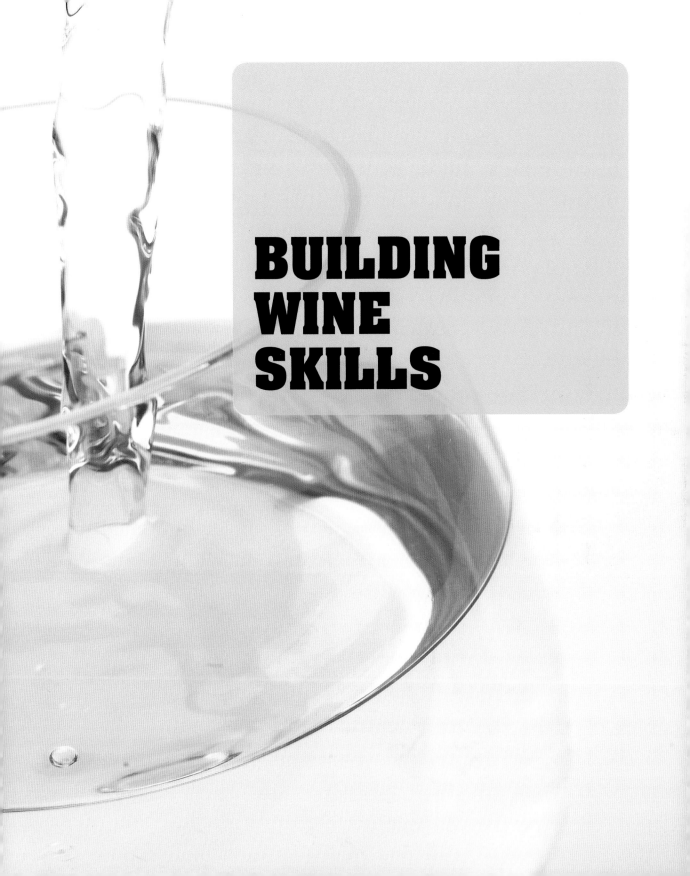

BUILDING
WINE
SKILLS

Do you count yourself among the wine-curious but find you are stumped in the wine aisle? If just trying to explain what you want to drink leaves you tongue-tied, memorizing grape names and wine regions won't do much good. It's a little bit like learning to drive: the first step is learning practical skills such as the rules of the road and how to steer, not theoretical knowledge like how to build a car or how the internal combustion engine works.

What wine lovers need above all is to get comfortable with real-world wine activities. Discovering what the wine world has to offer should be delicious fun, but it's hard to enjoy yourself when you're feeling stressed or apprehensive. A few lessons can make all the difference, starting with the most relevant topics: how to taste wine and describe it, how to shop for wine, and how to get the most enjoyment from each bottle. Once you feel more in control on everyday wine tasks, you will be inspired to take the driver's seat and explore the wonderland of wine on your own terms.

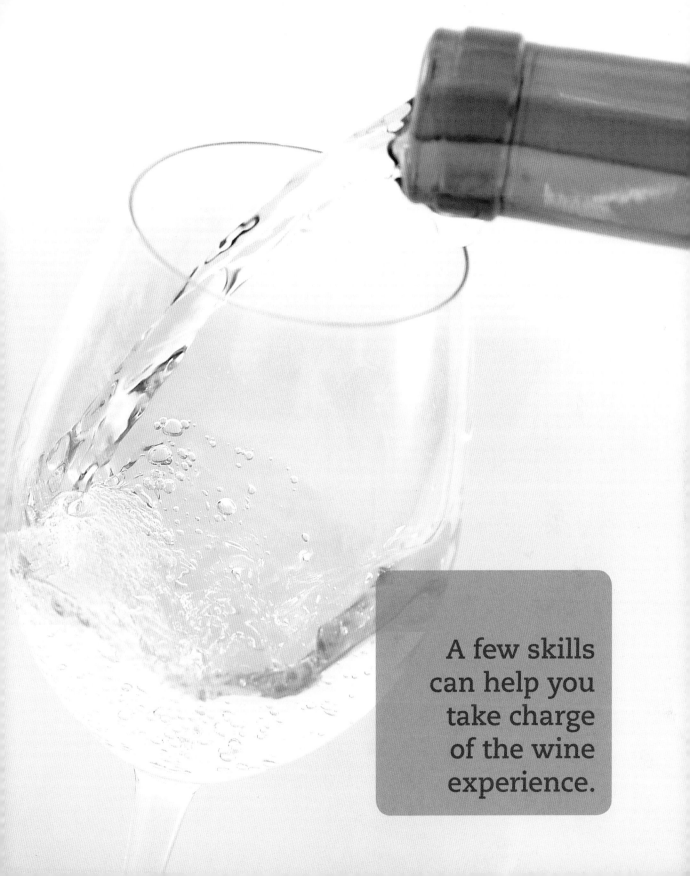

A few skills
can help you
take charge
of the wine
experience.

TALKING AND TASTING

The Insider's Sensory Tour

Wine is an amazing drink – but it is a drink that leaves many at a loss for words. Taking control of our wine experiences becomes much easier when we know what to look for as we taste and how to communicate about wine's variations in style. There is no need to adopt pretentious descriptive prose or to get lost in subjective perceptions. Wine's most fundamental qualities can be identified by taking one sense at a time. A simple sensory checklist enables us to evaluate new wines and to describe accurately what we like and don't like.

Wine Lingo and Geek-Speak

Enjoying wine is easy, but communicating about it is difficult. What people really want to know is what wines taste like and how they differ from one another. Unfortunately, our day-to-day vocabulary is weak in the realm of smells and tastes – the areas in which wine excels.

Rustic · Brambly · Barnyard · Leathery · Tight · Tar · Austere · Closed · Approachable · Flinty · Buttery · Grassy · Chewy · Short · Volatile · Cat Pee · Robust · Foxy · Stony · Flabby · Unctuous · Smooth · Meaty · Turgid · Vanilla · Vegetal · Chalky · Jammy · Tired · Hollow · Racy

Get with the jargon

Wine labels and restaurant wine lists rarely address the taste of wine, more often conveying ingredients and wine regions. The first step in making sense of wine is to learn how to talk about the experience of wine tasting and how to interpret what others say. For beginners, a handful of terms that describe wine's characteristics is all that's needed. The key is to approach the challenge in an organized way, with a sensory checklist of qualities that are reasonably objective.

The imaginative language used in wine reviews can be disorienting and sometimes even unappetizing.

Deal in descriptors

When we think of wine language, we tend to picture wine-label terms: grape names such as Chardonnay, or wine appellations like Bordeaux. But the most useful wine terms for the novice are descriptors. These words can help us describe the wine qualities we enjoy most and avoid those we don't. There are two main types of wine descriptor: indirect and direct. Neither is wrong. They are simply different ways of talking about wine.

Indirect

Subjective
Emotional
Imaginative
Metaphorical
Evocative
Effective

"This friendly, inky Syrah tastes of stewed boysenberries, with hints of pencil lead and forest floor."

Direct

Objective
Comparative
Qualified
Specific
Educational
Factual

"This Sauternes is full-bodied and sweet, with strong oak flavours and plenty of balancing acidity."

Indirect wine terms

Experts often paint a poetic "word picture" of a wine's flavour to convey complex ideas quickly to their audience. These terms:

- describe wine metaphorically by comparing it to other experiences;
- describe subjective features that may be perceived differently by each individual;
- are limitless in number and can include words that convey emotion and bias;
- often attempt, through evocative language, to capture elusive olfactory scents and flavours;
- are highly effective for motivating sales, as used in marketing and media;
- aid one-way communication from a wine professional.

Direct wine terms

To evaluate wines dispassionately, professionals use specific terminology for the most important of wine's sensory characteristics. These terms:

- describe wine's primary traits – like colour, sweetness, and strength – typically on a power scale;
- refer to reasonably objective features that most people perceive in the same way;
- are limited in number, tending to be concrete terms that convey less personal bias;
- pinpoint actual sensory qualities, such as how wine looks, tastes, smells, and feels;
- are highly effective for comparative analysis, as used in winemaking and education;
- help facilitate meaningful two-way communication.

Taste Wines Like a Pro

Our perception of wine is easily influenced by the environment in which we taste, so professionals try to be as objective as possible. A consistent tasting routine helps establish a baseline for comparison. The goal is to isolate and amplify the impact of wine's sensory characteristics – colours, scents, flavours – to distinguish one wine from another. This is best done by pouring yourself a glass of wine and following the steps below.

1	2	3
		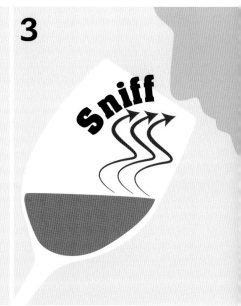

Look at the wine

Is the wine white, rosé (pink), or red? If the tasting environment is well lit, tilt the glass over a white surface, such as a sheet of paper, and look through the wine for useful style clues. How deep is the colour? Is it showing signs of browning with age?

See pp.22–5 for more on what to look for.

Swirl the wine in the glass

You swirl wine to smell it better – almost like turning up the volume on the stereo system. A wine's smells grow more intense when its aroma compounds are concentrated in the bowl of a wine glass. Swirling increases the wine's surface area, which in turn boosts its rate of evaporation and aromatic intensity.

Sniff the wine deeply

Smell is the main sense used in wine tasting, so sniffing wine before tasting is an essential step. Dip your nose into the wine glass, and take two or three deep sniffs. Think about what you are smelling. How intense is the aroma? Does it remind you of anything? Fruits or vegetables? Herbs or spices? Do you smell toasty oak barrels?

See pp.26–7 for more on what to look for.

TO SPIT, OR NOT TO SPIT? THAT IS THE QUESTION

Wine professionals often spit wine at large tastings, something that seems unnatural to most people, since spitting is rude in any other context. However, for those who must taste wine critically as part of their work, spitting is essential, since it minimizes alcohol absorption and prevents intoxication. At large wine-tasting events, in winery tasting rooms, and in wine classes, spittoons are always readily available.

Modern wine-tasting spittoon

4 Sip

5 Swish

6 Savour

Sip the wine

Take a slightly larger sip than usual. Instead of swallowing immediately, hold the wine in your mouth for 3–5 seconds, letting it coat every surface: tongue, cheeks, palate.

Swish it around

By swishing wine around as if it were mouthwash, you dramatically intensify the sensory perceptions of taste, smell, and "mouthfeel". Increasing surface contact makes tastes and tactile sensations more vivid. It also warms the wine; body heat increases wine's evaporation rate, concentrating its aromas for the olfactory nerves.

Savour the wine

Wine's flavour does not disappear when you swallow. Its aftertaste lingers for a minute or more, allowing you to assess its sensory qualities and make more personal judgments. Tick through the wine-tasting checklist to identify its style parameters. Decide whether you like the wine. Would you prefer it alone or with food? Would you buy it again?

See p.22 for the wine-tasting checklist.

Wine-Tasting Checklist

Think of each new wine you taste as an entry in a mental database. Deciding how it compares to others you've tried determines where it gets classified. The final step of tasting is to savour, assessing the main qualities that are reasonably objective as we commit the wine to memory. We'll use a checklist of sensory characteristics so we don't miss anything important.

Use your senses – well, most of them!

Four of our senses help us evaluate different wine attributes; the one sense that doesn't have any part to play in wine tasting is hearing. In the chart below, track any attribute across to the low, medium, or high column to find useful terms for describing how it manifests itself in a wine's style.

Put it in the vault
Describing a wine in words, even just to yourself, is the key to remembering its characteristics so you can compare them to those of wines you'll taste in the future.

SENSE	ATTRIBUTE	LOW	MEDIUM	HIGH
See	COLOUR	White	Pink	Red
	COLOUR DEPTH	Pale	Moderate	Dark
Taste	SWEETNESS	Dry	Lightly sweet	Fully sweet
	ACIDITY	Mildly acidic	Tangy	Tart
Smell	FRUIT INTENSITY	Mild	Flavourful	Bold
	OAK PRESENCE	No oak	Mild oak	Strong oak
Feel (mouthfeel)	BODY	Light	Mid-weight	Heavy
	TANNIN (red only)	Silky	Velvety	Rough
	CARBONATION	Still	Spritzy	Sparkling

How Wine Looks

The most obvious differences between wines are the ones we can see. People are so naturally focused on visual perception that wines on wine lists and in retail stores are usually classified by colour.

Figure out the colours

Wine colours range from nearly clear to inky purple-black, but the first step is to decide into which broad category they fit: white, pink, or red. A few rare wines are made in a specialized way that obscures their original colour; these are mostly russet-coloured sweet wines that are made from dried grapes. However, 99.9 per cent of the time, it will be quite obvious which wines are white, which are red, and which fall somewhere in between.

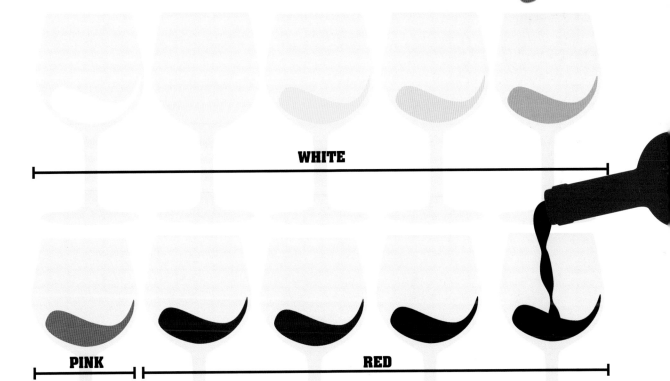

WHITE

PINK

RED

Rare rosés
Only a tiny percentage of wines fall into the pink middle ground of colour. These are called rosé wines, using the French word for "pinked".

Assessing wine by colour depth

The intensity of colour within each of the white, red, and rosé categories can give the drinker a hint about how a wine will taste. As a general rule, colour saturation tends to match flavour intensity, and it can also provide clues on other qualities. White wines with a golden hue, for example, are more likely to be oaky than those that are almost water white; and pale, translucent red wines are often lighter-bodied and less astringent than darker reds.

Light or faded?
Red wines grow paler over time. Their colours shift from pinky purple in youth, to a browner rusty orange in advanced age.

Showing some skin
Red wines are darker when they have had more grape-skin contact and been made from grapes with thicker skins and smaller berries. Grape skins supply not only colour but also flavour, so reds and rosés tend to taste bolder than whites.

Paler red

Heavy & bold

Mid-weight

Summery rosé

Oaky red

Oaky white

Mature white

Whiter shade of pale
Only the youngest white wines look nearly colourless, while those aged in barrels or bottles acquire pale yellow tones.

The golden rule
Deep colour in white wines is associated with older wines, oakier wines, and rich, sweet dessert wines.

Young white

Whites: What affects their colour?

The main colour source in white wines is oxidation: exposure to air deepens whites from faintest yellow to gold. The most common source of oxidation is barrel aging, so oaky Chardonnay tends to be darker and more golden than crisp, stainless-steel-fermented Sauvignon Blanc. Uncommonly intensely flavoured white wines will also display more colour saturation, as is the case with sweet dessert wines.

Darkened by barrels, age, or density

Reds: What affects their colour?

Just like whites, red wines look darker when they are more concentrated. However, while white wines darken with age, reds do the reverse, growing paler as their colour compounds succumb to gravity, settling as sediment. Colour behaves quite differently in red wine because of its source: dark grape skins.

The type of grape, degree of ripeness, and techniques used to extract colour from the skins all affect a red wine's colour depth. Thin-skinned grapes like Pinot Noir make paler wines than those from thicker-skinned varieties like Syrah; and fruit from sunny regions provides deeper colour than cooler-climate fruit.

Vintners extract more colour from the grape skins for premium age-worthy reds, while the hue of rosés is determined by limiting contact with the grape skins.

Darkened by grape-skin compounds

Lightened and browned by age

Are We Tasting or Smelling?

In everyday speech, we use the word "taste" for all sensations happening in the mouth. In the wine world, too, "taste" is mostly used in this generalized context. However, when we analyse wine, we make distinctions between wine characteristics based on which sense perceives them.

Know what taste is

By separating the three sensory threads – smell, taste, mouthfeel – that occur almost simultaneously when we take a sip, we can distinguish true tastes from the smells that constitute "flavour" and from the tactile sensations known as mouthfeel. For example, we might say that crème brûlée tastes sweet and creamy, or like vanilla and caramel. But in sensory science, only sweetness would be considered a true taste because it alone is detected by the tongue's taste buds. Vanilla and caramel "flavours" are really olfactory sensations, or smells, while creaminess is a tactile sensation, part of the dessert's mouthfeel.

TAKE A BIG SNIFF
Wine experts spend as much time sniffing wine as drinking it. This is because the aromas captured this way are far more distinct than their "flavour" counterparts in the mouth.

External smells register as **odours**

Smells
Olfactory nerves detect odours and flavours, such as wine's fruit and oak components.

Internal smells register as **flavours**

Mouthfeel
The flesh of the tongue, palate, cheeks, and gums detects tactile sensations, such as texture, carbonation, and tannic astringency.

Tastes
Taste buds on the tongue detect taste sensations, such as sweetness and acidity.

Perception of wine
As you drink wine, you take in its smells via the nose, tastes on your tongue, and feel on the fleshy parts of your mouth.

Understand aromas

Of all our senses, smell is the most important when it comes to wine tasting. Even if we don't sniff our wine, we still get an intense blast of aromas when we take a sip. We're used to thinking of this as flavour, as part of how wine tastes, but most of what we perceive as flavour is really olfactory stimulus – or smells.

Technically, there is no real difference between odours and flavours, except the direction from which they arrive. Olfactory nerves in the upper nasal cavity recognize smells as odours when sniffed through the nose from an external source. However, when those same smells reach the nose from the internal passage that connects the nose and mouth, they register as flavours, as part of how food or drink tastes.

Wine descriptors start to make a lot more sense once we grasp the fundamental difference between the taste sensations that are conveyed by the taste buds and the smell sensations delivered by the olfactory nerves. We taste a few rudimentary wine qualities – such as sweetness and acidity – on contact with our tongue. But we perceive a great many more complex wine characteristics as both scents and flavours when the volatile aroma compounds in wine reach our olfactory nerves.

The nose test

For a vivid illustration of the difference between taste and smell, try this little experiment.

- Plug your nose tightly, and take a sip of orange juice. Keep your nose blocked all the while, and don't let go for at least 5 seconds after you swallow.

- Notice how, when the nasal passage is blocked, you can discern only what your tongue can taste on its own – in this case, sweetness and acidity.

- Now unplug your nose. As soon as air can flow freely from your palate to your olfactory nerves, you will get a rush of citrusy orange "flavour".

There are at least 10,000 things we can smell…

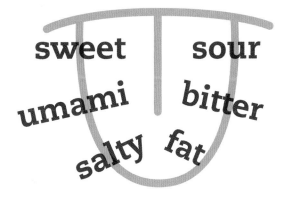

… but there are only six things we can truly taste.

sweet sour

umami bitter

salty fat

How Wine Tastes

Now that we know there are only six detectable taste sensations, we need to establish what impact that has on wine tasting. The most surprising thing is probably that only two "true" tastes are found in wine.

Know the sensations

Four of the six known taste sensations have been recognized for centuries: sweetness, sourness (or acidity), saltiness, and bitterness. The other two are far less apparent and were only discovered with more recent laboratory testing. The overall "yummy", or savoury, quality called umami, triggered by glutamates and amino acids, was first identified by Japanese researchers curious as to why seaweed and miso tasted so satisfying. More recently, another barely detectable taste has been found to be associated with fat in foods.

What to look for

Sweetness and acidity are the two tastes we look for and assess whenever we taste wine, and both are important in categorizing wine by style. We do not look for other tastes because wine has no salt, fat, or bitterness; and while many wines feature umami, it's not readily apparent.

Only two taste sensations are important in wine tasting: sweetness and acidity.

The 6 taste sensations are...

Sour = lemon
Bitter = tea
Fat = butter
Salty = soy sauce
Sweet = honey
Umami = MSG

Gauging sweetness
In the wine world, sweetness is measured in grams of sugar per litre of wine (g/l). This diagram gives an idea of how wines compare with some other beverages.

DRY MERLOT
2 g/l

TEA WITH ONE SUGAR
12 g/l

LIGHTLY SWEET RIESLING
15 g/l

Sweet or dry?

Sweetness is perceived as a sugary sensation on contact with the tongue, most vividly at the very tip, where taste receptors are more densely concentrated. Most wines have no perceptible sweetness and are described as "dry". This tends to be a confusing descriptor for beginners, because dry has a different meaning in wine than it does in everyday use. For centuries, winemakers around the world have called wines dry when their natural grape sugar has been fully converted to alcohol. *Sec* in French, *trocken* in German, and *secco* in

Italian all mean "not wet" in normal speech but "not sweet" when applied to wine.

A pleasing hint of sweetness can be found in varying degrees in wine, most often in mass-market bargain wines. Lightly sweet "off-dry" styles are particularly popular with wine novices, who appreciate their juice-like flavour. Fully sweet wines, or dessert wines, are seductive, but rare because they are challenging and expensive to produce. The vast majority of the world's wines are dry because they are simpler to make, have a longer shelf life, and work well with food.

HIGHS AND LOWS

This chart shows common terms for low-, medium-, and high-sugar wines, along with details of how each is perceived on tasting and examples of corresponding wines.

SUGAR	TERM	DESCRIPTION	WINE EXAMPLE
Low	Dry	No noticeable presence of sugar	Australian Chardonnay; French Côtes du Rhône
Medium	Lightly sweet; Off-dry	Slightly noticeable presence of sugar	German Riesling; California Old-Vine Zinfandel
High	Sweet; Dessert	Obvious, strong presence of sugar	Portuguese Port; Italian Moscato

ORANGE JUICE
85 g/l

SWEET PORT
100 g/l

WINE-GRAPE JUICE
225 g/l

Sour fresh-fruit acidity

Acidity is perceived as a sour sensation on contact, causing the mouth to salivate almost immediately, as with lemon juice or vinegar. Wine is more tart than most beverages, due to the high acidity of fresh grapes.

Newcomers often find wines too sour for their liking, in part because acidity always seems strongest on the first sip. But wine's acidic edge melts away as you continue to drink, especially if you're also eating. Since high levels of acidity can be a turn-off for the inexperienced, the wine profession treads carefully in describing it. Words such as "sour" and "acidic" carry negative connotations, so terms that sound more appetizing are more commonly used: tart or tangy, crisp or quenching, racy or refreshing.

A CHEF'S SECRET
Acidity makes everything it touches taste better. Chefs know this, and that's why so many restaurant dishes are made with a splash of wine, a squeeze of lemon, or a drizzle of vinegar.

HIGHS AND LOWS

This chart shows common terms for low-, medium-, and high-acidity wines, along with details of how each is perceived on tasting and examples of corresponding wines.

ACIDITY	TERM	DESCRIPTION	WINE EXAMPLE
Low	Mildly acidic; Flabby	Noticeable but modest acidity, as in baked apples	Oaky Chardonnay; Cream Sherry
Medium	Tangy; Crisp	Standard refreshing acidity, as in fresh apples	Italian Pinot Grigio; Chilean Merlot
High	Tart; Sharp	Prominent, aggressive acidity, as in underripe apples	French Sancerre; Italian Chianti

Acidity pH scale

The pH scale measures acidity, albeit in a different way than you might expect. The higher the number, the less acidic the sample, with water – a neutral point between acid and alkali – having a pH of 7.

WINE
pH 3–4

VODKA
pH 6–7

1   3   5   7   9   11

LIME JUICE
pH 2

ORANGE JUICE
pH 3.5

COFFEE
pH 5.5

WATER
pH 7

ANTACID
pH 10

THE TASTING
Identifying Sweetness and Acidity

Compare four wines at home

Sample the four white wine styles shown below.

1 Pay special attention to sensations on initial contact with your tongue.

2 Evaluate their levels of sweetness and acidity on a scale from low to high.

3 Consider which wine you prefer, whether alone or with food.

LOW SWEETNESS, HIGH ACIDITY	LOW SWEETNESS, MEDIUM ACIDITY	MEDIUM SWEETNESS, HIGH ACIDITY	HIGH SWEETNESS, LOW ACIDITY
1	**2**	**3**	**4**
FRENCH SAUVIGNON BLANC	CALIFORNIA CHARDONNAY	WASHINGTON RIESLING	FRENCH MUSCAT VIN DOUX NATUREL

For example...

Sancerre, Pouilly-Fumé, Bordeaux Blanc, or Touraine Sauvignon Blanc

Can you taste...?

Very Dry: very obvious absence of sugar

Tart Acidity: uncommonly high degree of sourness

For example...

Barrel-fermented styles from Sonoma, Monterey, or Central Coast

Can you taste...?

Dry: absence of sugar

Crisp Acidity: standard degree of sourness

For example...

Low-alcohol styles from Columbia Valley (particularly in German-style bottles)

Can you taste...?

Lightly Sweet or Off-Dry: noticeable presence of sugar

Tart Acidity: high degree of sourness

For example...

Dessert wines, such as Muscat de Minervois or Muscat de Beaumes-de-Venise

Can you taste...?

Sweet: obvious presence of sugar

Mild Acidity: uncommonly low degree of sourness

How Wine Smells

In wine tasting, "fruit" is the collective term for olfactory scents and flavours that come from the grapes used to make wine. Since all wines are made with 100 per cent fruit, almost all wine flavour fits this description.

Know your fruit from your oak

It is helpful to categorize wine's scents and flavours and assess their overall intensity. In wine tasting, the two main categories of wine's olfactory sensations are "fruit" smells and "oak" smells, each named after their part in the winemaking process.

Of all wine's smells, most come from the grapes.

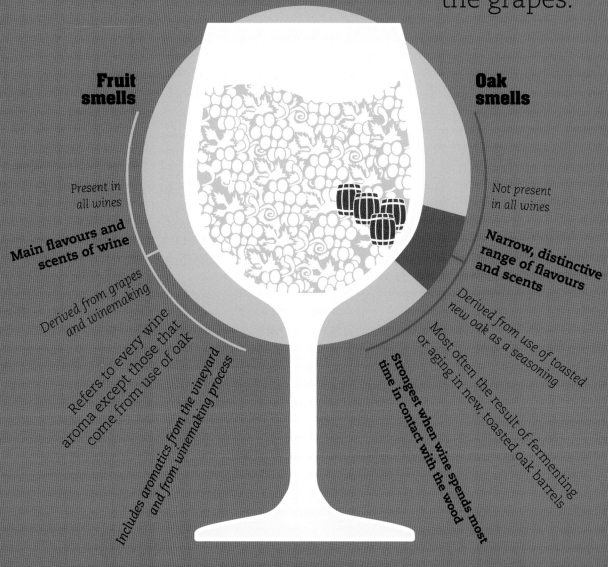

Fruit smells

Present in all wines

Main flavours and scents of wine

Derived from grapes and winemaking

Refers to every wine aroma except those that come from use of oak

Includes aromatics from the vineyard and from winemaking process

Oak smells

Not present in all wines

Narrow, distinctive range of flavours and scents

Derived from use of toasted new oak as a seasoning

Most often the result of fermenting or aging in new, toasted oak barrels

Strongest when wine spends most time in contact with the wood

HIGHS AND LOWS

This chart shows common terms for wines with low-, medium-, and high-intensity fruit, along with details of how each is perceived on tasting and examples of corresponding wines.

SCENT	TERM	DESCRIPTION	WINE EXAMPLE
Low intensity	Mild; Subtle	Understated flavour, as with chamomile tea	Italian Prosecco; French Chablis – rare outside of white wines
Medium intensity	Moderate; Flavourful	Standard flavour power, as with black coffee or tea	New Zealand Sauvignon Blanc; Spanish Garnacha
High intensity	Bold; Concentrated	Intense, powerful flavour, as with espresso	Napa Valley Cabernet Sauvignon, German *Eiswein* – rare outside of red wines and dessert wines

Understanding "fruit"

Many wine tasters try to identify specific aspects of a wine's fruit aromatics, with comparative terms like blackberry or lemon. For beginners, though, it is more useful to start by assessing the overall intensity of a wine's fruit on a simple power scale. Think of the fruit component as wine's flavour intensity: is it subtle and understated, or bold and over the top?

Professionals in the wine trade stretch the word "fruit" beyond its normal meaning. Fruit can encompass plenty of overtly fruit-like smells, such as the pineapple scent of Chardonnay or the blackcurrant aroma of Bordeaux. But in wine lingo, fruit is also a catch-all category that encompasses non-fruit flavours, too. Whether it's the peppery scent of Syrah, the herbal flavour of Sauvignon Blanc, or a floral aroma in Gewurztraminer, these would all be described as part of the wine's fruit component. However, when a wine is described as "fruity", it typically means that its scent is strong and dominated by ripe dessert-like smells of actual fruits.

In addition to the natural smells present in the raw grapes, the fruit component incorporates smells that are generated during winemaking. Complex chemical reactions create volatile aromatic compounds that can smell like all sorts of things – from bread dough, to leather; from cedar, to asphalt.

EARTH BECOMES "FRUIT"

Vineyard environments can contribute earthy aromatics, often called *terroir*, that are considered dimensions of a wine's fruit component.

POWER SCALE

- Over the top
- Pungent
- Bold
- Strong
- Flavourful
- Mild
- Under-stated
- Subtle

Fruit-intensity power scale
Use this power scale to help you identify the fruit intensity of a wine. Try to pick which term best suits any bottle you taste.

Understanding "oak"

The term "oak" describes a narrow range of wine scents and flavours, derived from contact with wood, usually toasted oak barrels. For centuries, oak barrels and vats were used to ferment and store wine for practical reasons, but they continue to be used today for the desirable flavours they impart. Oakiness is most commonly found in red wines and full-bodied whites, and it is particularly associated with premium aged styles.

Oak has the strongest impact when barrels are new, so wines made with older barrels may not have any oak traces. New toasted oak gives wine a range of flavours like those found in oak-aged spirits like cognac and bourbon.

OAKY SMELLS

In addition to a wood-like scent, wine aged in oak can pick up smells like vanilla, dessert spices, caramel, and nuts. Many wines are made without oak treatment, so these scents and flavours are not always present.

WINE IN OAK OR OAK IN WINE?

Oak flavour is imparted to wine by new toasted oak. In premium wines, the oak flavour comes from being aged or fermented in new wooden barrels. In bargain wines that are aged or fermented in stainless-steel tanks, it may come from flavouring agents such as oak chips or staves.

Traditional method

Flavour and scent from barrel

Industrial method

Flavour and scent from chips or staves

HIGHS AND LOWS

This chart shows common terms for wines with low, medium, and high levels of oak, along with details of how each is perceived on tasting and examples of corresponding wines.

OAKINESS	TERM	DESCRIPTION	WINE EXAMPLE
Low	Unoaked; Naked	Absence of oak scents and flavours, as with vodka	German Riesling; Italian Valpolicella
Medium	Mild Oak	Mild oak scents and flavours, as with young Canadian whiskey	French Bordeaux; Oregon Pinot Noir
High	Oaky; Toasty	Intense oak scents and flavours, as with premium aged cognac	Prestige Chardonnay; Spanish Rioja

THE TASTING

Identifying Fruit and Oak

Compare four wines at home

Sample the four wine styles shown below.

1 Pay special attention to the scents and flavours present before and after taking a sip.

2 Try to distinguish the overall wine smell, or "fruit", from the toasty scent of oak.

3 Evaluate the intensity of each on a scale from low to high.

LOW FRUIT, LOW OAK	MEDIUM FRUIT, MEDIUM OAK	MEDIUM FRUIT, HIGH OAK	HIGH FRUIT, HIGH OAK
UNOAKED FRENCH CHARDONNAY	BARREL-FERMENTED CALIFORNIA CHARDONNAY	BARREL-AGED SPANISH TEMPRANILLO	BARREL-AGED AUSTRALIAN SHIRAZ

For example...
Mâcon-Villages, Chablis, St-Véran, Bourgogne Blanc, or Viré-Clessé

Can you taste...?
Subtle Fruit: low-intensity wine flavour

No Oak: no detectable scent of oak barrels

For example...
Styles from Sonoma, Central Coast, Monterey, Santa Barbara, or Carneros

Can you taste...?
Moderate Fruit: medium-intensity wine flavour

Mild Oak: noticeable scent of oak barrels

For example...
Rioja, Toro, or Ribera del Duero of the *crianza* or *reserva* classifications

Can you taste...?
Moderate Fruit: medium-intensity wine flavour

Strong Oak: overt scent of oak barrels

For example...
Premium styles from Barossa, McLaren Vale, or South Australia

Can you taste...?
Bold Fruit: high-intensity wine flavour

Strong Oak: overt scent of oak barrels

How Wine Feels

Some sensory aspects of how wine "tastes" are neither tastes nor smells but "mouthfeel" – tactile sensations we discern with tongue, palate, lips, and gums. Mouthfeel incorporates some of our favourite food pleasures – from the crunch of potato crisps, to the creaminess of chocolate mousse.

In wine, we look for three types of physical sensation:

1. Carbonation, or bubbles
2. Weight, or body
3. Tannin, or astringency

Fizz and froth

The most obvious and instantaneous tactile sensation in wine is carbonation, since bubbles are immediately apparent on contact. Carbon dioxide is a natural by-product of fermentation, so all wines are bubbly at some point during winemaking. This natural fizz is usually allowed to escape, leaving the vast majority of wines "still", or non-carbonated. Sometimes, though, the bubbles are intentionally trapped and preserved to make a wine that is fully carbonated, or "sparkling".

Sparkling wines foam in the mouth like a fizzy soft drink and deliver a similar tingly shiver of refreshment on the palate. They need special bottles and corks to keep their carbonated contents under pressure. Occasionally, a milder prickle of carbonation, known as a spritz, may be present in wines that are not fully sparkling; these wines tend to be very young whites or rosés. Their bubbles typically dissipate quickly in the glass.

HIGHS AND LOWS

This chart shows common terms for wines with low, medium, and high levels of carbonation, along with details of how each is perceived on tasting and examples of corresponding wines.

CARBONATION	TERM	DESCRIPTION	WINE EXAMPLE
Low	Still; Standard	Total absence of bubbles or fizz	Pinot Gris; Sauvignon Blanc
Medium	Spritzy	Faint presence of bubbles or fizz	Vinho Verde; Basque Txakolina
High	Sparkling; Bubbly	Overt presence of bubbles or fizz	Champagne; Prosecco

Assessing weight

In wine terms, weight refers to texture or thickness – a physical sensation of viscosity on the palate that is also known as "body". In the same way that cream feels thicker than milk because it contains more fat, full-bodied wines feel heavier than light-bodied wines because they contain more alcohol. Most mid-weight wines have roughly 13.5% alcohol. The lower a wine's strength, the lighter it feels on the palate.

   Dessert wines are an exception to this rule, since dissolved sugar adds viscosity of its own. Wines that are both sweet and strong, like Port, are very heavy, feeling nearly as thick as syrup. Other factors, such as oak aging or yeast contact, can boost perceived weight but usually to a lesser extent than alcohol and sugar.

Fuller-bodied

Whiter, lighter
Most white wines tend to be lower in alcohol and feel lighter than most red wines, but there are a few exceptions to the rule.

13.5%

Scarce reds
Red wines are rarely made with less than 12.5% alcohol, so truly light reds are hard to find.

Lighter-bodied

CHECK OUT THOSE LEGS

A wine's weight becomes visible when wine slides down the sides of a glass after swirling. Known as "legs" or "tears", these drips fall slowest in the heaviest wines.

HIGHS AND LOWS

This chart shows common terms for low-, medium-, and high-texture wines, along with details of how each is perceived on tasting and examples of corresponding wines.

TEXTURE	TERM	DESCRIPTION	WINE EXAMPLE
Low	Light; Light-bodied	Sheer, delicate texture, as with skimmed milk	German Riesling, Italian Moscato – rare outside of sparkling, white, and rosé wines
Medium	Mid-weight; Medium-bodied	Standard medium texture, as with chocolate milk	French Bordeaux Blanc, Chilean Merlot
High	Heavy; Full-bodied	Rich, viscous texture, as with chocolate milkshake	California Old-Vine Zinfandel, Portuguese Port – rare outside red, dessert, and fortified wines

Discovering tannin

Red wines often dry out the mouth in the minute after tasting, blocking salivation and leaving a rough, leathery feeling on the palate. This is due to the presence of tannin, an astringent phenolic compound found in the skins, seeds, and stems of grapes.

• We find significant tannin only in red wines, because reds are fermented in contact with these solids, whereas white wines are not.

• Tannins add to a red wine's depth of colour and also tend to coincide with flavour intensity.

• Tannin is a strong antioxidant and natural preservative that helps wines age but breaks down over time.

• The youngest, darkest, most intense red wines designed for aging are typically the most tannic.

• Sometimes called a wine's "grip", tannin's mouth-drying effect is not always immediately apparent but gets stronger in the 30–60 seconds after tasting.

• Wines with mild tannin can feel plush, like velvet, while strong tannin can leave a harsher feeling, like suede.

Red wines get their tannin mainly from grape skins. These antioxidant compounds give red wine colour and flavour, as well as astringency.

MOUTH-DRYING, NOT DRY

Tannin is often confused with dryness because it makes the tongue feel dry. However, in wine lingo, "dry" refers to wines that are not sweet, while wines that dry out the mouth are described as tannic.

HIGHS AND LOWS

This chart shows common terms for low-, medium-, and high-tannin wines, along with details of how each is perceived on tasting and examples of corresponding wines.

TANNIN	TERM	DESCRIPTION	WINE EXAMPLE
Low	None	No detectable mouth-drying astringency	French Beaujolais; Dry rosé
Medium	Velvety; Soft tannin	Detectable, gentle mouth-drying astringency	California Merlot; French red Burgundy
High	Rough; Hard tannin	Obvious aggressive mouth-drying astringency	Italian Barolo; Australian Cabernet Sauvignon

THE TASTING
Identifying Body, Tannin, and Carbonation
Compare four wines at home
Sample the four wine styles shown below.

1 Pay special attention to how they feel in the mouth.

2 Look for weight, or thickness of texture, and for the telltale prickle of carbonation.

3 After swallowing the reds, consider the astringent, mouth-drying effect of tannin.

LIGHTWEIGHT, NO TANNIN, HIGH CARBONATION	**LIGHTWEIGHT, NO TANNIN, MEDIUM CARBONATION**	**MID-WEIGHT, MEDIUM TANNIN, NO CARBONATION**	**HEAVYWEIGHT, HIGH TANNIN, NO CARBONATION**
ITALIAN PROSECCO	**PORTUGUESE VINHO VERDE**	**NEW ZEALAND PINOT NOIR**	**CHILEAN CABERNET SAUVIGNON**

For example...	**For example...**	**For example...**	**For example...**
Simple affordable brands	Simple affordable brands	Moderately priced brands	Premium or moderately priced brands
Can you detect...?	**Can you detect...?**	**Can you detect...?**	**Can you detect...?**
Light: delicate, sheer texture	Light: delicate, sheer texture	Mid-Weight: standard medium texture	Heavy: dense, rich texture
Sparkling: vigorously carbonated	Spritzy: faintly carbonated	Soft Tannin: mildly mouth-drying	Strong Tannin: overtly mouth-drying
		Still: not carbonated	Still: not carbonated

Evaluating Wine Quality

One of the most difficult things for wine novices is figuring out how to assess the technical quality of a wine, rather than simply determine whether or not it suits their personal tastes.

Analyse the finish

Of all quality indicators, the length of a wine's "finish" is the most important and the easiest to discern. The term refers to the period of time after swallowing a wine during which its flavour sensations continue to resonate in the mouth; it's a fancy word for aftertaste. Lingering sensory impressions can last for anywhere from 30 seconds to 5 minutes, and their duration is a reflection of the wine's quality.

Wines made with impeccable ingredients and craftsmanship consistently display a longer, stronger, more pleasant finish than is found in less ambitious wines. A wine's finish is also where

the damaging effects of poor storage, faulty corks, or winemaking mistakes become apparent.

A fine wine's finish is perceived not simply as lasting tastes, smells, and mouthfeel but as an almost palpable vibrating energy that hums in the mouth after tasting. The finish of serviceable bargain wines will fade fastest; well-made wines with higher quality standards will hang around in the mouth for at least 1–2 minutes; and truly exceptional wines can dominate the palate for considerably longer. During this period, experts pay close attention, because each wine ebbs and flows on the palate in a unique way.

The quality of a wine can be measured by the length of time it resonates in the mouth.

Measuring quality
The old adage that you get what you pay for holds perfectly true for the intensity and length of finish in a luxury wine. This is one of the key elements lacking in bargain wines.

Long, like the enduring note of a tuning fork

Mid-length, like the lingering note of a piano

Short, like the quick clinking of two coffee cups

Modest bulk wine

Premium fine wine

Exceptional luxury wine

INTENSITY OF FINISH

DURATION OF FINISH

Assess cork taint

Wine bottles have been sealed with cork for centuries, but many vintners are now going cork-free because natural corks can sometimes degrade wine's flavour. Around 5 per cent of cork-sealed wines are noticeably contaminated by their cork, but the degree of damage varies widely. So-called corked wine has a characteristic fungus scent. In the worst cases, it can smell distinctly unpleasant, with odours reminiscent of mouldy cardboard or mildewed wool. In mild cases, though, it can be more apparent from the absence of good wine smells than the presence of bad ones. This insidious problem is hard to recognize unless more than one bottle of the same wine are compared side by side. The wine trade is well aware of this issue, so when in doubt, speak up. Restaurateurs and retailers should replace suspect bottles in most instances.

Identify heat damage

As with fruit, wine keeps longer when refrigerated. Wines all go bad eventually, but the colder they are, the more slowly they change. Heat increases the rate of the chemical reactions that take place as wine matures, most notably oxidation. Wine ages prematurely when kept too warm, leaving it seeming cooked – browned in colour and flattened in flavour. Extreme heat can alter the internal pressure of wine bottles, compromising their seal, which further speeds oxidation. Evidence of this is sometimes visible in seeping bottles or raised corks, but heat damage is usually less obvious. Short bursts of heat or longer storage at room temperature can permanently shorten a wine's potential life without showing obvious signs until it is tasted, showing in a short, dull, and lifeless finish.

WINE STORAGE

The optimum storage temperature for wine, to reduce spoilage as far as possible, is in the range of 10–15°C (50–60°F), and it should be kept away from light sources.

Chapter Checklist

Here is a recap of some of the most important points you've learned in this chapter.

✓ Wine **descriptors** help us explain wine qualities. They can be **indirect** and evocative, or **direct** and dispassionate.

✓ We evaluate wine attributes through the use of all of our **senses** except hearing.

✓ Most wine **colour** comes from **grape skins**. White wines pick up no colour, but the colour of rosés and reds depends on length of time in **contact** with dark-purple grape skins.

✓ Colour saturation tends to match **intensity** of flavour and indicate **oakiness** and **astringency**.

✓ We can truly taste just **six sensations** – sweet, sour, umami, bitter, salty, fat – with only the first two relevant to wine tasting.

✓ In the wine world, the term **"dry"** means "not sweet" rather than "not wet".

✓ The naturally **high acidity** of fresh grapes makes wine more tart than most beverages. This helps it flatter food, refresh the palate, and age gracefully.

✓ **"Fruit"** is the term given to all olfactory scents and flavours that come from the grapes used to make wine.

✓ **"Oak"** describes a narrow range of scents and flavours due to a wine's contact with wood.

✓ **"Mouthfeel"** describes the tactile sensations we discern with tongue, palate, lips, and gums.

✓ The lower a wine's **alcoholic strength**, the lighter it feels on the palate; the higher its strength, the heavier it seems.

✓ **Tannin** is an astringent phenolic compound present in the skins, seeds, and stems of grapes. Found only in **red wines**, it dries out the mouth after wine is swallowed.

BROWSING AND BUYING

Tricks of the Trade

Wine is harder to shop for than almost any other product. The options in stores and restaurants can paralyse even the most savvy. However, picking up a few strategies that wine professionals rely on can help banish doubts and build wine confidence. Labels may not tell us how wine will taste, but there's much to be learned between the lines. Wine packaging speaks volumes about what's inside, and three important numbers can simplify the shopping experience. A few restaurant rules of thumb make it easier to benefit from expert advice without breaking the bank.

Look at the Packaging

There is quite a lot we can learn about a wine without even reading the label – colours, fonts, and artwork speak volumes. Since wine-label terms and regulations can seem so disorienting to consumers, vintners often try to communicate style without words, through their package design.

Judging without tasting

In the modern self-serve retail environment, producers have every incentive to make sure their packaging evokes the wine's sensory profile and appeals to the appropriate audience.

Fun-loving and modern

Splashy colours, modern designs, and lighthearted names suggest ripe wines with dessert-like aromas, meant for immediate consumption.

Sophisticated classic

Sedate colours, traditional designs, and family names suggest more food-friendliness, tending towards leaner, drier wines with noticeable acidity.

Light equals bright

For whites, clear glass and bright labels suggest lighter-bodied, unoaked wines. Darker glass and autumn colours hint at a fuller body or oakier flavour.

Identify a wine by its bottle

Some wine regions use distinctive bottle shapes that have come to form part of their identity – an indicator of the style found within.

Burgundy

Bordeaux

Alsace

SUBLIMINAL LABEL MESSAGES
Packaging design reflects the vintner's style and philosophy and often hints at how the wine will taste.

So-called Burgundy bottles with sloping shoulders are most often used for Chardonnay, Pinot Noir, Syrah, and Rhône-style wines.

Square-shouldered Bordeaux-style bottles are used for most other styles, particularly Cabernet Sauvignon, Merlot, and Sauvignon Blanc.

Tall, fluted Alsace-style bottles are associated with white wines of German heritage, such as Riesling and Gewurztraminer, which may be sweet or dry.

PACKAGING INNOVATIONS

Some wines can age for decades, so wineries have been cautious in adopting modern packaging innovations. However, bottles with corks are not the most efficient containers, and today's vintners are exploring new options.

Alternative containers – like boxes

Bottles are no longer the only option for preserving wine. Improvements in food-packaging technology mean boxes, cartons, and cans are now viable containers. All of these can reduce shipping weight and protect wine from damaging light. Larger "bag-in-box" formats have the added advantage of extending wine's shelf life dramatically once they're "tapped"; the shrinking bag inside protects the wine from air, so it can taste fresh for up to six weeks.

Alternative closures – like screwcaps

Natural corks are still the norm for fine wine, but they can cause detectable flaws in a small percentage of the wines they are supposed to protect. Screwcaps, offering more consistency and a lower failure rate, are becoming more commonplace, particularly for wines designed to be drunk young.

Shopping by Numbers

Even when we know what style of wine we want – an Italian red or a California white – making a final decision can be complicated by the sheer number of choices. When faced with a proliferation of unfamiliar options or similar wines, professionals often compare three key numbers, each of which provides clues to how the contenders will taste.

Check the vintage

The year printed on the label is far more useful for learning how old a wine is than for whether it was made in a "good year" or "bad year".

The younger a wine is, the more fruit-driven it is likely to be. Young wines feature fresh-fruit flavours, and the youngest are often unoaked. They are also likely to be lighter-bodied, more refreshing, and more affordable.

Wines that are more than two years old are typically premium wines refined by aging, often in oak barrels. Mature wines feature flavours that are less vivid and fresh but more complex and multilayered, often with a distinctly toasty oak accent. Such wines are typically fuller-bodied, more opulent, and more expensive.

2000 2001 2002 2003 2004 2005 2006 2007 2008 2009 2010 2011 2012

Consider the alcohol

A wine's strength (its alcohol by volume, or ABV) can be used as a rough indicator of many important style parameters, especially body and flavour intensity. This idea is explored in greater detail in Section Two, but even a superficial overview can provide relevant insights when deciding on a wine to buy or drink. As a broad generalization, you can reasonably expect certain wine traits to vary proportionally with alcohol content.

UNDER 13.5%	13.5–14%	OVER 14%
THE LOWER THE ALCOHOL, THE MORE LIKELY A WINE WILL BE...	**STANDARD MID-WEIGHT WINES**	**THE HIGHER THE ALCOHOL, THE MORE LIKELY A WINE WILL BE...**
• lighter, or more sheer in texture; • paler in colour; • less intense in fruit and oak flavour; • higher in refreshing acidity; • younger and more fresh tasting.		• heavier, or thicker in texture; • deeper in colour; • more intense in fruit and oak flavour; • lower in refreshing acidity; • aged and richer tasting.

Look at the price

The most important number in buying decisions is always price. Many drinkers feel they need to spend more than they'd like on wine to get a "decent" bottle. Wine professionals know that the biggest jumps in quality are found among the most affordable wines and that quality is not always the biggest concern.

In wine, as with all consumer goods, higher prices correlate to higher quality. Making wine with better materials and craftsmanship yields more desirable traits, such as aesthetics, individuality, and durability, just as it would for making shoes or cars. However, there is a point of diminishing returns. (See the next page for more insight into shopping by price.)

IT COSTS HOW MUCH?!

We're used to paying more for quality in all consumer goods, but wine's lofty price tags can seem startling. In some instances, they seem to defy logic. A bargain Rioja might cost £6, while a great estate's top *gran reserva* could easily command £60. At auction, aged bottles might sell for £600 or more. Why? Finer wines are more expensive to make, but making better wines also means making fewer bottles at much greater expense, sometimes aging them for a decade or more before they're sold. The rest comes down to supply and demand.

Wines that retail at £60 are certainly higher in quality than wines that cost £6, but this does not mean they are ten times better or that you will like them ten times as much.

Beating the Budget

Wine has a reputation as a luxury product, but drinking well doesn't mean you have to break the bank. Wine professionals don't drink expensive wines every day, because they know how to get the most bang for their buck. Consider some of these insider tips next time you're shopping for wine.

Try a new price point

You don't have to spend a lot more per bottle to drink significantly better wine. For example, let's say the popular price for everyday wine in your area is £6 per bottle. Wines priced just above this, in the £7 to £10 range, will typically offer the best mileage per pound in terms of quality for the price. If they weren't worth more than the cheaper bottles in some way, they would be unable to command the higher price. As prices continue to rise from £12 to £25 and beyond, we can expect the wines to continue to improve, but we will have to pay a greater premium for each step up in quality.

SEEK ADVICE

When it comes to wine shopping, it's good to ask for advice. The salespeople will likely have more specific information than what is on the bottles' labels. At the very least, they should be able to help you zero in on options that suit your tastes.

Be clear up front about how much you want to spend. And if you don't know exactly what you want, just tell them what you're making for dinner, or name some wines that you've enjoyed in the past.

Cheap and cheerful but hit-and-miss

Safer bets, offering best value mileage

Superior versions for the quality-conscious

BARGAIN   **AFFORDABLE**   **PREMIUM**

Be an explorer

Famous wine regions such as Napa Valley will command higher prices than obscure ones like Paso Robles, and the same is true of legendary grapes, trusted brands, and brilliant package designs. These demand-driving factors do correlate to increased odds of better wine quality, if only by signalling that the vintner has the resources to pursue ambitious goals. However, there are many great wines that can be found by those willing to go off the beaten track. Although trying unfamiliar wines can seem risky, people often overestimate the danger. There's very little truly bad wine out there, and the only way to find out what you like is to jump in and explore.

Take reviews with a pinch of salt

Wine reviews can seem like lifesavers to the novice, but shopping according to point scores often results in overpaying. Since magazine scores don't take prices into account, there's a strong correlation between higher scores and wines that are more expensive to produce. Good scores also increase demand, providing an incentive for wineries, brokers, and retailers to raise prices on top-ranked wines – or, at least, to resist implementing discount strategies.

Decadent limited-production splurges

Rare specialities for when price is no object

LUXURY

COLLECTABLE

FILL YOUR TROLLEY?

Most retailers offer discounts to those shoppers who buy their wine in bulk, but this is not the only way for you to benefit from "volume pricing". Look for the items that your retailer purchases in greatest quantity. Floor stacks and feature bins show confidence in the product and probably have a lower markup than less well-stocked items.

Reading New World Labels

All wine labels list the vintner or brand identity along with their formal appellation, or region of origin. The most famous wine appellations tend to be small wine regions. However, political districts also qualify as wine appellations in many countries, ranging from large provinces to smaller counties and municipalities. Labels on wines from the New World – the Americas and the southern hemisphere – tend to be easier to understand, so that is where we will begin…

GRAPES UP FRONT
Most modern wine labels advertise the name of the grape variety from which the wines are made, as well as their vintage date; however, these details are not required by law.

What's on the label?

1 Wine appellation or region of origin – *mandatory*
A formal region-of-origin statement is required for all wines, indicating where the grapes were grown, which is not necessarily where the wine was made.

2 Brand name or wine producer – *mandatory*
Wines are most often sold under the name of the winery but may also be sold under a proprietary brand name.

3 Vintage date – *optional*
This specifies the year when the grapes were harvested.

4 Grape variety – *optional*
Wines are typically labelled by the type of grape used, in which case, they must contain at least 75 per cent of the specified variety.

5 Fine print
Legal requirements vary by country, but all wine bottles must indicate (on front or back label): bottle volume, alcohol content, and country of origin. The company or facility that made the wine must also be formally identified, along with its location.

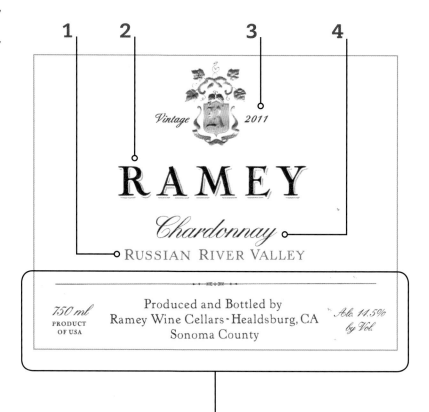

1 2 3 4

Vintage 2011

RAMEY

Chardonnay

RUSSIAN RIVER VALLEY

750 ml
PRODUCT OF USA

Produced and Bottled by
Ramey Wine Cellars · Healdsburg, CA
Sonoma County

Alc. 14.5%
by Vol.

5

Knowing what's what

Vintners often make more than one wine from the same grape and region – a basic version and a premium version, for example, or a sweet version and a dry version. To distinguish these from one another, they are given *cuvée* names that provide additional specificity on the label. (*Cuvée*, which is French for "vat", loosely means batch or blend in this context.) The optional extras that may appear in a wine's *cuvée* name include the following.

1 Vineyard site names
such as Dutton Ranch or Ornellaia.

2 Quality terms or certifications
such as "reserve" or "organic"
(some regulated, some not).

3 Wine-specific proprietary names
such as Penfold's Grange, or Insignia by Joseph Phelps.

4 Multi-wine brand names
such as Rothschild's Mouton Cadet or Coppola's Diamond Label.

5 Style references
such as "late harvest" or "unwooded".

Reading Old World Labels

Following centuries of tradition, top European wines are named according to their regions – Chablis and Chianti, for example – not their grapes. As a result, the European Union regulates wine-label statements in its own way. In "Old World" Europe, appellations are the organizing principle for wide-ranging quality standards, as well as their enforcement mechanism; elsewhere, appellations simply certify where a wine's fruit was grown.

Region over grapes

Vintners within top European appellations may grow only specified grapes. They also must conform to strict winemaking requirements in order to earn the right to use a place name on the label. Appellations formalize local traditions and are often organized as hierarchies, with smaller, premium appellations carving out the best sites within larger, less prestigious ones.

There are a few regions in Europe where naming grapes is traditional, such as Germany and northern Italy. Many up-and-coming appellations elsewhere also list grapes to appeal to international markets. However, in the French system that served as a model for EU wine law, a wine's region is its distinguishing feature and point of pride, not its grape. For example, the French Chablis below is made entirely with Chardonnay by law, but the label makes no reference to grape variety at all. This pattern is most often seen in the most traditional and ambitious wines.

HIDE THE GRAPE

Wines from Europe's prestigious regions have been named by their source for centuries – whether it's a large region or a tiny village. Their dominant grape is often not mentioned on the label.

European wine appellation

Pride of place
Region-of-origin statements are regulated differently in Europe and classified according to their quality standards. Premium appellations are typically prominent on labels, and the formal legalese is in small print immediately adjacent.

FONDÉE   EN 1859

CHABLIS
Appellation Contrôlée

750 ml

Élevé et mis en bouteilles par
LOUIS JADOT
F 21200 - FRANCE

12.5% vol.

PRODUCE OF FRANCE

Ranking of quality

Some European wine regions add their own special terms on labels as quality indicators. Such designations are tightly controlled, often recognizing multiple ascending ranks. Each region uses its own system, which can be based on one or more wine quality factors.

MYRIAD LAWS
Each wine-producing country in Europe has its own wine laws, making the Old World quite baffling for newcomers, especially those unfamiliar with the various languages.

1

2

3

1 Superior vineyard land
In some French regions, the best vineyards or wine estates are granted elite *grand cru* or next-best *premier cru* status. In Italy, *classico* signifies a superior subdistrict.

2 Extended barrel maturation
In Italy and Spain, legally defined terms such as *riserva* and *crianza* respectively are used to distinguish wines that spend extra time aging in oak barrels.

3 Degrees of grape ripeness
In Germany and Austria, full ripeness is not guaranteed, so a complex system of label terms like *Kabinett* and *Spätlese* is used to rank wines by the sugar content of their grapes at harvest.

PROS AND CONS

The upside of European wine labels is that they often include lots of information. However, most is only meaningful if you're already an expert. For example, the formal identity of this Champagne includes eight categories of information.

Cuvée name

Appellation

Producer

Sweetness level

Grape variety

Vineyard quality rank

Style category

Vintage

Buying in Restaurants

Restaurants provide an opportunity to sample multiple wines, both alone and with food, from a selection carefully chosen to complement their cuisine (see Chapter 7 for food-and-wine matching tips). However, restaurants can also present challenges for wine lovers – from poor wine service, to cynically high price markups.

Can you trust the venue?

Restaurants and bars can offer outstanding wine experiences tailor-made for sharing with friends and family – but only if the business cares about its wines and its customers. Take a quick look around. If the bar or restaurant takes pride in its wine service, you'll see the signs before you order. If their wine programme looks like an afterthought, or if they would clearly prefer to sell you beer or cocktails, proceed with caution.

Good signs
- Wine glasses already set on tables
- Large wine glasses filled less than halfway
- Clean, well-organized wine lists
- Many wines offered by the glass
- Extra wine details on the list, such as style descriptions

Bad signs
- No wine glasses visible
- Small wine glasses filled near the top
- Scruffy, poorly organized wine lists
- Few wines offered by the glass
- Incomplete wine listings – with no vintage dates, for example

SEEK OUT ADVICE

Not all restaurants have skilled, wine-savvy staff available to advise their guests, but when they do, you may as well take advantage. Whether it's a certified sommelier or a well-trained bartender, those who work most closely with their wines are great resources. Don't simply ask for their suggestions, unless you truly want to try the wines they like the most. If what you want is a wine closer to your personal tastes, provide them with more to go on. For example, one great strategy is to say, "I love Pinot Grigio but would like to try something different tonight. What can you recommend?"

Stay in control!

It's always in a restaurant's interests to boost wine sales, so sommeliers and servers will often favour premium wines and extra bottles unless otherwise directed. Many diners feel intimidated when ordering wine and go along with wine suggestions for fear of coming across as a stingy host. However, as the paying guest, remember that you are always in charge.

> No one can force you to spend more in a restaurant than you wish unless you cede control.

Provide a price target when asking for recommendations

Discreetly signal your budget by pointing to a price on the wine list. Without guidance, the server won't know whether you want to scrimp or splurge. Specifying a price point directs them to flavour options instead of quality levels.

Don't order a bottle when a glass will do

Wines by the glass and half-bottles are ideal for providing a palate-cleansing aperitif while reading the menu or for a final drink to finish off the main course or cheese plate. Bottles may feature the lowest margins, but they're only the best deal if you finish them.

Don't approve unlimited bottles in advance for large parties

It's tempting to tell servers to keep the wine flowing so you can relax and enjoy yourself. But doing so allows the staff to decide how much you'll spend. Expect to need one bottle for every two wine drinkers at dinner; less at lunches and brunches. If approving each new bottle is intrusive, authorize a set number.

Chapter Checklist

Here is a recap of some of the most important points you've learned in this chapter.

✓ The information printed on **wine labels** can be disorienting to the general public, so many producers try to communicate their **wine style** through their **packaging**.

✓ Bottles with **corks**, though traditional, are not the most efficient wine packages. **Screwcaps** are now often used instead of corks, and **boxes** are increasingly replacing bottles for everyday wines.

✓ When shopping for wine, three important **numbers** can serve as useful guides: vintage, level of alcohol, and price.

✓ Not even wine professionals drink expensive wine every day. Learn how to get the **best value** even on a budget, and don't feel under any pressure to **overspend**.

✓ **Wine labels** rarely reference **flavour**. Most give details that are more helpful for professionals than casual wine drinkers, such as a wine's **ingredients** and where the **grapes** were grown.

✓ The most useful **label-reading skills** are to recognize distinctions between the main types of label **statements**, and between grape-centric labels and European region-centric labels.

✓ When dining out, consider whether you can put your trust in the restaurant based on the amount of effort and pride they put into their **wine service**.

✓ At a restaurant where a **sommelier** or wine-savvy bartender is present, take full advantage and seek their **advice**.

✓ Be clear to your waiter about how much you wish to spend on wine and **don't be bullied** into spending more, whether by ordering a more expensive bottle than you would choose or by ordering more wine than is necessary.

POURING AND STORING

What to Drink When and How

Wine is an indulgence we can enjoy at home and share with friends and family. However, unlike beer and spirits, how to serve it and store it isn't always clear cut. Wine behaves differently at different temperatures, affecting how it tastes and how well it keeps. Understanding how and why makes it easier to get the most enjoyment from your wine purchases and to maximize their shelf life, even after the bottles are opened. Knowing how much to pour into what type of glass, or how many bottles you'll need, makes home entertaining with wine a breeze.

Entertaining with Wine

Whether you're dining out or entertaining at home, it's helpful to know how much wine you'll need and how to serve it. Here are some general guidelines.

How much wine is in a glass?

Internationally, an average glass of wine is about 150 ml (5 oz), and there are five such servings in a standard bottle. However, certain situations dictate pouring roughly half this amount:
• When a bottle is shared at the table, especially in fine-dining restaurants, or for multi-course meals that include more than one wine;

• When the wine's primary purpose is to raise a toast;
• When the wine is extremely sweet or extremely strong, as is the case with dessert wines and fortified wines;
• At wine tastings where multiple wines are being sampled.

Portion sizes

FULL-GLASS POUR (150 ML, OR 5 OZ)

This is the correct portion for:
• cocktail parties;
• wine before dinner;
• casual meals (single course, single wine);
• wines by the glass in restaurants.

HALF-GLASS POUR (75 ML, OR 2.5 OZ)

This is the correct portion for:
• toasts and wine tastings;
• after-dinner wines;
• fancy meals (multiple courses, multiple wines);
• wines by the bottle in restaurants.

HOW MUCH WINE DO YOU NEED FOR A PARTY?

Having 1 bottle per person on hand is wise when entertaining, to avoid running short, but average consumption is typically about half this amount.
• For social events and receptions: 1.5 glasses per person for the first hour, then 1 glass per person per hour thereafter.

• For dining out: 2.5 glasses per person, or 1 bottle for every 2 guests.
• For dinner parties: 2 bottles of reception wine, then 1 bottle per course for every 6–8 drinkers.
• For wine tastings (with 6–10 wines): 1 bottle of each wine for every 10–12 guests.

How much wine is in a bottle or a box?

Wine bottles look and feel substantial, so people often overestimate how much wine they contain. Standard bottles hold 750 ml of wine. The most common size for premium box wines is 3 litres; this is the equivalent of four standard bottles, but it occupies quite a bit less space.

3-litre wine box
3,000 ml

20 glasses

1,500 ml

750 ml

375 ml

187 ml

Split bottle

Half bottle

Standard bottle

Magnum, or double bottle

1.25 glasses

2.5 glasses

5 glasses

10 glasses

WHAT TO OFFER WHEN

It can be daunting trying to figure out just what people expect when you are hosting an event. Here are some points to remember.

• Traditionally, the reception drink, served to guests on arrival, is sparkling wine, because it is light and piques the appetite.

• Wine preferences (white or red) tend to be roughly 50/50, so guests tend to expect both types to be available. Choose crowd-pleasers: mid-weight wines have the broadest appeal.

• Offer a lightly sweet option at larger events, especially those that attract multiple generations of guests. Many people never acquire a taste for dry wines and prefer sweeter styles.

• Daytime events call for lighter wines. Look for younger, lower-alcohol styles and expect less total consumption than for evening affairs.

• For multi-course, multi-wine dinners:

1. Serve sparkling wine as an aperitif and/or with first courses.

2. Serve white wines before reds – lighter before heavier if more than one.

3. Finish with dessert wines or fortified wines.

Know Your Glasses

Wine tastes good enough to be enjoyed from any vessel, even sipped straight from the bottle, but it is usually served in specialized wine glasses. Much as darkened cinemas flatter movies by focusing our attention on the bright screen, stemmed glasses with large bowls flatter wines by focusing our attention on their aromatics.

Wine-glass anatomy

Most glasses and cups are designed for efficiency and convenience, like tumblers that get filled to capacity. Wine glasses are not; they are designed to please your nose. Every feature is oriented around swirling, sniffing, and maintaining wine's temperature – all to enhance wine's scent. There are all sorts of glasses, some made for specific styles of wine. But a single multipurpose wine glass is all you need to enjoy everything from Prosecco to Port.

Headspace
This part of a wine glass stays empty for two reasons: to allow the wine to be vigorously swirled without spilling, increasing its surface area and its rate of evaporation; and to retain and concentrate the resulting aroma compounds.

Rim
Wine glasses are most fragile at the lip, so practical glasses often feature sturdy rolled rims. Deluxe glasses have thinner cut rims that can feel amazingly sheer on the lips but make them easy to break.

Wine
Wine glasses are designed to hold 15–18 cl (5–6 oz) of wine. As a rule, they should not be filled more than halfway, or above the widest point of the bowl, to maximize the impact of the wine's aroma. As a result, 30–35-cl (10–12-oz) glasses are ideal.

Bowl
Wine glasses should feature large bowls that narrow at the top to concentrate wine's aromas. The most versatile are widest near the bottom and have a total capacity of roughly 30–35 cl (10–12 oz).

Stem
The stem of a wine glass serves as a handle, designed to keep your fingers off the bowl. Body heat is easily transferred, and wine's flavour changes greatly with even small shifts in temperature. The stems should comfortably accommodate the width of your hand at the knuckles.

The sum of its parts
Wine glasses are unusual in that their component parts are designed more for smelling than for drinking.

Base
Well, you may need to put the glass down. Possibly.

Choose the right size

White wines are often served in smaller glasses than reds because they smell milder; their pleasing scent can seem weak when there is too much headspace. Conversely, reds can smell too strong in too small a glass, since they contain more aroma compounds. When using one all-purpose glass, compensate by filling it higher for whites and lower for reds.

In casual cafés, wine often comes in tiny 18–24-cl (6–8-oz) "Paris goblets" filled near the rim, limiting your ability to smell it properly. In fine-dining restaurants, expensive wines may be served in huge crystal glasses that could accommodate a whole 75-cl bottle. Specialized stemware for particular grape varieties is beautiful but unnecessary for appreciating a fine wine.

| **White wine style** | **Red wine style** | **Café style** | **Luxury style** |

A glass apart

Two styles of wine benefit from different glasses entirely: sparkling wines and highly concentrated wines. Bubbly wines lose carbonation faster with a larger surface area, so they are served in tall, thin flutes. High-sugar dessert wines and high-alcohol fortified wines are served in half-size 7–9-cl (2.5–3-oz) portions. Their aromatics are typically strong enough to enjoy in a standard wine glass, but they look nicer served in smaller glasses.

Sherry glass and Champagne flute

WHY DECANT WINES?

Many premium wines that are designed to improve with age may benefit from being removed from their bottle before being served. There are two reasons to decant:

• **To remove sediment in older red wines**
After ten years or more of aging in bottles, red wines throw a fine sediment, or sooner if the wine is unfiltered. Pouring gently into a decanter can separate the clear wine from these solids.

• **To aerate and mellow younger wines**
For premium wines that have yet to reach their peak, a little air can help flavours bloom and intensify, replicating the flavour changes that would develop with longer cellaring.

Wine and Temperature

Wine's flavour is dependent on volatile components that are temperature-sensitive, so we try to serve it at the most flattering temperature and maintain that ideal by pouring small amounts, keeping bottles on ice, and holding the glass by its stem. We have easy access to room temperature and refrigerator temperature, but most people prefer their wines somewhere in between: a little cooler than the room for reds and a little warmer than the fridge for everything else.

Your wine, your rules!

As with all things, individual preferences in wine temperature can vary widely, and the most important thing is to drink your wine the way you like it. If that means icing your reds or warming your whites, ignore the snobs and go for it!

Remember, though, that if your wine seems a little too bland, it may just need to warm up a little; and if it seems a little too boozy or lacks refreshment, it may just need a little chill.

WHY DON'T WE CHILL REDS?

The only wines that aren't routinely served cold are red wines, because the tannins and other grape-skin compounds that give them colour seem more astringent and bitter at low temperatures.

Try this

Open two bottles of wine – one chilled white and one red at room temperature.

- Pour two glasses of each wine, and put one of each in the refrigerator.
- After 5 minutes, taste each pair side by side, looking for the differences in taste.

Both wines from the fridge will seem less aromatic and less flavourful than the same wine in the warmer glass – but also more refreshing and less boozy. The colder red's tannin will seem harsher and more raspy. The reverse will be true of the warmer pair, seeming more flavourful and fragrant, as well as more alcoholic and less refreshing. And the red's tannins will feel smoother.

Most people will find the cold red to be unappealing and the white better once it has been out of the fridge a little while.

FREEZING WINE

Freezing unopened wine bottles is a bad idea, because they will explode and make a mess. But it is a great way to preserve leftovers: more effective than vacuum pumps, which flatten wine's flavour, and longer-lasting than wine-protecting sprays, which break down over time. Wine spoils in two ways after the cork is pulled. Oxidation starts it on the path to vinegar, and its flavours are lost to evaporation, never to return. Both processes grind to a halt in the freezer, with the only ill effects being a minor degree of flavour loss in all wine and the formation of a colour-fading sediment in reds. Wines that are sparkling, very mature, or very subtly flavoured aren't good candidates, but others freeze very well. Tilt bottles upwards so frozen wine doesn't touch the cork, though, since that can impart a bitter taste into the wine.

Optimum temperatures

It is perfectly acceptable for you to drink wine at whatever temperature you like – even chilling your reds, for example. However, you may wish to follow standard practice when you have guests.

Serving advice for reds

• Red wines taste best at 15–21°C (60–70°F).

• Serve lighter reds colder and heavier reds warmer.

• Keep reds at room temperature, then chill briefly immediately before serving: 5–15 minutes in the refrigerator. For example, chill lighter French Beaujolais for 15 minutes before serving, but give heavier Argentinian Malbec just 5 minutes.

• Port wines are an exception to this rule: although they are red and strong, they taste more balanced when chilled as for whites.

Serving advice for other wines

• White, rosé, sparkling, fortified, and dessert wines taste best at 4–10°C (40–50°F).

• Serve lighter wines colder and heavier wines warmer.

• Keep these wines refrigerated, "warming" them briefly immediately before serving: 5–15 minutes at room temperature. For example, let heavier Australian Chardonnay shed its chill on the table for 15 minutes before serving, but give lighter Italian Pinot Grigio just 5 minutes to warm. Serve the lightest wines, like Spanish Cava, straight from the fridge.

• Sweet dessert wines are an exception to this rule: they taste best quite cold, regardless of their alcoholic strength.

Warmer by weight
Within any given category, the heaviest wines tend to taste better a little warmer, and the lightest wines tend to shine with more of a chill.

Over 26°C (80°F)
– Danger zone for all wine
– Heat-damage alert!

18–24°C (65–75°F)
– Room temperature
– Human comfort zone

Best for serving red wines

10–15°C (50–60°F)
– Cellar temperature
– Ideal wine storage

Best for serving other wine styles

1–4°C (34–40°F)
– Refrigerator temperature
– Safe food preservation

0°C (32°F)
– Freezing point

Wine and Aging

Any wines that will be drunk within a couple of months can be stored in the refrigerator or at room temperature, but long-term storage requires more wine-friendly conditions – specifically a cool temperature and protection from light. Wine is a perishable product that changes over time in a slow march towards spoilage. It may take them longer to go bad than fresh grapes, but eventually all wines will succumb to oxidation, turn brown, and die.

Not all wines age well

Contrary to popular belief, most wines do not improve with age. Many can be kept quite a while before they deteriorate, but their fresh-fruit qualities will fade, and very few wines are concentrated enough to develop new flavours and smells to replace them over time.

The distinctive, complex scents of mature wines arise from chemical reactions that take place in the bottle between components like phenols and esters. Wines that don't have enough such "stuffing" from the start will tire and lose intensity rather than becoming more interesting with age. And wines that can't fend off the onslaught of oxidation with preservative components like antioxidant tannins or high levels of acidity don't stand a chance. Only uncommonly concentrated wines reward patient cellaring, and these tend to be expensive styles.

RATIO OF WINE AGEABILITY

Over 90% of all wines are designed to taste best immediately.

THE FACTS:

- This is especially true of white, rosé, and sparkling wines.

- Any necessary aging is done at the winery before release.

- Well-made wines won't decline immediately but rarely improve.

- Value-oriented wines tire fastest.

- Pink rosé wines and *nouveau*-style reds are the least stable and should be drunk within 6 months.

Less than 10% of wines are designed to taste better after 5 years.

THE FACTS:

- They must be high enough in concentration to develop new flavours.

- Most in this bracket are red wines or dessert wines, since high levels of tannin and sugar can act as preservatives.

- Typically, these are premium and luxury wines, usually made in a traditional style.

Less than 1% of wines are designed to taste better after 10 years.

THE FACTS:

- The finest high-tannin reds may not taste pleasant when very young, because they tend to need a few years to "soften".

- These types of wine are usually exceptional collector's wines, both rare and expensive.

INSIGHT ON AGING

Decades ago, it was easier to predict which wines needed to be laid down: you just needed to remember a few grapes and styles! Nowadays, the market prefers wines that are ready to drink, and most vintners do whatever it takes to comply. But making wines to taste better sooner means they will also decline faster. The only way to be sure a wine will improve with age is to open a bottle and see what happens. Pour yourself a glass or two, and leave the rest of the bottle sitting out on the counter. If the wine tastes better the next day, it can improve with age; and the longer it continues to taste pleasing, the more likely it is to reward a few years of cellaring. But if the wine's flavour flattens or becomes less pleasant, drink it over the next few months.

HOW TO STORE WINE

For wine, the ideal storage conditions are like those found in a natural basement: dark and damp, still and chilly. A temperature range of 10–15°C (50–60°F) is ideal for wine's development, but since few people can afford a cellar or wine fridge, it may be necessary to compromise. Pantries and closets that don't get too hot or dry can work for laying wines away – ideally, sealed in boxes and laid on their sides on the floor. Natural corks shrink when they dry out, and this allows damaging air in. Storing bottles horizontally keeps them wet and plump, maintaining their protective seal.

Chapter Checklist

Here is a recap of some of the most important points you've learned in this chapter.

✓ An **average glass of wine** is 150 ml (5 oz), so a standard-size bottle holds about **five glasses**.

✓ Standard bottles hold **750 ml**. The most common size for box wines is **3 litres**, the equivalent of four standard bottles.

✓ Wine is delicious enough to drink from any vessel, but it tastes better served in specialized **wine glasses**.

✓ Wine glasses are designed to please your nose, their shape based on **swirling, sniffing, and maintaining** wine's temperature – all to enhance the scent of the wine.

✓ There are two reasons for **decanting**: to remove **sediment** in older reds; and to **aerate** and mellow younger wines.

✓ The flavour of wine depends on **volatile components** that are sensitive to temperature. This is why it is best to serve it at the most **flattering temperature** and maintain that while drinking, too.

✓ **Individual preferences** in wine temperature can vary greatly. Ultimately, you should drink your wine the way you like it.

✓ The only wines not routinely served cold are reds, because the tannins and other grape-skin compounds tend to seem more **astringent and bitter** at low temperatures.

✓ **Red wines** taste best at 15–21°C (60–70°F). All other wines – whether **white, rosé, sparkling, fortified, or dessert wines** – taste best at 4–10°C (40–50°F).

✓ Many wines can be kept quite a while before they **deteriorate**, but very few are **concentrated** enough to develop new flavours and smells to replace those lost over time.

NAVIGATING WINE BY STYLE

The huge number of wine options and impenetrable information on labels can be enough to make anyone's head spin. Our natural instinct is to study them one by one, but this is a losing strategy for beginners – there are simply too many wines out there. Rather than zooming in on what distinguishes one particular wine from the pack, it's far more useful to zoom out and learn about what all wines share in the big picture.

Grasping a handful of central wine truths can help even a wine novice visualize how wines relate to one another in sensory terms: in how they look, taste, smell, and feel in the mouth. For instance, grapes pass through predictable stages of development as they ripen, and not all wines are made from grapes of equal ripeness. Degrees of ripeness correlate with many sensory factors – from wine's alcohol content, or weight, to oakiness and acidity. This kind of expert-level insight is the key not only to making educated guesses about how different wines will taste but also to predicting how they will pair with various foods.

Labels can be
confusing, but
how wines
taste makes
perfect sense.

VISUALIZING WINE STYLE

The Ripeness Factor

One advantage wine professionals have over other wine drinkers is that they can picture how wines relate to one another in terms of how they taste, not just by their ingredients or regional provenance. The inherent biology of grapes and yeast limits the range of possible winemaking outcomes, creating consistent patterns in flavour profile that anyone can learn to recognize. A few basic insights into factors like how grapes ripen can help beginners make educated guesses about which wines will be lighter or heavier, milder or bolder, sweeter or drier, before they open the bottle.

The Wine Style Spectrum

Professionals know that there are clear and consistent patterns that govern wine style, and they use this knowledge to make educated guesses about how wines will taste before they open the bottle. You don't need to memorize dozens of grapes or regions to be able to use the same generalizations when you shop for wine.

Mapping wines by style

Navigating the wine world requires a sense of its range and boundaries. Wines can be loosely classified by their two most important power scales: weight and flavour intensity. Charting them on a classic grid can provide any wine drinker with expert-level insights into the big picture – into how wine styles relate to one another on a sensory level.

But why weight and flavour? Both are key sensory characteristics that are highly relevant to personal tastes and easy for beginners to identify. These traits correlate strongly with one another, as well as with other relevant wine qualities, such as acidity, oak, and tannin. Most importantly, though, they also have reasonably direct relationships with wine features that we can observe before we open the bottle, like colour and alcohol content.

Cracking wine's code

Charting wine styles by weight and flavour reveals some consistent patterns. Paler wines are often both lighter-bodied and milder in flavour than darker ones. White wine styles range more widely than reds. Pink rosé wines share territory with both whites and lighter red wines. Wines with bubbles are usually low in alcohol.

Such conclusions might seem banal, but just scratch the surface. Looking deeper into how wine styles relate to one another from a sensory perspective helps explain which factors have the greatest impact on relevant characteristics. These fundamentals help wine professionals navigate the wine world – and they can help you make more informed wine decisions, too.

CHARTING MAIN TRAITS

For the novice, it's very useful to picture where wines fall on a spectrum of style defined by wine's weight and flavour intensity. This provides a meaningful context for comparing wine options and for remembering how they taste.

WEIGHT

Heavier wines are:

Higher in alcohol • Richer in texture.
They are also often but not always:
Bolder in flavour • Given oak treatment • Aged before bottling • Lower in acidity • From warmer regions • May be fortified with distilled spirit

Lighter wines are:

Lower in alcohol • More sheer in texture.
They are also often but not always:
Milder in flavour • Unlikely to be given oak treatment • Bottled and sold young • High in acidity • From cooler regions • May be carbonated – sparkling or spritzy

FLAVOUR

Milder wines are:

More subtle in flavour and scent, often with herbal/earthy flavours • Rarely oaked.
They are also often but not always:
Lower in alcohol • Paler in colour • Bottled and sold young • High in acidity • From cooler regions

Bolder wines are:

More intense in flavour and scent, often with baked/spicy flavours • Often given oak treatment.
They are also often but not always:
Higher in alcohol • Deeper in colour • Aged before bottling • Lower in acidity • From warmer regions

Recognizing patterns in how wines taste and relate to one another can help us make informed decisions without getting bogged down in excessive details.

White wine
like Chardonnay
and Pinot Grigio

Sparkling wine
like Champagne
and Prosecco

Rosé wine
like Anjou
and Tavel

Red wine
like Shiraz
and Chianti

Fortified wine
like Port
and Sherry

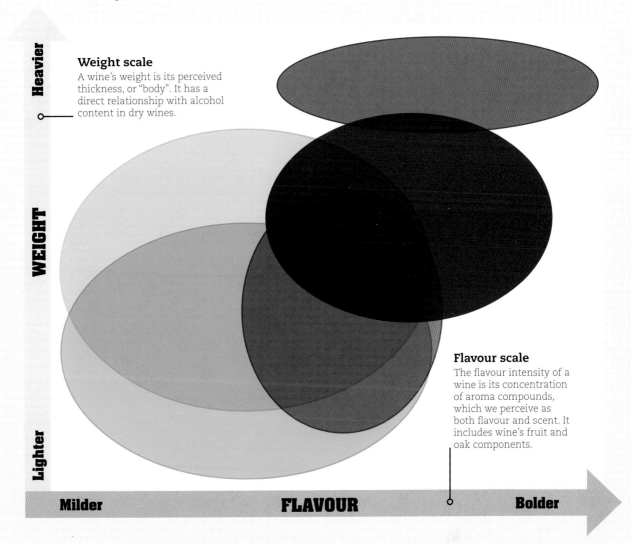

Weight scale
A wine's weight is its perceived thickness, or "body". It has a direct relationship with alcohol content in dry wines.

Flavour scale
The flavour intensity of a wine is its concentration of aroma compounds, which we perceive as both flavour and scent. It includes wine's fruit and oak components.

Heavier

Lighter

WEIGHT

Milder

FLAVOUR

Bolder

The Three Flavour Factors

Wines are often labelled by grape variety, but ingredients alone can't tell you how a wine will taste. There are two additional factors that can play just as strong a role in shaping wine's flavour and style.

Same grape; different taste

In any wine's taste, the type of grape is just a starting point that will be shaped and changed by two more powerful forces: the vineyard's ambient natural environment and human vintner's active interventions. Consequently, wines made from the same grape variety can taste very different when grown in different regions and made using different methods. The three variables that control how any given wine will taste are:

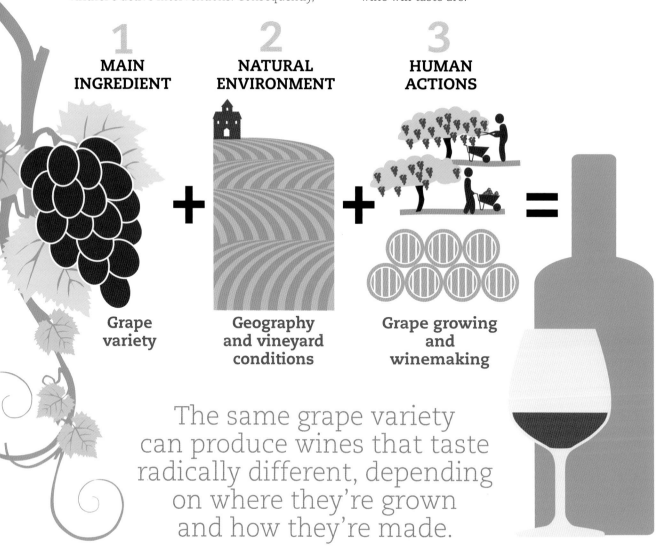

1

MAIN INGREDIENT

Grape variety

+

2

NATURAL ENVIRONMENT

Geography and vineyard conditions

+

3

HUMAN ACTIONS

Grape growing and winemaking

=

The same grape variety can produce wines that taste radically different, depending on where they're grown and how they're made.

Unexpected similarities

We latch on to grape varieties when we shop for wine because they are prominent on wine labels, but also because they seem to offer a clear-cut way to decode wine. However, navigating solely by grape doesn't take into account the other two flavour factors. For instance, Pinot Noir and Syrah make vastly different wines. However, a French Pinot Noir from Burgundy and a French Syrah from the nearby Rhône will resemble each other more closely than they would New World versions from California and Australia respectively. Common ground between the French wines in culture and climate will outweigh the family resemblance that is conveyed by the grape variety.

For similar reasons, a rich Chardonnay from California will be closer in flavour profile to Alsace Pinot Gris than it would to a lighter Chardonnay such as French Chablis simply because both Alsace and California are sunny and warm. Chilly Chablis produces wines with more in common with other cool-climate whites, like northern Italian Pinot Grigio.

All over the map
Wines from different grapes grown in nearby regions or similar climates often taste more alike than wines from the same grape grown in vastly different regions or climates.

THE TASTING
Identifying the Style Spectrum
Compare eight wines at home

Sample these four white wine styles and four red styles side by side, noting how they compare to one another in terms of body and overall flavour intensity.

VERY LIGHT, BOLDEST FLAVOUR	**LIGHTWEIGHT, MILD FLAVOUR**	**MID-WEIGHT, MEDIUM FLAVOUR**	**HEAVYWEIGHT, MEDIUM FLAVOUR**
1	**2**	**3**	**4**
MOSCATO D'ASTI	**PROSECCO**	**SAUVIGNON BLANC**	**BARREL-FERMENTED CHARDONNAY**

For example...
Italian, or Italian-style Moscato from Australia or California

About this wine
This outlier on the spectrum is made from an uncommonly aromatic variety. Moscato's unusual pungency leads to flavourful wines even at low levels of alcohol.

For example...
Look for sparkling Italian styles from the Veneto or Venezie

About this wine
A delicate, subtle-tasting, low-ripeness style – ideal for refreshing the senses in warm weather and daytime drinking.

For example...
Look for styles from the New Zealand region of Marlborough

About this wine
Noticeably richer in texture and more intense in aroma and flavour, thanks to greater ripeness and an aromatic grape variety.

For example...
Look for premium California styles from Sonoma County, Russian River Valley, Santa Barbara, or Carneros

About this wine
Opulently rich in mouthfeel, thanks to ample sunshine, and flavour-boosted with the help of toasty new oak barrels.

BODY

FLAVOUR

④ ⑧ ⑦ ⑥ ⑤③ ② ①

Wine lover's treasure map

Here, some popular wines are plotted on our chart of weight and flavour intensity. Where do your favourites fall: bigger and bolder, at top right; or milder and more refreshing, at lower left? As you encounter wines, visualizing how they relate to others in sensory terms will help you look beyond grapes and regions in exploring your personal tastes.

MID-WEIGHT, MEDIUM FLAVOUR

5

MID-WEIGHT, BOLD FLAVOUR

6

HEAVYWEIGHT, BOLD FLAVOUR

⑦

VERY HEAVY, BOLDEST FLAVOUR

⑧

For example...
Bourgogne (Burgundy), or similar styles such as Mercurey or Santenay
·····················

About this wine
This classic style is rather light and low in ripeness for a red, though mid-weight in the big picture, with restrained but seductive aromas.

For example...
Rioja Crianza, or similar but stronger Rioja Reserva
·····················

About this wine
Riper and stronger, but not much heavier in weight. The flavour intensity is amplified by a strong presence of new oak scent.

For example...
Premium Australian Shiraz from the Barossa or McLaren Vale
·····················

About this wine
Extreme flavour density and body for a non-fortified wine, thanks to exceptional ripeness in sun-drenched South Australia.

For example...
Portuguese Late-Bottled Vintage Port, or a Port-style fortified red California Zinfandel
·····················

About this wine
This outlier is spiked with distilled grape brandy, making for a potent wine with added alcohol that turbo-charges its heft and concentration of flavour.

Why Regions Trump Grapes

Wine characteristics such as colour, flavour, and alcohol content are almost direct reflections of the colour, flavour, and sugar content of the grapes used. Geography and climate affect the development of these traits in the vineyard as the fruit grows and ripens on the vine.

The sliding scale of ripeness

As a general rule, most wine characteristics grow stronger together, regardless of the grape variety used to make them. A few others tend to decrease in similar progression. This pattern relates directly to the amount of sun grapes get in the vineyard and its effect on the ripening process.

Weight increases

along with: Flavour intensity • Colour • Colour depth • Jammy, "baked fruit" flavours • Exotic, "spicy" flavours • Oak flavours • Tannin

Sparkling wine

White wine

Rosé wine

Red wine

Fortified wine

Acidity decreases

along with: Herbal, "green fruit" flavours • Outdoorsy, "earthy" flavours • Carbonation

Compared to grape varieties and winemaking, the sun has a more dramatic impact on grape ripeness and, therefore, on a wine's final style.

For red wines and heavier wines, grapes must be very ripe

Because their grapes need lots of sunshine and warmth, red wines and full-bodied wines tend to come from places that are very sunny, warm, and dry.

To maximize ripeness and flavour potential, vintners usually let the fruit hang on the vine as long as possible.

For white wines and lighter wines, grapes should not be too ripe

Since their grapes can suffer from too much sunshine and warmth, white wines and light-bodied wines more often hail from places that are cooler, cloudier, and more humid.

To avoid excessive ripeness and retain freshness, vintners often harvest the fruit earlier.

Ripeness: A Key Concept

There is no single idea as powerful as ripeness for explaining how the wine world works and predicting how different wines will taste.

From tasting "green" to tasting great

Ripeness is the final stage of fruit development, when it becomes ready to pick, with the right balance of flavours to taste fresh and delicious. Ripening shifts fruit from a hard, sour immature stage towards a sweet, juicy state, accompanied by a colour change from green to the fruit's proper colour. We use the word "green" to describe the tastes associated with underripeness – sourness, bitterness, and the leafy flavour of vegetables – even though some fruits, like Granny Smith apples or white grapes, are still green in colour when they are ripe and sweet. Plants get their energy from sunlight, through photosynthesis, so the degree of ripeness achieved by any fruit will depend on how much sun it gets in the final weeks before harvest.

MORE HOURS OF SUNLIGHT AND WARMTH

MANY SHADES OF RIPENESS

For winemakers, picking grapes at exactly the right moment is critical, because it locks the flavour profile of their raw material in place. Sugar content is the main consideration in deciding when to harvest, since it determines wine's potential alcoholic strength. However, many other components are also evaluated, such as the fruit's levels of acidity, flavour compounds, and tannins.

Technically, there is no single universal definition of "perfect ripeness" among

Moving targets
Many changes occur as grapes ripen. Their berries become bigger, softer, and juicier, tasting sweeter and less sour; their flavours shift from mild and vegetal to intense and fruity; and if they are of a purple variety, their skins deepen in colour.

ACIDITY

SWEETNESS

SKIN COLOUR

FRUIT FLAVOUR

The final phase of any fruit's growth is to become ripe – sweet and ready to eat.

winemakers, since each grape component responds a little differently to changes in geography, weather, and farming techniques. Grapes with as little as 18 per cent sugar would be considered fully ripe for Riesling grown in Germany's chilly Mosel, but not for California Cabernet Sauvignon, where anything under 24 per cent sugar would be seen as underripe. Also, winemakers can and do harvest earlier or later depending on what styles they want to make, picking earlier for white or sparkling wine to retain refreshing acidity, or

waiting longer for colour and flavour to develop in the skins when making red wines.

Luckily, wine drinkers do not need to adopt the winemaker's nuanced view of ripeness. For the purpose of navigating wine by style, you'll be better served making a useful generalization: think of the grapes used for lighter, cooler-climate wine styles like Riesling or Prosecco as being less ripe, and those used for heavier, warmer-climate styles like Cabernet Sauvignon or Port as being more ripe.

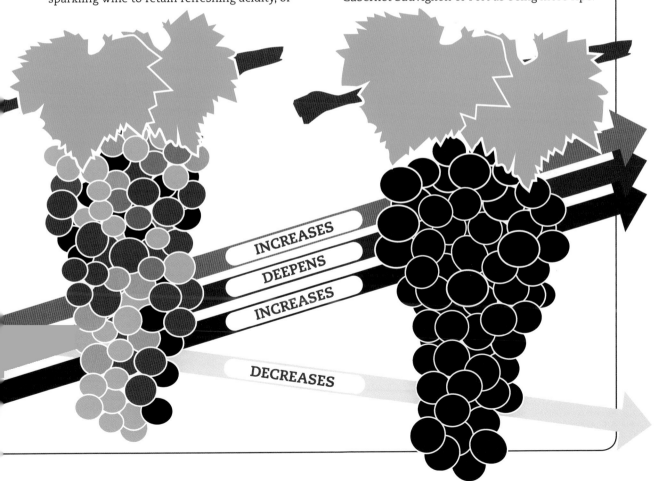

INCREASES

DEEPENS

INCREASES

DECREASES

Predicting Ripeness

It's often possible to deduce a wine's degree of ripeness from label clues like alcohol content, an essential step in cracking the code of the confusing wine world.

Give flavour a boost

Grapes that receive more sun become riper, which increases the overall sensory impact of their wine on multiple levels. Sweeter grapes produce wines with higher alcohol when they are fermented all the way to dryness. Such wines feel heavier in the mouth but also amplify flavour by definition. Riper grapes tend to taste stronger because they have more flavour compounds such as aromatic esters but also because alcohol vaporizes easily. Even at low temperatures, a little extra alcohol acts as a scent and flavour booster in wine, just as in perfumes. Greater ripeness also deepens the colour of red wines.

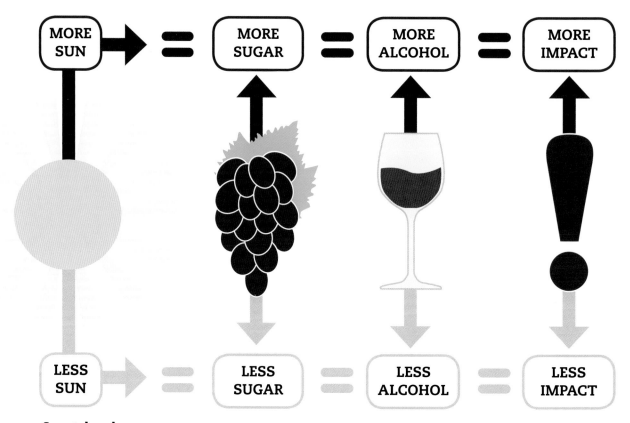

MORE SUN = MORE SUGAR = MORE ALCOHOL = MORE IMPACT

LESS SUN = LESS SUGAR = LESS ALCOHOL = LESS IMPACT

Secret decoder
One of the most useful pieces of information on any wine label is hidden in the small print. Alcohol content correlates well enough to many wine traits to serve as a rough style indicator.

BELOW 13%

WINES TYPICALLY FEATURE LOW-RIPENESS TRAITS:

Always lighter in texture
Usually higher in acidity
Often milder in flavour
Often paler in colour
Rarely oaked
May be carbonated

EXAMPLES:
French Champagne
Spanish Albariño
Italian Chianti

BETWEEN 13% AND 14%

WINES TYPICALLY FEATURE MODERATE-RIPENESS TRAITS:

Mid-weight in texture
Moderate in acidity
Moderate in flavour
Moderate in colour
May be oaked
Rarely carbonated

EXAMPLES:
Australian Chardonnay
French red Bordeaux
Oregon Pinot Noir

ABOVE 14%

WINES TYPICALLY FEATURE HIGH-RIPENESS TRAITS:

Always heavier in texture
Usually lower in acidity
Often bolder in flavour
Often deeper in colour
Often oaked
Rarely carbonated

EXAMPLES:
California Zinfandel
Argentinian Malbec
French Châteauneuf-du-Pape

What alcohol can tell you

In dry wines, where no grape sweetness is preserved, there is a nearly direct relationship between ripeness and alcohol content, and alcohol content must be listed on virtually all wine labels. We can predict a fair amount about how a given wine will taste just by knowing that 13.5% is the norm. We know that wines with higher alcohol will, by definition, be heavier in mouthfeel than average, but we can guess that they will also taste less tart and smell more intense and fruity due to greater ripeness. Dry wines with lower alcohol will usually be the reverse: lighter, milder, and more herbal.

The predictive power of alcohol content doesn't stop there. Some wine factors that are entirely under human control, such as degrees of oak and carbonation, are associated with higher or lower degrees of ripeness, and therefore alcohol content, for aesthetic reasons. The likelihood that a wine will be oaky increases greatly with higher-than-average alcohol, for example, while a lower-than-average alcohol level increases the chances of encountering carbonation. There are exceptions to these rules of thumb, of course, and wine qualities are least foreseeable in the crowded middle ground between 13% and 14%. But the patterns hold true enough to provide helpful guidance when wine shopping, and their predictive power becomes more ironclad the further alcohol levels deviate from the norm.

How Grape Varieties Fit In

The type of grape used to make wine is a major style factor. Each has its own unique characteristic and flavour profile. Some grape varieties are very distinctive, while others are less easily recognizable. Like different varieties of apples or mangoes, wine grapes will look different and taste different when fresh. But since all vines depend on sunshine and ripeness for their fruit's development, grapes are not always wine's sole flavour factor.

Organizing varieties

In the same way that children's personalities become more apparent as they grow older, grape varieties often resemble one another at very low ripeness, but grow more and more distinct as they get riper.

The traditional way to organize grape varieties is according to their native region – for example, Cabernet Sauvignon and Sauvignon Blanc

both come from Bordeaux in France and are genetically related, while Chardonnay and Pinot Noir come from Burgundy. This certainly helps us navigate wine lists and retail stores, but from the wine drinker's perspective, it can be more helpful to classify grapes according to sensory qualities, particularly similarities in their overall flavour and scent.

White grape varieties

Grapes with high flavour intensity are shown in **BOLD**.

APPLE FAMILY

CHARDONNAY
ALBARIÑO
PINOT BLANC/PINOT BIANCO
CHENIN BLANC
VIURA/MACABEO
GLERA/PROSECCO
VERMENTINO

FLORAL FAMILY

MOSCATO/MUSCAT
GEWURZTRAMINER
VIOGNIER
FIANO
MALVASIA

PINOT GRIGIO/
PINOT GRIS

TORRONTÉS
TOCAI FRIULANO

RIESLING

VERNACCIA
SEMILLON

SAUVIGNON BLANC
GRÜNER VELTLINER
VERDEJO
VERDICCHIO

HERBAL FAMILY

Examining white relationships

In white wines, there is a broad apple/pear resemblance between wines made from the most popular grape varieties; this is most obvious in the likes of Chardonnay and Pinot Grigio. But a few stand out with aromatics that are unusually distinct, like the leafy green scent of Sauvignon Blanc or the florality of Moscato. Some grapes combine elements of more than one family, such as Riesling, the charming appley flavours of which seem to incorporate a touch of both flowers and herbs, like jasmine tea. In general, the stronger a white wine's aromatics, the less likely it is to be barrel-fermented and overtly oaked. For white wines, winemakers use new oak like a chef uses spices: to add personality to wines that have a subtle neutral scent.

Most white wine grapes feature an apple-like flavour, but some project more intense scents, like flowers or green herbs.

Floral fragrances

Apple flavours

Leafy green scents

Examining red relationships

Despite higher flavour intensity, red grapes can be harder to categorize aromatically than white grapes. Where white wines have simpler scents, reds are more complex, and most feature a layer of oak to some degree. However, red wine grapes can be sorted into a few broad "families".

Most red wines smell of fruits with deep colours, such as berries and cherries. Many of the most popular grapes smell and taste most like the darkest black fruits – say blackberry or blueberry – as with Cabernet Sauvignon and Malbec. A smaller number, like Pinot Noir and Sangiovese, taste more like brighter red berries, with scents reminiscent of strawberry or sour cherry. While most red wines tend to

fall somewhere on the red fruit/black fruit continuum, some feature an unusual concentration of additional scents – appetizing aromas and flavours that don't register as fruit, like black pepper and star anise. Since these grapes make wines that smell like they've been seasoned from the spice rack, such as Syrah and Grenache, we'll call this the spiced-fruit family.

LEFT TO STEW
Red wines get most of their flavour from steeping with dark grape skins during winemaking, a process that leads to stronger flavours and scents than those found in white wines.

Red grape varieties

Grapes with high flavour intensity are shown in **BOLD**.

BLACK-FRUIT FAMILY

CABERNET SAUVIGNON
MERLOT
TEMPRANILLO
BARBERA
CARMENÈRE
MONTEPULCIANO
CORVINA
PETITE SIRAH

SPICED-FRUIT FAMILY

SYRAH/SHIRAZ
AGLIANICO
MONASTRELL/MOURVÈDRE
NERO D'AVOLA
NEGRO AMARO
PINOTAGE

MALBEC
ZINFANDEL

**GRENACHE/
GARNACHA**

NEBBIOLO

**CABERNET
FRANC**
SANGIOVESE

PINOT NOIR
DOLCETTO
GAMAY

RED-BERRY FAMILY

Many popular red wine grapes project dense black-fruit flavours, but some feature brighter red-berry scents or a spiced-fruit aromatic profile more prominently.

Spiced-fruit flavours

Black-fruit flavours

Red-berry flavours

Chapter Checklist

Here is a recap of some of the most important points you've learned in this chapter.

✓ Clear, consistent patterns govern **wine style**, and they can be used to make educated guesses about how a given wine will **taste**.

✓ A wine's taste is shaped by **three main factors**: the grape variety, the vineyard environment, and the impact of the winemaker.

✓ Wines from different grapes grown in **similar regions or climates** often taste more alike than wines from the same grape grown in very **different regions or climates**.

✓ Most wine characteristics grow **stronger** together, while a few others tend to **decrease** together. This relates to the amount of **sun** the grapes receive and its effect on the **ripening**.

✓ For red wines and **heavier wines**, grapes must be very ripe. For white wines and **lighter wines**, grapes should not be too ripe.

✓ **Ripeness** is the final stage of fruit development, when it becomes ready to pick and has the right balance of flavours to taste **fresh and delicious**.

✓ The ripening process shifts fruit from being hard and sour to a **sweet, juicy state**. There are also changes in colour and flavour as grapes get more sun leading up to the harvest.

✓ Winemakers do not all share the same notion of **"perfect ripeness"**. Each grape component responds differently to changes in geography, weather, and farming techniques.

✓ Riper grapes tend to taste stronger because they have more **flavour compounds** such as aromatic esters, but also because **alcohol vaporizes easily**.

✓ By knowing that **13.5% alcohol is the norm**, you can predict a fair amount about how a wine will taste based on its alcohol level.

THE WHITE WINE SPECTRUM

Exploring Beyond the Pale

White wines are incredibly diverse – they range from the most subtle Muscadet, to the most pungent Moscato; from the lightest, palest Riesling, to the heaviest Sherry, as dark as molasses. If we sort them by grapes and regions alone, as wine lists do, whites can seem like a disjointed and confusing category full of contradictions. But if we look at them from a different perspective, focusing on how they taste and relate to one another in sensory terms, clear patterns emerge. It becomes easier to explore and discover new wines to enjoy.

Mapping White Wines by Style

Visualizing the relationships between wine styles is a helpful way to find and follow patterns in the tastes of any given subset of wines. Taken together, factors like grape and region, climate and winemaking approach, can give us a sense of which wines are likely to have the most in common in terms of sensory traits and flavour profile.

Plotting for weight and flavour

The graph below reveals helpful patterns among popular white wines, assessed by approximate weight and flavour. Notice that wines placed lower or to the left are from cool regions, while heavier and more intense wines shown further up and to the right come from warmer places.

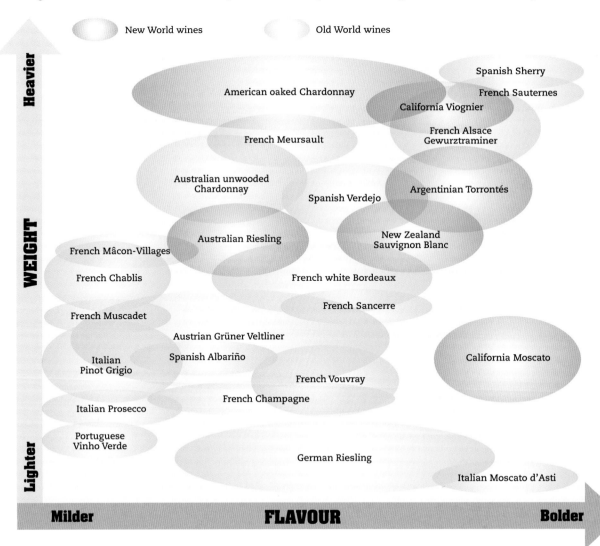

Ramping up flavours

Some grapes naturally taste more intense and distinctive than others, but sunshine and warmth develop flavours in all grapes as they ripen. Generally speaking, the lower a wine's alcohol content, the milder and more neutral its flavour is likely to be. With the exception of a few hyper-aromatic grapes, this is particularly true of whites, which can taste quite pleasant at very low degrees of ripeness.

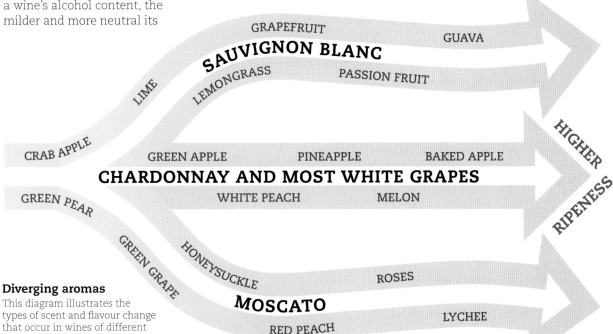

Diverging aromas
This diagram illustrates the types of scent and flavour change that occur in wines of different grape varieties as they ripen.

Underripe grapes all share similar flavours. Sun and ripeness bring out the unique character of individual varieties.

Becoming individuals

In colder regions or when harvested early, wines made from most white grapes share a similar low-ripeness aromatic profile, featuring mild, simple apple and pear flavours. Such wines also share other low-ripeness features – like low alcohol, high acidity, and absence of new oak flavours. As a result, these qualities almost always go hand in hand in the lower-left corner of the grid opposite.

When grapes achieve greater ripeness, either through warmer climate conditions or by delaying harvest, the individual aromatic personality of each variety becomes more apparent. Most white grapes get peachier and more tropical in flavour as they ripen, moving towards the top-right corner of the grid. Some may eventually reach a stage where their fruit tastes cooked or dried. Those varieties with the most distinctive aromatic character, like floral Moscato or herbal Sauvignon Blanc, get more intense with ripeness, too, but will progress in their own direction.

Chardonnay's Style Range

Chardonnay, the most popular wine grape on earth, is a great illustration of how wines made from the same variety can fall in different zones on the style chart. The primary controlling factor is the degree of ripeness, so geography and climate play a major role. However, winemaking decisions can further diversify the results, especially when flavour-boosting techniques are used.

Strength and weakness

Like many white wine grapes, Chardonnay is understated in flavour and scent, delivering familiar appley flavours that vary based on ripeness. Unlike most grapes, Chardonnay can provide wines of seductive texture with balanced acidity at radically different degrees of ripeness, making it capable of producing world-class wine in both the coldest and warmest wine regions. Its

greatest weakness is a relatively neutral flavour profile, so winemakers often add flavour to bring its aromatic intensity in line with its tactile richness. For still wines, barrel fermentation and aging add the toasty, dessert-spiced flavour of oak. For sparkling wines, a similar aging strategy is used, but with the winemaking yeast sediments, or lees, providing a bready, baked-goods flavour.

PURE CHARDONNAY FLAVOURS

CHARDONNAY PLUS OTHER FLAVOURS

Hot climate
American Napa Valley Chardonnay
• Very high ripeness (think apple pie plus toasty oak)
• Heavyweight, modest acidity, and baked-fruit flavour, with caramel and vanilla oak accents

Warm climate
South Australian unwooded Chardonnay
• Highish ripeness (think pineapple)
• Mid-weight, moderate acidity, and mild fruit flavour, with tropical and creamy accents

Cool climate
French Meursault
• Lowish ripeness (think golden apple plus toasty oak)
• Mid-weight, high acidity, and mild fruit flavour, with hazelnut and vanilla oak accents

Cold climate
French Chablis
• Very low ripeness (think green apple)
• Lightweight, very high acidity, and subtle fruit flavour, with herbal and chalky accents

Frigid climate
French Champagne
• Underripeness (think crab apple plus yeasty dough)
• Very lightweight, very high acidity, and subtle fruit flavour, with brioche and French-toast yeast accents

FLAVOUR BOOSTED BY NEW OAK BARRELS

FLAVOUR BOOSTED BY YEAST SEDIMENT

THE TASTING
Identifying Chardonnay's Stylistic Range

Compare three Chardonnays at home

Sample these wines side by side, paying special attention to which characteristics change as you move from colder to warmer wine regions and, therefore, from lower to higher degrees of grape ripeness within the same variety.

Contributory factors

These Chardonnays are plotted on the chart above according to their weight and flavour, which vary based on factors such as grape ripeness, winemaking practices, and cultural traditions.

LOW RIPENESS, NO OAK

FRENCH WHITE BURGUNDY

For example...

Chablis or other unoaked white Burgundy, such as Mâcon-Villages, Rully, or Beaujolais Blanc

Can you detect...?

Pale colour;
Very low sugar/very dry;
High acidity/tart;
Low fruit intensity;
No oak flavour;
Light to medium alcohol

MEDIUM RIPENESS, NO OAK

NEW WORLD UNOAKED CHARDONNAY

For example...

Australian unwooded or an unoaked New World option from California, Chile, or South Africa.

Can you detect...?

Pale colour;
Low sugar/dry;
Medium acidity/tangy;
Low fruit intensity;
No oak flavour;
Medium to high alcohol

HIGH RIPENESS, NEW OAK

NEW WORLD OAKED CHARDONNAY

For example...

Napa Valley Chardonnay or other barrel-fermented New World example over 14% from Sonoma, Monterey, Washington, Chile, South Africa, or Australia

Can you detect...?

Golden colour; Low sugar/dry;
Medium acidity/tangy; Medium fruit intensity; Overt oak flavour;
High alcohol

Exploring Lighter White Styles

Truly light-bodied wines are those with 12.5% alcohol or less – wines that are almost invariably white and consistently share a sheer, delicate mouthfeel. When dry, lightweight wines are made from low-ripeness fruit by definition, but many are lightly sweet wines in which fermentation was stopped to retain some sugar. However, fully sweet dessert wines are an exception: many are heavier than their alcohol would suggest.

If you enjoy these lighter white wines...

LIGHTWEIGHT, MILD FLAVOUR	LIGHTWEIGHT, MEDIUM FLAVOUR	LIGHTWEIGHT, BOLD FLAVOUR
①	②	③
FRENCH BRUT CHAMPAGNE	GERMAN MOSEL RIESLING	ITALIAN MOSCATO D'ASTI

About this wine

Sparkling wines are a speciality of cool regions, like Champagne in northern France. Their refreshing fizz and acidity, as well as their subtlety of flavour, are hallmarks of grapes of low ripeness, often a mix of both green- and red-skinned varieties.

About this wine

Mosel Rieslings are the lightest of the world's truly noble wines. Most feature very low alcohol and a sweet/tart flavour profile. Riesling is an aromatic variety producing wines that taste stronger as its grapes grow riper and sweeter.

About this wine

Moscato grapes are freaks of nature that deliver an uncanny perfume-like intensity of flavour at even modest degrees of ripeness. Asti styles are only partially fermented, so their grapes ripen further than alcohol alone might suggest.

Sheer delights

The lightest white wines typically feature high degrees of refreshing acidity, and the category includes almost all sparkling and semi-sparkling wines. Those that are driest tend to be mildest in flavour, because they are made with fruit of low ripeness. To acquire bolder flavours, lightweight wines must be made either from an aromatic grape variety, such as Moscato or Riesling, or in a lightly sweet style, where greater ripeness is achieved but not all grape sugar gets converted to alcohol – or sometimes both at once.

try these wines with similar sensory profiles.

LIGHTWEIGHT, MILD FLAVOUR

SPANISH CAVA

LIGHTWEIGHT, MEDIUM FLAVOUR

FRENCH VOUVRAY

LIGHTWEIGHT, MEDIUM FLAVOUR

PORTUGUESE VINHO VERDE ROSADO

About this wine

Catalan sparkling wines are made with native Spanish grapes but follow the methods pioneered in France for making Champagne. The resulting wines often feature less finesse but can deliver their own unique rich appeal and have more tempting price tags.

About this wine

The Chenin Blanc grape of Vouvray shares many of Riesling's distinctive traits. Grown in the chilly Loire Valley, it makes wines that are not as delicate as the Mosel's but are similar in sweet/tart balance and appley aromatic intensity.

About this wine

No other wine has Moscato's flavour profile, but its fans often enjoy these pink fizzy refreshers from northern Portugal. Milder in flavour and less overtly sweet, they are made from red grapes harvested while still "green".

Exploring Mid-Weight White Styles

Given the right growing conditions, any white grape can produce a mid-weight wine, and at least three out of every four white wines will fall into this category, over 12.5% alcohol but below 14%. This represents the natural range of dry wines from grapes of normal ripeness and includes styles that are very popular, thanks to their emphasis on refreshment and food-flattering qualities.

If you enjoy these mid-weight white wines...

MID-WEIGHT, MILD FLAVOUR

NORTHERN ITALIAN PINOT GRIGIO

MID-WEIGHT, MEDIUM FLAVOUR

FRENCH BOURGOGNE BLANC

MID-WEIGHT, BOLD FLAVOUR

NEW ZEALAND SAUVIGNON BLANC

About this wine

White wines are prized more for refreshment than richness in Italy, so this style is harvested early. The wines feature modest alcohol and snappy acidity as a result, as well as mild, understated flavours.

About this wine

Many popular white Burgundies feature a light kiss of toasty oak to supplement Chardonnay's subtle flavour. They are lighter and more understated than New World Chardonnays and are known for their finesse.

About this wine

Sauvignon Blanc is grown throughout the New World but most notably in this island nation. Its cool climate is perfectly suited for developing intense citrus and tropical flavours in this aromatic grape variety.

Happy medium

Being the most crowded of white wine categories, this is also the most diverse and the one where the grape variety plays the strongest role. Mid-weight wines are almost always dry and range from moderately tangy to very tart in acidity. Fruit flavour intensity in this category depends largely on the grape's aromatic power, but some wines are flavour-boosted during winemaking with oak or aging. A mild touch of new oak flavour from barrel fermentation is common for mid-weight Chardonnays but less so for wines made with other grapes.

try these wines with similar sensory profiles.

MID-WEIGHT, MILD FLAVOUR	**MID-WEIGHT, MEDIUM FLAVOUR**	**MID-WEIGHT, BOLD FLAVOUR**
SPANISH ALBARIÑO	**AUSTRIAN GRÜNER VELTLINER**	**ARGENTINIAN TORRONTÉS**

About this wine

This sophisticated white comes from Galicia on Spain's Atlantic coast and is tailor-made for seafood. It is similar to Pinot Grigio in body and subtlety, but it has sharper acidity and more fragrant aromatics.

About this wine

This Austrian grape is known for its "green" scents and vibrant acidity. Aromas of celery and white pepper distinguish the wines, which range from sappy, fruity refreshers to deluxe wines of substance.

About this wine

Rarely seen outside Argentina, the Torrontés grape makes wines that share the intensity of flavour and dryness associated with Sauvignon Blanc but smell more like floral Moscato.

Exploring Heavier White Styles

There are far fewer white wines than reds in the heavyweight category, at 14% alcohol or higher, because to reach this level they must be either made from hyper-ripe grapes or strengthened with distilled spirit. Chardonnays dominate the dry range of full-bodied whites, but this segment also includes most sweet dessert wines and all fortified whites, which can contain up to 20% alcohol.

If you enjoy these heavier white wines...

HEAVYWEIGHT, MEDIUM FLAVOUR

①

AUSTRALIAN OAKED CHARDONNAY

HEAVYWEIGHT, BOLD FLAVOUR

②

FRENCH ALSACE GEWURZTRAMINER

HEAVYWEIGHT, BOLD FLAVOUR

③

SPANISH MEDIUM SHERRY

About this wine

Chardonnays from sunny New World regions are often oaked – through barrel fermentation for premium wines, and oak chips for modest wines. This is warranted by the fuller body and greater ripeness routinely achieved in places like Australia.

About this wine

The sunny Alsace region's most aromatic wine is the peach-and-lychee-scented Gewurztraminer. Here, this grape makes lush, powerhouse wines with overtly floral flavours and uncommonly low levels of acidity.

About this wine

The world's strongest white wines are fortified Sherries from Andalusia in Spain. They are spiked with brandy, then flavour-boosted with yeast and oxidation in a unique aging process. Some are also sweetened with raisin syrup to complement their nutty taste.

Heavy hitters

White wines in this category always feature dense, rich texture but can range all over the map in sweetness – from completely dry, to syrupy sweet. Acidity is rarely high outside the finest wines. The near-direct connection between alcohol content and fruit flavour in wine naturally skews heavyweight wines towards the bolder end of the aromatic spectrum. Flavour intensity may be inherent to the grape in some cases but is more often amplified in the winery or vineyard – by fermenting in new oak barrels, for example, or using super-ripe, late-harvest fruit.

try these wines with similar sensory profiles.

HEAVYWEIGHT, MEDIUM FLAVOUR	HEAVYWEIGHT, BOLD FLAVOUR	HEAVYWEIGHT, BOLD FLAVOUR
SOUTH AFRICAN OAKED CHENIN BLANC	**CALIFORNIA VIOGNIER**	**PORTUGUESE RAINWATER MADEIRA**

About this wine

Few wines can deliver the one-two punch of alcohol and oak of Chardonnay without losing acidity and balance. Chenin Blanc can do it with grace in warm, dry regions, such as South Africa's coastal winelands, and some are lightly sweet.

About this wine

Viognier is a French grape from the Rhône region but is now more often grown in New World regions like California. Like a mash-up of Chardonnay and Gewurztraminer, it makes gorgeously luscious wines with effusive floral aromas.

About this wine

The tropical island of Madeira makes a unique fortified white wine with Sherry-like flavours that are intensified and caramelized by applying heat during aging. This uncommon technique gives the wine a sharply nutty taste.

THE RED WINE SPECTRUM

Exploring the Dark Side

There are just as many distinct and delicious red wine styles as there are white. However, the logistics of making red wines look red mean they have more in common with one another in terms of alcohol content and flavour intensity. Winemakers blend multiple grape varieties together more often in red wines than whites, making it even harder to decide what to drink. Luckily, a few key concepts can help wine drinkers anticipate what qualities they'll find in the glass – whether it's pure, pale Pinot Noir or inky, blended Cabernet Sauvignon; cool-climate Chianti or sun-loving Shiraz.

Mapping Red Wines by Style

There is no doubt that red wines have lots of personality and individual character, but they have less stylistic diversity than whites in terms of body and flavour intensity. A handful of whites can be as bold or heavy as the heftiest reds, but no red wines are as subtle or delicate as the lightest, mildest whites. Therefore, in discussing red wines, we'll focus on the upper right-hand quadrant of our style-plotting grid – red wine's bolder-flavoured, richer-textured territory.

Skins limit red wine range

The purple peels of dark grapes give red wines their colour, as well as the flavours that make red wines so aromatically diverse. However, the growing conditions needed to develop these compounds and the logistics of transferring them from the grape skins to the wine rule out the possibility of making as broad a range of red wine styles as we see in white.

• **Flavour Intensity** The same compounds in dark grape skins that supply colour in red wines also supply flavour. Since both come from the same source and can't be separated, wines that look red cannot taste as mild as whites can.

• **Weight** Purple grapes need more sun to ripen than green grapes. At the low degrees of ripeness that make truly light-bodied wines, the peels of dark grapes are low in colour and fruit flavour and high in bitterness and vegetal flavours. As a result, there is little commercial demand for red wines below 12.5% alcohol.

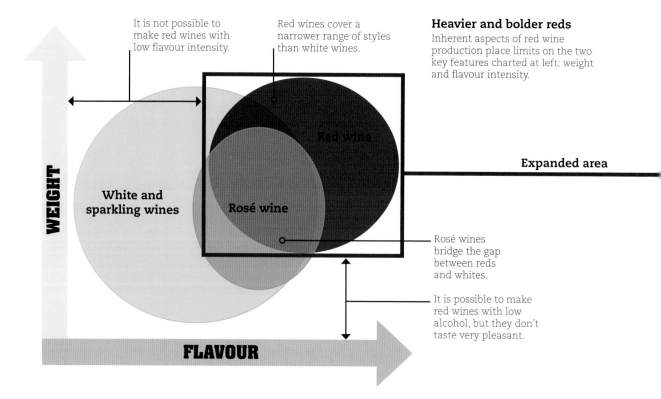

It is not possible to make red wines with low flavour intensity.

Red wines cover a narrower range of styles than white wines.

Heavier and bolder reds
Inherent aspects of red wine production place limits on the two key features charted at left: weight and flavour intensity.

Expanded area

WEIGHT

White and sparkling wines

Red wine

Rosé wine

FLAVOUR

Rosé wines bridge the gap between reds and whites.

It is possible to make red wines with low alcohol, but they don't taste very pleasant.

Plotting for weight and flavour

On the graph below, the relationships between key red wine styles are illustrated, with circles approximating their stylistic range. There are always exceptions, of course, with top wines often being heavier and more intense than the averages shown.

New World wines   Old World wines

Heavier

WEIGHT

Lighter

Portuguese Port

Italian Barolo

California Zinfandel

Spanish Priorat

California Cabernet Sauvignon

Australian Shiraz

Argentinian Malbec

Washington Merlot

South African Pinotage

French Bordeaux

Chilean Merlot

French Côtes du Rhône

California Pinot Noir

Spanish Rioja

Oregon Pinot Noir

French red Burgundy

Italian Chianti

Canadian Cabernet Franc

New Zealand Pinot Noir

Italian Valpolicella

German Spätburgunder

French Beaujolais

Italian Lambrusco

Milder   **FLAVOUR**   **Bolder**

Red Wine Flavour Progression

Red wines have more in common with one another in "big picture" traits like body and flavour intensity than whites. However, they tend to be more aromatically distinct because most grape flavour compounds are found in the peel, and only red wines are fermented with their skins (see pp.142–3). Much of the variation derives from the particular grape variety used, but the familiar pattern of ripeness also comes into play when considering red wines as a group.

Making educated guesses

The alcohol content of red wines is a better proxy for grape ripeness and associated characteristics than it is in whites because reds are more reliably fermented dry. The standard pattern – low-ripeness wines smelling more subtly of sour fruits and green herbs, and high-ripeness wines smelling more intensely of cooked fruit and dessert spices – is also more apparent because red wines taste stronger overall, and being served warmer amplifies their aromatics. The colour saturation of red wines is also an indicator of ripeness, reducing the need to rely on alcohol alone.

COMMON RED WINE SCENTS AND FLAVOURS

Many aspects of a wine go hand in hand. This diagram shows which general categories of scents and flavours are associated with different levels of ripeness in red wines, as well as how these correlate to other style factors.

LOWER RIPENESS — HIGHER RIPENESS

SOUR RED BERRIES	SWEET BLACK FRUIT	DRIED/COOKED FRUIT
HERBS	SPICES	DESSERTS

Associated with:
Alcohol below 13.5%
Colder wine regions
Traditional European wines

Often occur alongside:
High levels of acidity
Pronounced dryness
Low levels of new oak flavour
Harsh "green" tannins (think astringent tea)

Associated with:
Alcohol over 14%
Warmer wine regions
Modern New World wines

Often occur alongside:
Lower levels of acidity
Moderate dryness
High levels of new oak flavour
Velvety "soft" tannins (think plush hot cocoa)

Keeping it in the family

The most obvious common ground in red wine flavours is found in closely related grapes, such as the three main Bordeaux varieties. Recent genetic studies show a parent/offspring relationship between Merlot and Cabernet Franc, and that Cabernet Sauvignon's parents are Cabernet Franc and Sauvignon Blanc. Wines from these grapes share a leafy, vegetal flavour profile in cold regions and wet vintages but become easier to tell apart with more sunshine and ripeness.

Common scents
The smells and flavours of red wines change with ripeness, as shown for these five well-known grape varieties (above and below).

Uneven ripening

Not all grapes ripen alike. Even at their ripest, cool-climate varieties like Pinot Noir rarely achieve the same levels of flavour development routinely reached in warm-climate grapes like Shiraz.

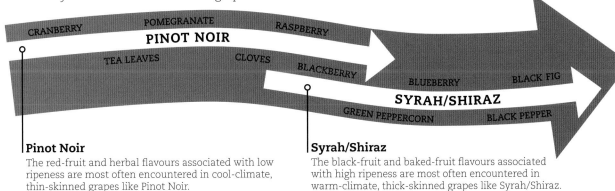

Pinot Noir
The red-fruit and herbal flavours associated with low ripeness are most often encountered in cool-climate, thin-skinned grapes like Pinot Noir.

Syrah/Shiraz
The black-fruit and baked-fruit flavours associated with high ripeness are most often encountered in warm-climate, thick-skinned grapes like Syrah/Shiraz.

Cabernet Sauvignon's Style Range

Wines made with Cabernet Sauvignon provide a great example of how and why winemakers often combine multiple grapes. Since this variety makes darker, more flavourful wines than most others, it is often used in blends. Cabernet Sauvignon reliably boosts wine's weight, flavour intensity, colour depth, and ageability, allowing vintners more creative control.

Bordeaux blends

Blending grapes is traditional in the Bordeaux region, where native Cabernet Sauvignon is most respected but its milder cousin Merlot is more widely planted. Cabernet Sauvignon struggles to ripen in cooler zones, making wine that is dark and strong but tannic. In sites with more ripening potential, such as Bordeaux's Left Bank, it can thrive and make wines that are even darker and stronger but taste more fruity and less harsh. Over centuries, vintners have adapted to this environment – using small amounts of Cabernet Sauvignon to intensify lighter Merlot-based wines in cooler sites and modest wines, and small amounts of Merlot to mellow the brute force of Cabernet Sauvignon in warmer sites and premium wines.

CABERNET SAUVIGNON CONTENT IN BLENDED WINE

Most wines labelled Cabernet Sauvignon are not 100 per cent Cabernet Sauvignon, because most wine-labelling laws require only 75–85 per cent of the named grape to be present. Only in the warmest, sunniest regions does this variety ripen thoroughly enough to be pleasing unblended.

Traditional Bordeaux blend – *modest*

A small proportion of Cabernet Sauvignon adds colour, body, and flavour without dominating. Typically it boosts lighter wines in cooler regions, as in Merlot-based Bordeaux but also many Tuscan and Spanish reds.

Traditional Bordeaux blend – *premium*

Cabernet Sauvignon is the primary ingredient but is partnered with grapes that can soften and flesh out its austere qualities. Many of the world's finest reds follow this model but cannot be labelled as Cabernet Sauvignon.

New World Cabernet Sauvignon blend

When this grape ripens more fully, it becomes more intense and less harsh, as is common in the Americas and the southern hemisphere. Blending is still the norm, but it is not always mentioned on labels.

Pure unblended Cabernet Sauvignon

Cabernet must reach a high degree of ripeness to taste balanced on its own, especially in a premium wine. The combination of its natural intensity and high ripeness makes for some of the world's most concentrated wines.

THE TASTING
Identifying Cabernet Sauvignon Traits
Compare three blended red wines at home

Sample these wines side by side, paying special attention to how characteristics change between them. While percentages of Cabernet Sauvignon will vary, they are likely to be higher in heavier wines from warmer regions, where grapes ripen more fully.

WEIGHT

FLAVOUR

Blending to control weight

In cool regions like its native Bordeaux, small amounts of Cabernet Sauvignon are typically used to strengthen a mid-weight wine. In sunnier regions, like Chile or California, the roles are often reversed.

UP TO 75% CABERNET SAUVIGNON

① FRENCH LEFT BANK BORDEAUX

For example...

Château wines from modest appellations like Graves, Haut-Médoc, Listrac, or Moulis

· ·

Can you detect...?

Medium colour; Very low sugar/very dry; High acidity/tart; Medium fruit intensity; Mild oak flavour; Medium alcohol/mid-weight; Rough tannic mouthfeel

UP TO 75% CABERNET SAUVIGNON

② CHILEAN BORDEAUX-STYLE BLEND

For example...

Blends where a grape variety is not named on the front label but where Cabernet Sauvignon is mentioned on the back label

· ·

Can you detect...?

Dark colour; Low sugar/dry; Medium acidity/tangy; High fruit intensity; Mild oak flavour; High alcohol/heavy; Softer velvety mouthfeel

MORE THAN 75% CABERNET SAUVIGNON

③ AMERICAN SONOMA CABERNET SAUVIGNON

For example...

A premium Sonoma appellation, like Alexander Valley or Knights Valley, or other California sources, like Napa Valley

· ·

Can you detect...?

Very dark colour; Low sugar/dry; Medium acidity/tangy; Very high fruit intensity; Strong oak flavour; High alcohol/heavy; Softer velvety mouthfeel

Exploring Lighter Red Styles

Since very few red wines are truly light-bodied, those that we think of as "lighter" in style tend to be those below 13.5% alcohol – a touch stronger than the range for lightweight whites. Outside some niche wines for entry-level audiences, vintners overwhelmingly ferment their red wines to dryness. This results in a fairly consistent relationship between alcohol content and ripeness among reds and fewer sweet exceptions.

If you enjoy these lighter red wines...

LIGHTER WEIGHT, MILDER FLAVOUR	LIGHTER WEIGHT, MEDIUM FLAVOUR	LIGHTER WEIGHT, BOLDER FLAVOUR

① FRENCH BEAUJOLAIS-VILLAGES

② ITALIAN CHIANTI

③ AMERICAN OREGON PINOT NOIR

About this wine

The Beaujolais district of Burgundy is known for its very light red wines made with Gamay grapes. Gamay has uncommonly low tannin, so its wines are among the few reds that taste pleasant chilled.

About this wine

This popular Italian red is made primarily with Sangiovese grapes, known for their high levels of acidity and tannin. While everyday Chianti may see little or no aging, the finest are stronger, more intense, and often aged longer.

About this wine

Pinot Noir makes wines that are lighter and paler than the average red but are some of the world's most sought after. Known for its seductive aromatics and silky texture, red Burgundy's noble grape thrives in cool regions like coastal Oregon.

WEIGHT

FLAVOUR

On the bright side

Almost all lightweight reds are from cool climates, where lower-than-average grape ripeness is the norm. They generally feature elevated acidity and bright flavours that lean towards the red-berry and herbal end of the aromatic spectrum. Many are young value-oriented wines that spend little or no time in barrels to preserve fruity freshness. But premium wines are likely to be oak-aged, just as for heavier reds. When vintners want to retain light sweetness or obtain lower alcohol, they usually opt to make rosé instead of red.

try these wines with similar sensory profiles.

LIGHTER WEIGHT, MILDER FLAVOUR

④

FRENCH
TAVEL ROSÉ

LIGHTER WEIGHT, MEDIUM FLAVOUR

⑤

PORTUGUESE
DOURO

LIGHTER WEIGHT, BOLDER FLAVOUR

⑥

SPANISH
RIOJA

About this wine

To find wines as slurpable as Beaujolais, it's best to look to rosé wines like those made in the south of France. These medium-bodied Grenache-based blends are dry, with a flavour profile that is closer to red wine than white.

About this wine

Few regions produce red wines with enough acidity and tannin to rival Italian reds, but northern Portugal is one to watch. Douro wines are dry reds made in the same district as Port and from the same mix of native grapes.

About this wine

Spain's Tempranillo grape often makes denser, darker wines, but in cool Rioja its wines have a brighter, Pinot Noir-like appeal. The region's tradition of barrel aging results in some of the oakiest of lighter red wines.

Exploring Mid-Weight Red Styles

The middle ground in red wines encompasses the majority of reds and skews a little stronger than in whites, with most containing between 13.5% and 14.5% alcohol. The modern consumer's preference for rich, flavourful reds leads vintners to shoot for this weight range, which has become the "new normal" only in recent decades. A century ago, the average red wine was considerably lighter than it is today.

If you enjoy these mid-weight red wines...

MID-WEIGHT, MILDER FLAVOUR	MID-WEIGHT, MEDIUM FLAVOUR	MID-WEIGHT, BOLDER FLAVOUR
① CHILEAN MERLOT	② FRENCH CÔTES DU RHÔNE	③ FRENCH BORDEAUX

About this wine

Merlot is often overshadowed by its famous cousin Cabernet Sauvignon. Softer and fruitier, it nonetheless makes some of the world's finest red wines. Merlot thrives in Chile's sunny climate, where it grows riper than in its native Bordeaux.

About this wine

Grenache grapes dominate the blend in these flavourful Mediterranean wines, providing their signature flavours of strawberries and white pepper. The region's stronger premium wines are named after their villages, like Châteauneuf-du-Pape.

About this wine

All but the mightiest red Bordeaux fall in the mid-weight category. It can be hard to tell whether they contain more Merlot or more Cabernet Sauvignon, but all are known for being lean, dry, and flavourful, with herbal aromatic accents.

WEIGHT

FLAVOUR

World of difference

Mid-weight reds are the most diverse, because so many grapes and appellations contribute to this popular category. Most are dry wines, but they can be all over the map in aromatic character, colour depth, and degree of oak flavour. A fairly consistent pattern of distinctions can be found, however, between most Old World styles and those from the New World. In general, the driest wines that are most austere, earthy, and acidic tend to come from Europe, while those from elsewhere more often feature riper, more dessert-like flavours, as well as more overt oak (see Chapter 10).

try these wines with similar sensory profiles.

| **MID-WEIGHT, MILDER FLAVOUR** | **MID-WEIGHT, MEDIUM FLAVOUR** | **MID-WEIGHT, BOLDER FLAVOUR** |

④

ITALIAN BARBERA

⑤

ITALIAN MONTEPULCIANO D'ABRUZZO

⑥

SPANISH RIBERA DEL DUERO

About this wine

Barbera from Piedmont used to be known as light, tart, fish-friendly reds. Some are still made the traditional way, but many are now ripened longer and aged in barrels, resulting in a richer and more intense blackberry-scented wine.

About this wine

Fans of Côtes du Rhône will find that these wines from Italy's Adriatic coast share many Rhône traits. They are modestly priced wines that deliver generous flavour and texture and a touch of rusticity, without feeling heavy.

About this wine

Tempranillo is Spain's most noble grape. It ripens brilliantly on the arid plains of Castilla that line the Duero river, making some of Spain's most age-worthy red wines, which see French-style aging in new oak barrels.

Exploring Heavier Red Styles

Red wines must reach higher alcoholic strength than whites to be heavyweight contenders: typically 14.5% alcohol or more. For standard wines, grapes must achieve uncommonly high ripeness to reach this level, from either very warm vineyards or by hanging extra-long on the vine. But this category also includes fortified red wines, the alcoholic strength of which is enhanced with added brandy – strong, sweet Port, for example.

If you enjoy these heavier red wines…

HEAVIER WEIGHT, BOLDER FLAVOUR

① PREMIUM AUSTRALIAN BAROSSA SHIRAZ

HEAVIER WEIGHT, BOLDER FLAVOUR

② PREMIUM AMERICAN NAPA VALLEY CABERNET SAUVIGNON

MUCH HEAVIER WEIGHT, MUCH BOLDER FLAVOUR

③ PORTUGUESE PORT

About this wine

Thick-skinned Shiraz, aka Syrah, can make wines of epic intensity in regions like South Australia's Barossa and McLaren Vale. These inky wines have potent aromas of jam, bacon, and black pepper.

About this wine

Cabernet Sauvignon makes some of the world's most intense and long-lived red wines. The heaviest examples come from sun-drenched New World regions like California and feature flavours such as mocha and cassis liqueur.

About this wine

The world's heaviest red wines are the fortified dessert wines of Portugal's Douro Valley. Spiked with distilled spirit mid-fermentation, they taste like a delicious mix of red wine, fresh grapes, and grappa.

WEIGHT

FLAVOUR

Ripe old age-worthy wines

Heavyweight reds are naturally concentrated in flavour, and many are premium wines. Since high-alcohol reds tend also to be high in tannin and flavour compounds, these wines often require time in barrels, and many are released years after the harvest. Flavours lean towards the black-fruit to baked-fruit range in this category, reflecting the taste of hyper-ripe fruit. Many wines feature spiced aromas such as pepper, cocoa, or clove, some derived from the grapes and others from maturation in new oak barrels.

try these wines with similar sensory profiles.

HEAVIER WEIGHT, BOLDER FLAVOUR	HEAVIER WEIGHT, BOLDER FLAVOUR	MUCH HEAVIER WEIGHT, MUCH BOLDER FLAVOUR

④

PREMIUM ARGENTINIAN MALBEC

⑤

PREMIUM SPANISH PRIORAT

⑥

AUSTRALIAN TAWNY

About this wine

Argentina's arid Mendoza plateau flanks the Andes at high elevation and makes intense red wines from the French Malbec grape. Premium bottlings can be blockbusters, with flavours of blueberries, five-spice, and violets.

About this wine

This Catalan appellation is a treasure trove of ancient Garnacha and Cariñena vines that can make wines with an incredible concentration and power. Often blended with Syrah and Cabernet Sauvignon, they feature flavours of figs and anise.

About this wine

Australia, as a British colony, was weaned on fortified Ports and Sherries and has a strong tradition of making delicious "stickies" – strong, sweet dessert wines. Tawny is an aged style with russet colour and nutty, caramelized flavours.

MATCHING WINE AND FOOD

The Sommelier's Secrets

Wine is an excellent food partner, like a special sauce on the side, and most foods taste better with wine than with other drinks. For everyday meals, aligning your wine with the time of year or time of day is enough. But for real wine-and-food harmony, thinking like a sommelier can help you match recipes with flattering wines. Professionals know that the ways a dish are seasoned and cooked are often more important than its main ingredient. Discover some surprising quirks of sensory science that will change how you think about pairing wine and food.

What to Drink When

Outside of fine dining and fancy dinner parties, it's rarely necessary to worry about pairing specific wines to specific foods. Choices based on factors such as time of day and time of year often make more sense than trying to tailor a wine to a particular dish. The season affects what we're likely to be eating anyway, and most meals combine all sorts of diverse foods, whether served for lunch or dinner.

WHITE WINES ON WARM DAYS

Wines that deliver refreshment and can be served chilled fit the bill in summer for the same reason we wear shorts and eat salads: they help us cool off.

Offset weather with wine

The same factor that has such a dramatic impact on wine style has a strong influence on our wine cravings. We instinctively seek lighter, younger wines (usually chilled) while the sun is up or the weather is hot. And when the sun goes down or the temperature drops, stronger, more complex wines make us feel warm and cosy.

Drinking aged, full-bodied wines – particularly reds served at room temperature – is the beverage equivalent of pulling on a sweater. Essentially, bold, strong warm-climate wines provide a little bottled sunshine that has the power to banish a wintry chill, while light, brisk cool-climate wines help us beat the heat.

WHEN THE SUN IS HIGH OR THE WEATHER IS WARM

WE TEND TO CRAVE WINES THAT ARE:

Lighter
Lower in alcohol
Younger and fresher-tasting
Lower in oak flavour
Served colder
Paler in colour

Simple young sparkling wines,
like Italian Prosecco

Crisp unoaked whites,
like New Zealand Sauvignon Blanc

Light refreshing "chillable" reds,
like French Beaujolais

Pale, brisk fortified wines,
like Spanish Manzanilla Sherry

WHEN THE SUN GOES DOWN OR THE WEATHER IS COOL

WE TEND TO CRAVE WINES THAT ARE:

Heavier
Higher in alcohol
Mature and complex-tasting
Higher in oak flavour
Served warmer
Deeper in colour

Complex aged sparkling wines,
like French Champagne

Rich barrel-fermented whites,
like California Chardonnay

Strong, flavourful "warming" reds,
like Australian Shiraz

Opulent, jewel-toned fortified wines,
like Portuguese vintage-style Port

Matching on many levels

Most wines taste great with most foods, so it's hard to go too far wrong: taking cues from the season, time of day, and degree of formality is usually all that's necessary to improve wine-and-food harmony. However, when the occasion calls for something special, borrow a few pairing strategies from wine professionals to tilt the odds in your favour.

Consider which types of wine offer similar flavours or textures and so might harmonize with your meal's main ingredient. Paying attention to seasoning and cooking methods allows sommeliers to create pairings in which both the wine and food magically seem to taste better together than they did apart. You don't need encyclopedic wine knowledge to get there; all you need is a little insight into how our senses work when wine and food interact.

PLAYING WITH MATCHES

GOOD

Everyday occasions
Suitability for event, based on season and time of day

BETTER

Home entertaining and dining out
Basic matching to main ingredient

BEST

Sommelier-style refinements
Pairing to specific recipe, based on food chemistry

Pairing Wine with Main Ingredients

When choosing a specific wine to go with a certain meal, most people have excellent natural instincts. Successful wine pairings are based on the same principles that lead us to drink lemonade with summer salads or espresso with chocolate desserts. Pairing wines that share similar sensory qualities with the food being served – light with light, rich with rich – is a very effective way to find mutually flattering combinations.

Match weight and texture

The lightest foods, like delicate shellfish, usually taste best with the lightest wines, such as sparkling whites, while the heaviest foods, like red meats, usually taste best with stronger, heavier wines, like intense reds. Both fat in food and alcohol in wine register as texture in the mouth; fatty meats and high-alcohol wines both seem thicker and heavier than low-fat seafood and low-alcohol wines.

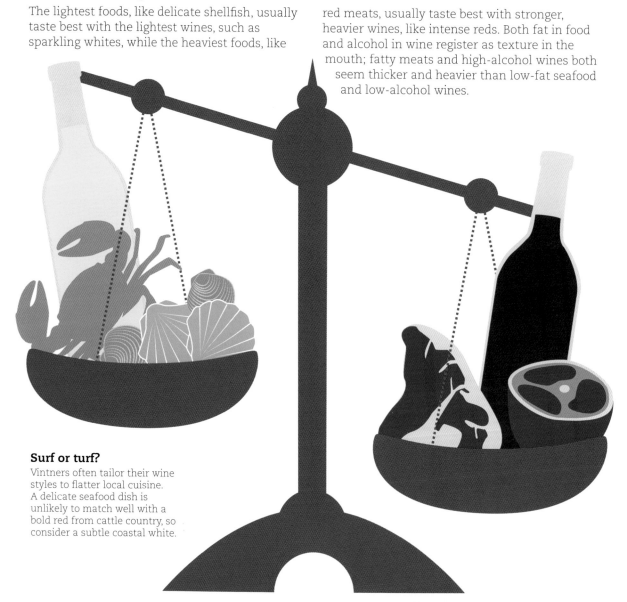

Surf or turf?
Vintners often tailor their wine styles to flatter local cuisine. A delicate seafood dish is unlikely to match well with a bold red from cattle country, so consider a subtle coastal white.

WHY IS MATCHING FLATTERING?

When we drink wine with our dinner, it's a balancing act in which the food and wine both compete for our attention. Sticking to drinks of similar weight and flavour density levels the playing field, like organizing wrestlers by weight class. When one is heavier or tastes stronger than the other, it can detract from our appreciation of the lighter partner, and the dining experience as a whole suffers. The ideal is for neither element to overpower the other, allowing their flavours to mix and mingle on equal terms.

Match flavour intensity

Understated foods with mild flavour, like oysters or omelettes, generally taste best with mild white wines, such as Muscadet or Pinot Grigio. Foods that are higher in flavour intensity, like smoked salmon or blue cheese, tend to taste better with wines of similar aromatic amplitude, like Gewurztraminer or Cabernet Sauvignon.

Match colour depth

Absence of colour tends to signal low flavour intensity, while deep colour tends to coincide with high flavour impact (though there are exceptions, of course). Think of the difference in flavour power between flounder and tuna, chicken and duck, or veal and venison. Foods with minimal colour, like goat's cheese or scallops, tend to taste best with transparent white or sparkling wines, while foods with intense colour saturation, like lamb or chocolate, tend to taste better with red wines.

MILD FLAVOURS
Sushi;
Noodles

LIGHT COLOURS
Goat's cheese;
Scallops

BOLD FLAVOURS
Sausages;
Curries

STRONG COLOURS
Lamb;
Chocolate

Think flavour; think colour
Consider the main ingredients, and think about which wine styles might have a broad resemblance in terms of weight, flavour intensity, or colour.

Pairing Tricks of the Trade

Compared to wine, the foods we eat are far more complicated: more ingredients and recipe combinations lead to more possibilities. If we want to choose a wine for a particular meal, it helps to understand how foods relate to one another in weight and flavour intensity, in the same way that we assess wine styles.

Assess how foods relate

Thinking about how foods relate to one another allows us to predict which wines will best suit any given meal. Between core proteins and side dishes, sauces and garnishes, though, it can be hard to know where to focus. And in a restaurant, everyone at your table may be eating a different dish, so it helps to think in terms of dominant features and cuisine styles.

Lighter or heavier?

When we look at menu items in restaurants or recipes in cookbooks, we instinctively consider their "weight". We might want something light, like a salad, or something heavier, like a steak. Regardless of portion size, fat content is the main feature that drives perceived weight in food. The mouth-coating richness of fats and oils gives food added texture in the same way alcohol makes wine feel heavier.

Milder or bolder?

Flavour intensity is something we think about less often, but it plays a major role in personal taste. Some foods are inherently more flavourful than others. Tomatoes have a stronger taste than cucumbers, for example, while chicken tastes milder than lamb.

Mapping foods and wines by weight and flavour intensity can help you identify those with similar qualities.

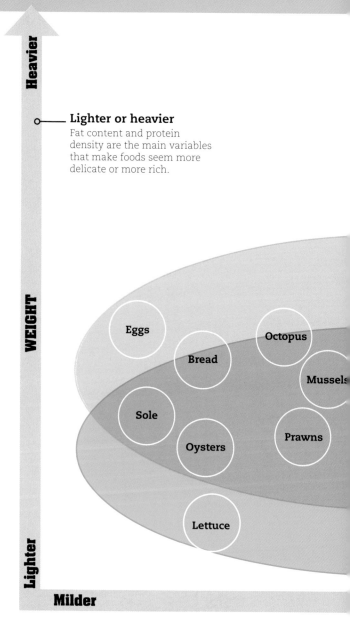

Lighter or heavier
Fat content and protein density are the main variables that make foods seem more delicate or more rich.

Heavier

WEIGHT

Lighter

Milder

Eggs

Bread

Octopus

Mussels

Sole

Oysters

Prawns

Lettuce

Factor in the recipe

Cooking methods and seasonings often boost flavour and enrich texture, which can push any of the items on the chart below higher or further to the right. (The items on the chart are only examples, and it should not be considered an exhaustive list.) Chicken will feel heavier if fried, and bolder if grilled, than it would if it were steamed. The seasonings, sauces, and marinades associated with Thai cooking consistently add a spicy-sweet flavour boost, regardless of whether they are added to prawns or beef.

White wine
like Chardonnay
and Pinot Grigio

Sparkling wine
like Champagne
and Prosecco

Rosé wine
like Anjou
and Tavel

Red wine
like Shiraz
and Chianti

Fortified wine
like Port
and Sherry

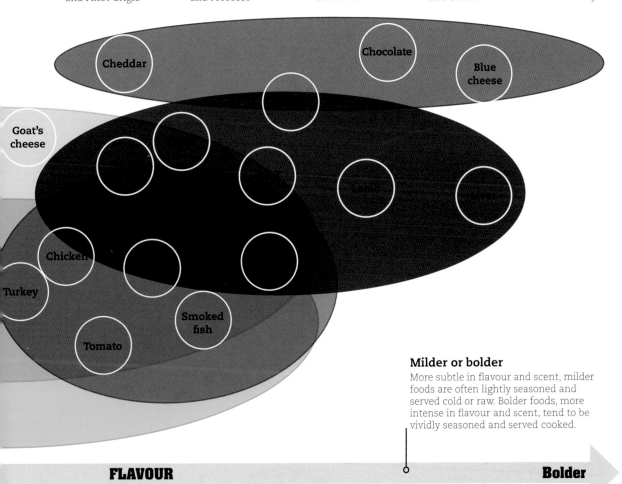

Cheddar

Chocolate

Blue
cheese

Goat's
cheese

Lamb

Chicken

Turkey

Smoked
fish

Tomato

Milder or bolder
More subtle in flavour and scent, milder
foods are often lightly seasoned and
served cold or raw. Bolder foods, more
intense in flavour and scent, tend to be
vividly seasoned and served cooked.

FLAVOUR

Bolder

Pairing Wine to Specific Recipes

While matching by main ingredient works reasonably well, it is possible to take your wine-pairing skills to the next level by learning a few tricks of the trade. Professional sommeliers almost always rely on the "like with like" strategy for making pairing recommendations, but they achieve better results because they take it a step further.

Match to strongest flavours

Wine drinkers usually work around main ingredients when choosing wine – for example, picking a Pinot Grigio for scallops or a Cabernet Sauvignon for beef. Sommeliers pay more attention to overall flavour. If the recipe is tangy or herbal or smoky or sweet, they will generally choose wines with similar flavour profiles, regardless of the main ingredient. They look beyond the protein at the heart of a dish and consider how the recipe makes it look, taste, smell, and feel in the mouth.

PRO MATCHING
When sommeliers match wine and food, they assess the total sensory experience of each dish, including how it's cooked, sauced, and seasoned.

EVERYDAY MATCHING BY INGREDIENT

Scallops are delicate and pale.
*Pair them with delicate white wines,
like Italian Pinot Grigio.*

Beef is stronger dark-red meat.
Pair it with heavier red wines, like
California Cabernet Sauvignon.

SOMMELIER-STYLE MATCHING BY PREPARATION

Scallop ceviche is tangy, citrusy, and herbal.
*Pair it with a tangy, citrusy, herbal white wine,
like New Zealand Sauvignon Blanc.*

Beef carpaccio is raw and barely seasoned.
*Pair it with a young, refreshing white wine with
subtle flavour, like Spanish Albariño.*

Seared truffled scallops are rich,
earthy, and caramelized.
*Pair them with a rich, toasty, earthy white wine,
like French Meursault (Chardonnay).*

Steak au poivre is dark,
intense, and peppery.
Pair it with an inky-purple, black-pepper-scented
red wine, like Australian Shiraz.

Match oaked wines to browned foods

The distinctive flavour of new oak in wine has a strong similarity to the flavours found in foods that have been browned during cooking. Roasting, frying, or grilling a chicken breast will deepen its colour and intensify its flavour in a way that steaming or boiling will not. Aging or fermenting wine in new oak barrels can add a similar set of flavours and scents, since wood is "toasted" in the barrel-making process. The aromatic resemblance between browned foods and barrel-aged or barrel-fermented wine provides them with a natural affinity.

Colour matching
In general, foods that are raw or cooked without browning pair best with wines that are young, unoaked, and fresh. Foods that are browned in cooking – roasted, grilled, or sautéed, for example – tend to be better with oakier wines.

Lighten up a little

In restaurants, wine is not the star of the show. Wines are designed to work in a supporting role to highlight the food. Just as background harmonies shouldn't obscure a lead singer's melody, wine shouldn't interfere with our ability to appreciate a chef's handiwork.

Lighter, milder wines are more forgiving food partners. Not only do they pair pleasantly with lighter, milder foods, but they can also provide a palate-cleansing counterpoint even when outmatched by heavier meals. Strong, intense wines may taste impressive alone, but their forceful traits can get in the way when paired with food, unless the dish is equally hearty and flavourful.

Lighter, milder wines
If you are looking for a wine that will "go with anything", something lighter and milder is the safest bet. For sommeliers, the rule of thumb is, "When in doubt, pair Champagne."

Food Chemistry

Sommeliers know that seasonings in food can skew our sensory perceptions of wine in predictable ways. Salt and sugar in particular can significantly alter how we perceive the tastes of acidity and sweetness in any wine served alongside our meals.

Salt: Dry wine's friend

Salt is present in most things we eat, and we tend to add more in cooking because it helps emphasize other flavours. Salt blocks our ability to discern acidity in wine, and wine returns the favour by blocking perceived saltiness in the food without compromising overall flavour.

Wines need to taste a little too acidic alone to taste just right with most foods. In fact, one reason wines are so tart is that winemakers know they will be drunk with salted food. Tart wines designed to taste their best in this context – like Italian Chianti or French Sancerre – are often called food-oriented wines.

Sugar: Dry wine's enemy

Also a universal flavour enhancer, sugar is less wine-friendly than salt. Sweet food makes wine taste far more sour than it seems alone. Since wine is naturally tart, the result is usually unflattering, like the shocking sourness of orange juice after brushing your teeth.

A wine needs to be at least as sweet as a dish to avoid this problem. Foods with faint sweetness are far kinder to fruity modern wines than to drier styles. Overt sweetness, as found in fruit-based sauces, works well with lightly sweet wines like Riesling. Fully sweet desserts call for sticky-sweet dessert wines.

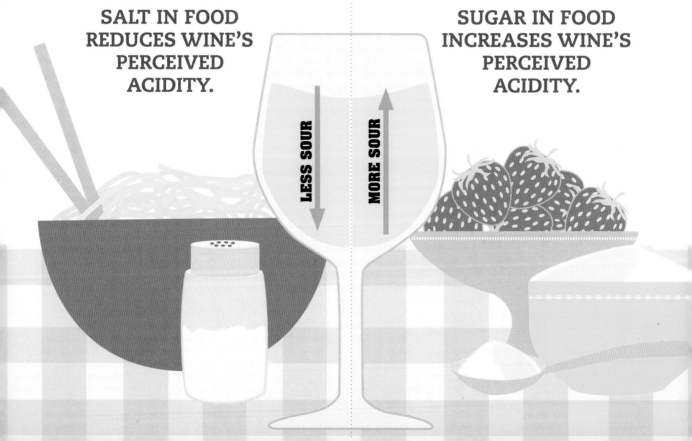

SALT IN FOOD REDUCES WINE'S PERCEIVED ACIDITY.

LESS SOUR

MORE SOUR

SUGAR IN FOOD INCREASES WINE'S PERCEIVED ACIDITY.

THE TASTING
Identifying the Effects of Salt and Sugar
Compare two wines at home

Prepare a glass of each of the wine styles below.

1 Sample the wines, paying special attention to first impressions of sweetness and acidity.

2 Taste a pinch of salt, and taste the Sauvignon Blanc again after it dissolves. Note how the perception of acidity is significantly reduced, making the wine seem softer and fruitier.

3 Repeat step 2 with the Riesling. Notice how the same acid-blocking effect takes place and that suppressing acidity makes it seem a little sweeter.

4 Wait 5 minutes to allow your taste buds time to recover, then repeat step 1.

5 Taste a dab of honey, and sample the Sauvignon Blanc again. Note how the acidity is amplified, making the wine seem extremely sour and one-dimensional.

6 Repeat step 5 with the Riesling. Notice how the same acid-boosting effect takes place but that the wine now seems significantly less sweet than it did alone or after salt. The honey's sweetness overpowers the wine's, making it seem much drier.

FRENCH SAUVIGNON BLANC

For example...
Bordeaux Blanc, Sancerre, Pouilly-Fumé, or Touraine

By itself, notice...
Low sweetness/very dry; High acidity/very tart

After salt, notice...
Marginally less dry; Dramatically less acidic

After honey, notice...
Marginally less sweet; Dramatically more acidic

AMERICAN RIESLING

For example...
Styles from Washington State's Columbia Valley or California that do not say "dry" on label

By itself, notice...
Medium sweetness/lightly sweet; Medium acidity/tangy

After salt, notice...
Marginally sweeter; Dramatically less acidic

After honey, notice...
Dramatically drier/less sweet; Dramatically more acidic

Seasonings other than salt and sugar

Most sensations don't "add up" to seem stronger together; they balance and neutralize each other as our senses adjust. Sights and sounds seem most vivid when isolated, and any competing stimulus reduces their perceived intensity – that's why we can hear a whisper in a quiet room but must shout to be heard in noisy restaurants. The same holds true for most tastes, smells, and textures, but we are much less likely to notice the pattern.

In sensory perception, 1 + 1 ≠ 2.

We don't turn on the lights to see the TV better, because two competing light sources make each other seem dimmer. A similar neutralizing effect takes place when wine and food share a dominant feature.

Sensory adjustment

When wine and food share a similar sensory characteristic, your senses adjust and perceive both as weaker together than they were apart. The result is nearly always pleasant and harmonious, allowing us to apply the broad "like with like" approach to tastes, smells, and textures across the board.

Not only do we pair light with light, and heavy with heavy, but we can also pair tart with tart, oaky with smoky, and sweet with sweet, with terrific results. This effect is usually most obvious and immediate with taste-bud sensations.

Tangy foods – tomatoes or pickles, say – and tart wines – like Chianti or Sauvignon Blanc – will seem *less* acidic together, not more acidic.

Sweet foods – such as fruit salad or crème brûlée – and sweet wines – like Riesling or Sauternes – will seem *less* sweet together, not more sugary.

A similar pattern occurs with many olfactory and tactile perceptions, too, though less vividly:

FINE DINING IS NOT AN EXTREME SPORT

Sommeliers often recommend wines that share a dominant feature with the food that is being served. The goal is to deliberately allow these strong features to tone each other down – that is, not to exaggerate the shared trait but to help it melt into the background in a pleasing way. Pairing wine and food is not like watching movies or going to rock concerts, where isolating and amplifying sensations can push the envelope to thrilling extremes. Harmony between wine and food is almost always about seeking comfort and balance.

Spicy-heat exception

"Like with like" is a sound pairing strategy, but it doesn't work for spicy foods and "spicy" wines. The same word may be used for both, but it describes very different qualities. Foods that are spicy trigger a physical sensation of burning, like that of hot chillies, whereas wines that are spicy have intense aromatics that resemble spices or seasonings, like those of peppery Syrah. Since wine aromatics come mainly from grape skins and intensify with ripeness, the wines with the spiciest flavours are most often red and full-bodied.

Sommeliers tend to avoid heavier reds with spicy heat and, more often, recommend lightly sweet white and rosé wines with low alcohol – an Italian Moscato or German Riesling, for example.

Spicy heat in food and high alcohol in wine amplify each other's dominant features instead of balancing and neutralizing. Alcohol acts as an irritant that briefly makes the burn of spicy food seem more intense and painful, like rubbing salt into a wound. And full-bodied wines seem heavier and more alcoholic when tasted after eating something spicy, too. Neither effect is flattering.

DOWNPLAY THE SPICE!
The high alcohol level of heavy wines can make them painful to drink with foods that have a piquant kick, so avoid pairing them with the hottest spicy dishes.

Upping the ante
Low-alcohol wines tame the "flames" of spicy food and soothe the senses, while heavier wines seem to turn up the heat.

Spicy heat in food

High alcohol in wine turns up the heat

THE TASTING
Identifying Sensory Competition
Compare four wines and four foods at home

Try this simple taste test at home to get a clear idea of how your senses operate when they encounter competing sources of similar sensation.

1 Sample all the wines alone first, paying special attention to your first impressions of their sweetness and acidity, fruit and oak flavour, and body and tannin.

2 Take a bite of fresh tomato, then retaste wine 1. Notice how eating something equally tangy makes the wine seem less tart than it did alone, not more acidic.

3 Retaste wine 2; then take a bite of smoked almond, and taste it again. Notice how eating something roasted or smoked with an equally woody flavour makes the wine seem less oaky than it did alone, not more so.

4 Retaste wine 3 both before and after a dab of butter. Notice how tasting something equally rich and heavy makes the wine seem lighter than it did alone, not heavier.

5 Retaste wine 4 before and after a bite of dark chocolate. Notice how eating something equally sweet makes the wine seem less sweet than it did alone, not more sugary.

6 Wait 5 minutes to allow your taste buds to recover from all this stimulation.

7 Retaste any combination of wine and food in the same before-and-after format. You should notice two things:
a) the effects of tongue-based tastes, like sweetness and acidity, are more dramatic than olfactory and tactile sensations; and
b) the food items generally seem most harmonious with the wines that most resemble them in taste, smell, or texture.

1 YOUNG ITALIAN SANGIOVESE

2 TEMPRANILLO-BASED SPANISH RESERVA

For example...
Chianti Classico or any young, modestly priced Tuscan Sangiovese-based wine that is less than three years old

For example...
Rioja Reserva or any *reserva*-level Spanish Tempranillo-based wine, such as Ribera del Duero or Toro

On its own, you should detect...
Low sweetness/very dry;
High acidity/very tart;
Medium fruit intensity;
Low oak flavour;
Mid-weight;
Medium tannin

On its own, you should detect...
Low sweetness/dry;
High acidity/tart;
Medium fruit intensity;
High oak flavour;
Mid-weight;
Medium tannin

Make it less acidic
Acidic foods like tangy tomatoes, citrus, or vinegar will make wine tasted alongside seem dramatically less acidic.

Make it less oaky
Smoked almonds or other foods with roasty, cooked flavours will make wine tasted alongside seem much less oaky.

3

PREMIUM
NEW WORLD
CABERNET
SAUVIGNON

For example...

Chilean, or any
premium Cabernet
Sauvignon-based wine
from the Americas or
southern hemisphere
....

**On its own, you
should detect...**

Low sweetness/dry;
Medium acidity/tangy;
High fruit intensity;
High oak flavour;
Heavy;
High tannin
....

Make it less heavy

Fatty foods like dairy
products or meats
will make wine tasted
alongside seem
noticeably lighter.

4

FORTIFIED
RED DESSERT
WINE

For example...

Portuguese Port or any
sweet, fortified dessert
red wine over 15%
alcohol, such as
Australian Tawny or
French Banyuls
....

**On its own, you
should detect...**

Very high sweetness;
Mild acidity/soft; Very
high fruit intensity;
Variable oak by style;
Fortified/very heavy;
Medium tannin
....

Make it less sweet

Sweet foods like candy,
desserts, or fruit will
make wine tasted
alongside seem
dramatically less sweet
and more acidic.

Chapter Checklist

*Here is a recap of some of the most important
points you've learned in this chapter.*

✓ Don't worry about pairing **specific wines
to specific foods**. It is often better to make
choices based on such factors as **time of
day and time of year**.

✓ **Lighter, younger wines** (usually chilled) are
ideal in hot weather, while **stronger, more
complex wines** are perfect for cooler seasons.

✓ The most flattering combinations come when
you pair wines with **similar sensory qualities**
as the food being served: light with light, and
rich with rich.

✓ Match wine and food according to **intensity of
flavour or depth of colour**, and you'll get it
right more often than you might expect.

✓ **Seasonings and sauces** often influence a
dish's flavour more than the main ingredients,
and this is key to how sommeliers work,
assessing the **total sensory experience** of
each dish – even down to the cooking methods
used – to find the best wine match.

✓ Generally speaking, raw foods and foods
cooked without browning match best with
young, fresh, unoaked wines. Browned foods –
roasted, grilled, or sautéed, for example – tend
to work better with **oakier wines**.

✓ When in doubt, pair **Champagne**.

✓ **Salt and sugar** in a dish alter your perception
of acidity and sweetness in any **accompanying
wine**. Salt in food reduces wine's perceived
acidity; sugar increases wine's perceived acidity.

✓ **"Like with like"** is a sound pairing strategy;
however, spicy foods don't work with so-called
spicy wines. These **big, bold reds** seem to
magnify the **fiery burn** of a dish, while low-
alcohol white wines **soothe** the senses.

MASTERING WINE VARIABLES

Wine is an incredibly complicated consumer product, even when we have a few rules to guide us. Wine labels emphasize grapes and regions, brands and vintages, but none of these spells out how a wine will taste. It can feel like they're written in code. Wine beginners often wish they knew more about each wine – the proportions of the blend, or the number of months it ages in barrels – but that's rarely helpful information. Imagine watching a complicated sport for the first time: you can't make sense of what's happening on the field by learning the players' names, positions, or stats. First, you must learn the rules of the game.

Experts know that a short list of variables shapes wine's flavour, such as vineyard climate and winemaking decisions. This lets them make useful generalizations. For the wine novice, it's more fruitful to get acquainted with how these controlling factors work than it is to get bogged down in brand-specific details. There will always be exceptions, of course, but discovering tasty surprises is what keeps wine interesting.

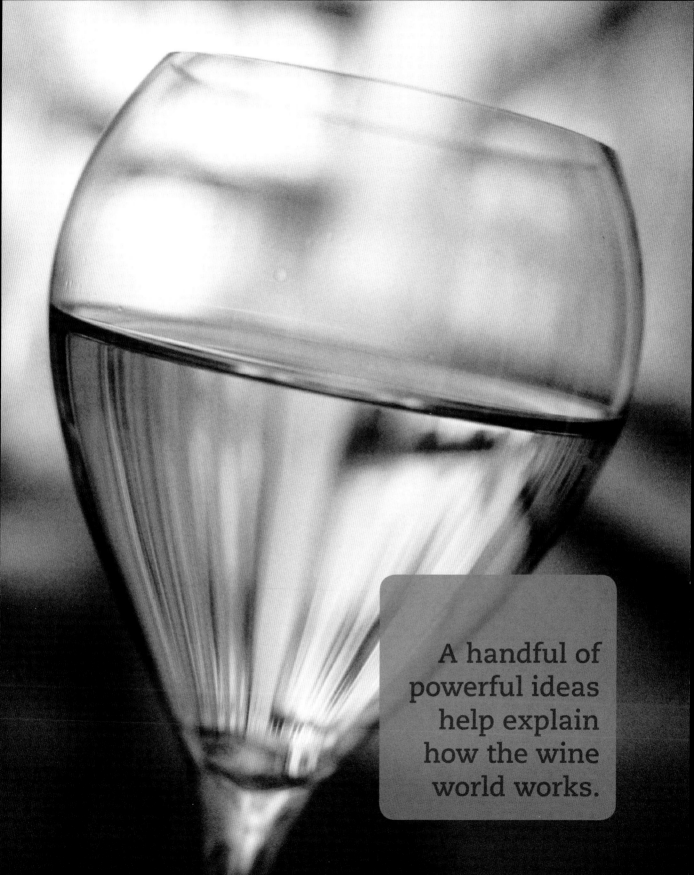

A handful of
powerful ideas
help explain
how the wine
world works.

WINEMAKING DECISIONS

Sweetness, Colour, and Oak

A vineyard's climate may control its potential for ripening fruit, and grape varieties may have distinct flavour profiles, but these are only wine's raw materials. Human decisions at the winery also play a major role in a wine's flavour. Like a chef given fresh ingredients, the winemaker decides what to do with them – whether to make sweet wine or dry, red wine or white, wine that is fresh and unoaked or barrel-aged and refined. By manipulating the winemaking process, he or she can also turn the grapes into sparkling wine with bubbles or fortified wine with extra alcohol.

Fermenting Grapes into Wine

Wine is produced through fermentation, a process in which living yeasts convert sugar into alcohol. In fresh foods, this natural occurrence is the first step on the road to spoilage. However, for thousands of years, mankind has taken control of the fermentation process – and not only for making wine and beer. Fermentation turns flour into bread, milk into cheese, and cocoa beans into chocolate. Think of yeast as the magic pixie dust that transforms simple fresh grapes into much more complex, flavourful wine.

Sugar breakdown

Many types of yeast occur naturally in our environment, particularly those of the sugar-eating *Saccharomyces* genus that is used in baking, brewing, and winemaking. These yeasts consume sugar and break it down into alcohol and carbon dioxide (CO_2). Fermentation always begins spontaneously, thanks to the presence of wild yeasts in the vineyard and winery. Nowadays, though, many modern vintners prefer to inoculate with cultured yeast strains for more predictable results.

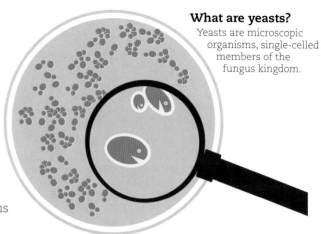

What are yeasts?
Yeasts are microscopic organisms, single-celled members of the fungus kingdom.

EQUATION OF ALCOHOLIC FERMENTATION

Alcoholic drinks begin with fermentation, where living yeasts consume and metabolize sugar, converting it into alcohol. It also generates carbon dioxide, heat energy, and flavours and aromas.

RAW MATERIAL

Sugar

+

FERMENTATION AGENT

Yeast cultures

=

XXX

Alcohol (ethanol)

Flavours from beyond the grape

Wines smell and taste of far more than just grapes. During fermentation, countless smaller chemical reactions are triggered, adding new flavours and scents that may not have been present or detectable in the fruit.

Fermentation is what makes wine so aromatically complex and enjoyable, much the way it does for cheeses. The unique flavours of French Brie, Wisconsin Cheddar, and Italian Gorgonzola derive from fermentation and aging, not from their raw material (cow's milk). Yeast significantly alters the flavours and scents found in fresh grapes, too.

CHOCOLATY OR PEPPERY WINE?

Exotic terms are often used to describe non-grape aromatics in wine, usually by naming other fruits, foods, or spices they resemble. These are not ingredients, though; they are simply metaphors to describe wine's diverse scents.

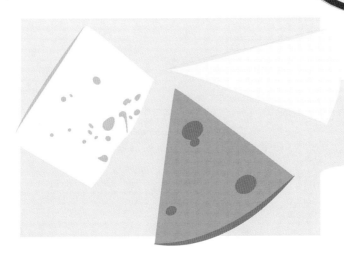

Importance of cultures

Just like cheesemakers, vintners choose their yeast strains carefully to exert control over how the finished wine will taste and smell.

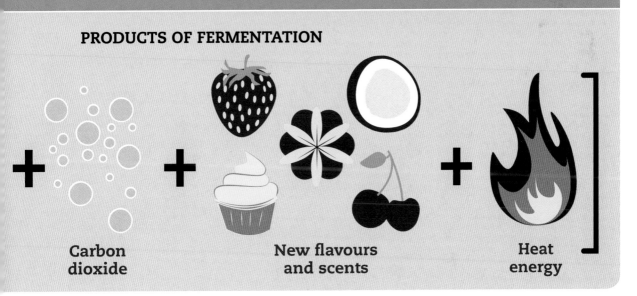

PRODUCTS OF FERMENTATION

+ **Carbon dioxide**

+ **New flavours and scents**

+ **Heat energy**

Controlling Sweetness

Grapes are sweet, but most wines are not, and the historic reason for this is entirely practical: early winemakers wanted to increase alcohol and reduce sugar to prevent spoilage. Sweet wines and low-alcohol wines are most susceptible to microbiological decay, whereas more alcoholic wines that are drier – that is, less sweet – have a longer shelf life.

Sugar/alcohol balance

Wines are traditionally fermented dry, because this has been the easiest way to make wine for thousands of years. Once fermentation begins, yeasts feed and reproduce until their sugar supply is depleted, and it is difficult to halt the process prematurely.

Sugar is potential alcohol
Sugar's primary role in winemaking is to be converted into alcohol. Most wines are dry, not sweet, especially those with more than 13% alcohol.

Sweet grape juice — Fermentation — Dry wine

Lightly sweet wines / Fully dry wines

18% sugar / 0% alcohol

10% alcohol / 3% sugar

Sugar (%) / **Alcohol (%)**

Sweet winemaking dreams

Sweet wines may be outnumbered, but they have always been desirable because they taste delicious. Most European wine regions have developed their own methods for making sweet wines, each an adaptation to their environment.

Modern technology now makes these wines more stable than ever. Most follow one of three winemaking strategies, each of which can make wines that range from lightly sweet "off-dry" wines to candy-sweet dessert wines.

Method 1: Stop fermentation early

Cold   Alcohol

Yeast

Interrupting the yeast life cycle can preserve some natural grape sugar. There are two main options.

(a) Reduce temperature
Yeasts slow and die in near-freezing conditions. Retaining sugar this way means sacrificing potential alcohol, so the sweetest wines will have the lowest alcohol content.

Examples: lightly sweet Rieslings and rosés; fully sweet Italian Moscatos

(b) Add distilled spirit
Yeasts cannot tolerate alcohol over 15%, so fortifying wine with brandy can stop fermentation.

Examples: fully sweet Portuguese Ports; French Vin Doux Naturel Muscats

Method 2: Concentrate grapes before fermenting

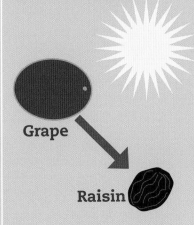

Grape

Raisin

Reducing the water content of grapes increases the proportion of all that remains, including sugars, acids, and flavour compounds. In warm regions, grapes may be sun-dried after the harvest; in cooler zones, delaying harvest is more common. "Late-harvest" grapes shrivel and concentrate on the vine, yielding rich, sweet wines. In cold climates, grapes may hang until midwinter, freeze-concentrating remaining juice.

Examples: sun-dried Italian Vin Santo and Spanish Moscatel; late-harvest French Sauternes and German Auslese; freeze-concentrated Austrian Eiswein and Canadian Icewine

Method 3: Sweeten the wine after fermenting

Sugar

Wine

Many bargain wines that aren't fully dry are made by blending small amounts of grape juice (or concentrate) into a dry wine. Many fine sweet wines are also made by variations on this theme. Most use grapes as their sugar source, but some – like *demi-sec* Champagne – use cane sugar.

Examples: German Liebfraumilch (grape juice); French Champagne (cane sugar); Spanish Cream Sherry (raisin syrup); Hungarian Tokaji Aszú (late-harvest grapes)

THE TASTING

Identifying Stages of Fermentation

Compare grape juice and wine at home

All wines start as sweet grape juice, such as example 1, and most end up as dry wines with no perceptible sugar but plenty of alcohol, like example 4. However, winemakers can interrupt the fermentation process to make a sweeter wine. Wines 2 and 3 are made by disrupting fermentation.

1 Sample these four drinks side by side. As you do so, consider how fermenting with yeast changes grape juice into wine.

2 Pay particular attention to the palpable variations in sweetness and body as the wines grow heavier in weight.

3 Notice that the presence or absence of sugar and alcohol are not obvious when smelling but become very apparent on the palate when you take a sip.

> Most wines are fermented fully dry, but vintners sometimes stop fermentation early to retain grapey sweetness.

1

WHITE GRAPE JUICE

Sugar

For example...
Any mass-produced juice, or squeeze your own
· ·

Contains
100% table grapes
    18% sugar (approx)
    0% alcohol (approx)
· ·

Can you detect...?
Very sweet;
Very tart;
Grapey scents and flavours
· ·

Explanation
Grape juice is the sweetest of all fruit juices, which is why it is ideal for winemaking. Wines made from other fruits are lower in alcohol and have a shorter shelf life. Wine is rarely made from the kinds of table grape used for juice and jam, but they are similar enough in sweetness to help us picture the raw material vintners use to make white wines.

2

SPARKLING MOSCATO

Ferment halfway; stop by chilling

3

FORTIFIED DESSERT MUSCAT

Ferment halfway; stop by adding brandy

4

DRY MUSCAT

Ferment completely, depleting all sugar

For example...

Italian Asti or any sweet, sparkling Moscato that contains less than 10% alcohol.

....

Contains

100% Moscato (aka Muscat)
5% sugar (approx)
7% alcohol (approx)

....

Can you detect...?

High sugar/fully sweet; High acidity/tart; High fruit intensity; No oak flavour; Low alcohol/ light; High carbonation

....

Explanation

Fizzy sweet Moscatos taste like what they are: a halfway point between grape juice and wine. Such wines are made by stopping fermentation before it is complete, leaving lots of grape sugar unfermented and sacrificing potential alcohol. Their bubbles are a natural by-product of fermentation.

For example...

Muscat de Beaumes-de-Venise, Muscat de Minervois, or Muscat de Frontignan

....

Contains

100% Moscato (aka Muscat)
15% sugar (approx)
15% alcohol (approx)

....

Can you detect...?

High sugar/very sweet; Low acidity/not refreshing; High fruit intensity; No oak flavour; High alcohol/ heavy; No carbonation

....

Explanation

This is a fully sweet style in which fermentation is interrupted before grape sugars are depleted – but through a different method. Adding distilled spirit mid-fermentation kills off the yeasts, creating a sweet, strong liqueur-like dessert wine.

For example...

French Alsace Muscat or any Muscat labelled "dry" from Australia or the USA. Alternately, Argentinian Torrontés. (Do not choose French Muscats labelled *vendange tardive, sélection de grains noble,* or *vin doux naturel.*)

....

Contains

100% Moscato (aka Muscat)
0.5% sugar (approx)
13% alcohol (approx)

....

Can you detect...?

Low sugar/dry; High acidity/tart; High fruit intensity; No oak flavour; Medium alcohol/ mid-weight; No carbonation

....

Explanation

Fermented to dryness, leaving no significant residual sugar, most dry wines do not taste at all sweet. They usually have at least 12% alcohol, which prevents spoilage.

Determining Colour and Style

White and red wines are typically made with different types of grape, but this isn't the source of the biggest differences in how they taste. White and red wines are made using two completely different processes.

Two wines, two methods

Consider following two recipes with the same ingredients: tomatoes, onions, and peppers. Peeling the tomatoes and chilling the mixture creates a delicate gazpacho that retains a garden-fresh taste without any bitterness from the skins. Keeping the tomato skins on and simmering the mixture changes the result dramatically, yielding a thicker, stronger-tasting pasta sauce. Grapes behave similarly. Making white wine involves eliminating grape skins and preserving the fresh taste of the juice through refrigeration; making red wine involves grape-skin contact and controlled heat to extract as much colour and flavour as possible.

The red method

Red wines taste stronger and more "bitter", like the peels of grapes.

This is because red wines are made from whole grapes, including skins, seeds, and pulp. Red wine can only be made from dark-skinned grapes, because the skins are their source of colour and flavour.

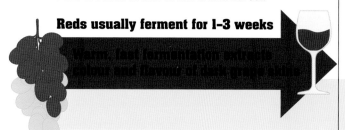

Reds usually ferment for 1–3 weeks

Warm, fast fermentation extracts colour and flavour of dark grape skins

Fermented warm and fast

Vintners harness the heat generated during fermentation to help extract colour and flavour compounds from grape skins, and astringent antioxidant tannins come along for the ride. Warmth speeds the yeast life cycle, so red wines ferment to dryness quickly and vigorously, generating more of the chemical reactions that create new flavours and scents that weren't present in the grapes.

The white method

White wines taste milder and more "juicy", like the flesh of grapes.

This is because white wines are made from grape juice only – skins, seeds, and pulp are all discarded. Only clear juice is used in white-wine making. All grape solids, including the colourful skins, are removed before fermentation begins.

Whites usually ferment for 2–6 weeks

Cold, slow fermentation preserves fresh taste of clear grape juice

Fermented cold and slow

Winemakers use refrigeration to preserve the delicate flavour of the milder grape juice. Without grape-skin antioxidants present, they must also shield the juice from air in sealed tanks or barrels to prevent oxidation. Chilling slows the metabolism of yeasts, so fermentation proceeds much more gently. The rate of chemical reactions that generate new aromatic compounds is significantly reduced.

Reds, whites... and a bit of both

A critical distinction between wine styles is when their grapes are pressed, separating liquid from solids: before fermentation for whites, after fermentation for reds, and mid-fermentation for rosés.

Red wine

Crush grapes (dark only)

Ferment juice and solids (warm and fast)

Squeeze wine from solids

Wine

Red

White wine

Crush grapes (any colour)

Squeeze juice from solids

Juice

Ferment juice only (cold and slow)

White

Rosé wine

Crush grapes (dark only)

Ferment for up to 48 hours

Squeeze juice from solids

Juice

Ferment juice only (cold and slow)

Pink

START AS FOR RED

FINISH AS FOR WHITE

Fermenting or Aging in Oak

Wines were once made and sold in barrels, but nowadays the vast majority are fermented in inert stainless-steel tanks and sold in bottles. However, winemakers still use traditional oak barrels to refine and improve most premium wines. In the same way that chefs use butter and spices to enrich and season recipes, vintners use oak barrels to add texture and flavour to their wines.

The barrel effects

There are three ways in which wine is changed by the time it spends in oak barrels.

All barrels intensify wine

Water and alcohol are absorbed through wood's pores and evaporate when they reach the surface. What remains – tannins, flavour compounds, and acids – becomes more concentrated, increasing the quality and aging potential of the wine.

All barrels soften and enrich wine's texture

Air enters through wood's pores, exposing the wine to very slow, continuous oxidation. This causes small-scale chemical reactions that soften harsh young wines and make them feel smoother on the palate.

Only new barrels add oak flavour and tannin to wine

Oak contains soluble flavour compounds and tannins, which are imparted to wine over time. New barrels give wine a strong toasty flavour, like that found in cognac or bourbon. However, just like a tea bag, a barrel will lose its flavour gradually with each use, approaching a neutral state by its fourth year. For most wines, 100 per cent new oak is too strong, so vintners typically rotate in only 20–50 per cent new barrels with each vintage.

BARRELS OR CHIPS?
The taste of oak is appreciated by many wine drinkers, so a shortcut is often taken for cheaper brands: oaking wine with wood chips.

What oak barrels do to wine

Let water and alcohol out

Let air and oxygen in

Transfer oak flavour

Oak barrels vs steel tanks

For the full trifecta of concentrated flavour profile, rich mouthfeel, and oaky flavour, only wood barrels will suffice. But not all wines can justify the inherent costs of patient aging in barrels.

Inert vessels – *no oak effects*

Wines that are unoaked are fermented in vessels that impart no flavour, such as stainless-steel tanks. Most white and rosé wines are unoaked, but only the lightest, youngest, and least ambitious red wines are made this way.

INTENSIFIES WINE

ENRICHES TEXTURE

ADDS OAK FLAVOUR

Oak barrels – *all oak effects*

Premium red wines are fermented in steel tanks, then matured in oak barrels before bottling. Since reds are more harsh when young, they need anywhere from 3 months to 3 years to mellow in barrels, depending on the wine's style and ambition. Only the heaviest white wines see oak at all, but those that do are usually fermented in barrels from the start, as with Chardonnays. For both red and white wine, newer barrels and longer aging strengthen their oak flavours. However, older, "neutral" barrels will impart no obvious oaky taste.

Oak treatments – *oak flavour only*

Many people enjoy cognac-like oakiness in their wine, but getting it there the traditional way is time-consuming and expensive. Modern winemakers can add an oaky taste with wood chips or planks. However, this cannot replicate the other effects of aging wine in breathable barrels – enriching and concentrating wine – so it is rarely used other than for bargain wines.

NEW OAK: VANILLA, CARAMEL, DESSERT SPICE, COCONUT...

New oak is naturally high in dessert-like aromatic compounds, especially vanillin. The toasting process that is used to bend the wood into rounded shapes produces nutty lactones and caramelizes its surface. Winemakers use oak as a seasoning for wine and pay close attention to the type of oak used and how it is toasted.

For vintners, French and American oak are as distinct as Ethiopian and Colombian coffee. The degree of "toast" that the wood is given has a similar effect to the type of roast those coffee beans might receive. Smaller barrels also guarantee a stronger oak flavour in wine for the same reason that a fine espresso grind increases coffee's intensity: more surface contact between wine and oak means more flavour is transferred.

THE TASTING
Identifying Grape Skins and Oak Barrels
Compare four wines at home

All four of these wines are made with dark-skinned grapes in the Pinot family, but their degree of colour is determined by how long the grape juice remains in contact with grape skins. Red and purple grapes can be made into white wines if their skins are removed before fermentation begins. Brief skin contact adds just a blush of colour and flavour. Only the red wines receive oak-barrel treatment.

1 Taste wine 1 (white) and wine 2 (rosé). Notice how fresh they taste. This is because they are fermented chilled, with minimal skin contact, then bottled unoaked and released while young.

2 Now sample the red wines 3 and 4. Notice how fermenting warmer, with grape skins, alters their flavour. Being premium reds, both wines have been aged in oak barrels to soften and enrich their mouthfeel. But wine 4 is intense enough to benefit from the stronger flavour of newer oak, and that should be apparent on tasting.

Fermenting with the skins extracts not only colour and flavour but also harsh bitter components that soften and mellow when aged in oak barrels.

UNOAKED WHITE FROM RED GRAPES

1

PINOT GRIGIO

Squeeze immediately, then discard solids

For example...

Italian Pinot Grigio, German Grauburgunder, American Pinot Gris, or Canadian Pinot Gris

Can you detect...?

Low sugar/dry;
High acidity/tart;
Low fruit intensity;
No oak flavour;
Low alcohol/light;
No tannin.

Explanation

Pinot Grigio is a paler-skinned variant of Pinot Noir. While Pinot Noir looks dark purple, Pinot Grigio looks reddish pink on the vine. Since it isn't dark enough to make good red wine, its grapes are immediately squeezed, and only the clear juice is cold-fermented, making a white wine.

UNOAKED PINK FROM PURPLE GRAPES	RED AGED IN OLD BARRELS FROM PURPLE GRAPES	RED AGED IN NEW BARRELS FROM PURPLE GRAPES

2

PINOT NOIR ROSÉ

Squeeze early in fermentation, then discard solids

3

FRENCH PINOT NOIR

Ferment with solids, then age in "neutral" oak

4

PREMIUM PINOT NOIR

Ferment with solids, then age in new oak

For example...

Try for an Australian one, or substitute any pink Pinot Noir, such as French Burgundy Rosé or New Zealand Pinot Noir Rosé

Can you detect...?

Lowish sugar/medium-dry;
High acidity/tart;
Moderate fruit intensity;
No oak flavour;
Low alcohol/light;
Negligible tannin.

Explanation

Making pink wine combines elements of both red- and white-wine making. Dark grapes are crushed and spend 6–48 hours soaking with the skins. When they have picked up just enough colour and flavour, the pink juice is separated from the grape solids and cold-fermented.

For example...

Select a modestly priced Bourgogne Pinot Noir or another young, affordable French Burgundy, such as Mercurey or Santenay

Can you detect...?

Very low sugar/very dry;
High acidity/tart;
Moderate fruit intensity;
Mild oak flavour;
Medium alcohol/mid-weight;
Mild tannin.

Explanation

Red wines extract colour and flavour from the dark grape peel, along with harsh astringent tannins. Vintners typically age all but bargain reds in barrels to let them mellow before bottling. The mildest and most affordable European reds are often aged in older barrels that have largely lost their new-oak taste.

For example...

From a California appellation such as Sonoma County or Monterey, or a substitute from Oregon, New Zealand, or Canada

Can you detect...?

Low sugar/dry;
Moderate acidity/tangy;
Higher fruit intensity;
Strong oak flavour;
Medium alcohol/mid-weight;
Moderate tannin.

Explanation

Premium New World wines are typically made from riper grapes, and vintners try to maximize colour and flavour extraction. Making reds more intense makes them harsher, too, so longer barrel aging is needed to soften them. Bolder grape flavours merit a stronger "seasoning" with newer barrels.

Speciality Styles: Fortified Wine

The alcohol in most wines results from natural fermentation; however, a handful of styles are "fortified" with distilled spirits – usually with a crude grape brandy resembling grappa that is nearly pure alcohol. Fortified wines have more alcohol than standard wines, typically 15–20%. This makes them smell stronger and feel heavier, which is why they're served in small portions. They can be white or red, but the most popular are sweet.

And now for the history bit

Fortified wines are historic relics that have survived because we like the way they taste. Wine casks were originally spiked with spirits by wine merchants and sea captains, not winemakers, as a preservative before shipping. Like salting fish or pickling vegetables, measures for preventing spoilage were routine for long-distance transport, especially in hot climates. This helps explain why the most popular fortified wines – from Port and Sherry, to Madeira and Marsala – were all innovations of British merchants stationed in warm-climate ports, tasked with supplying wine for a global seafaring empire. In the wineries they owned or controlled, stabilizing wine by adding alcohol was integrated into winemaking to improve quality. Strong demand for these products in Britain and the colonies led local Portuguese, Spanish, and Italian vintners to follow suit.

HOT-CLIMATE WINES
Fortified wines are specialities of unusually hot wine regions, where grape sugar and alcohol are easily available, thanks to ample sunshine.

Style out of necessity

Take the historical practice
Fortify the finished wine with brandy in order to prevent spoilage during transport to distant markets.

Adapt it to making wine
Fortify the wine after fermentation but before aging, to preserve it in the traditional "Sherry method".

Refine it to making sweet wine
Fortify mid-fermentation to kill yeasts, retain grape sugar, and preserve the wine in the "Port method".

Sherry method:

Fortified after fermentation

Wines made by this older method are almost always white wines that are fermented to dryness first. The resulting "base wine" is then fortified with spirit and aged. Such wines may or may not be sweetened afterwards, so they can range from bone-dry wines like Fino Sherry to sweet, sticky wines like Cream Sherry.

Sherry-style wines are almost always flavour-boosted to balance their strong alcohol. Wines made by the Sherry method include those below.

Port method:

Fortified during fermentation

This technique, also known as *mutage*, is a more recent innovation and makes only sweet wines, which may be white or red. Distilled spirit is added much earlier, during the fermentation stage. Since yeasts cannot tolerate alcohol levels of more than 15%, adding brandy stops the fermentation process abruptly and guarantees a sweet dessert wine. Wines made by the Port method include those below.

Spanish Sherry

Flavour is amplified with either oxidative aging for stronger brown Sherry or aging with special flor yeasts for paler, lighter-bodied Fino Sherry (or both for Amontillado Sherry).

....

Portuguese dry Madeira

Flavour is amplified with oxidative aging at high temperature, known as maderization, for dry Sercial and Verdelho Madeiras.

....

Italian dry Vermouth

Rarely sold as wine, Vermouth is, in fact, wine that is fortified and flavoured through the infusion of herbs and other botanicals.

....

Portuguese Port

Most Ports are red and come in two main styles. Russet-coloured Tawny Ports are barrel-aged and nutty, while the more classic purple Ports are protected from oxidation to stay jammy and vivid.

....

French Vins Doux Naturels

White Muscats are sweeter and drunk young, but Grenache-based reds like Banyuls are drier and often given barrel aging.

....

Spanish Vinos de Licor

Andalusian Moscatels and Pedro Ximénez from Sherry country start with sun-dried white grapes before fortification.

....

Other styles made this way include sweet Madeira and Moscatel from Portugal, Marsala and sweet Vermouth from Italy, and Malaga and Montilla-Moriles from Spain.

....

ADDED GRAPE SUGAR (OPTIONAL): RAISIN SYRUP OR JUICE CONCENTRATE

ADDED ALCOHOL: DISTILLED SPIRIT (GRAPE BRANDY)

NATURAL ALCOHOL: PRODUCED DURING FERMENTATION

NATURAL GRAPE SUGAR: PRESERVED FROM FRESH GRAPE JUICE

ADDED ALCOHOL: DISTILLED SPIRIT (GRAPE BRANDY)

NATURAL ALCOHOL: PRODUCED DURING FERMENTATION

Speciality Styles: Sparkling Wine

Carbon dioxide and alcohol are by-products of fermentation, so all wines are bubbly at one stage. This fizz is usually allowed to dissipate, but some wines taste better with a little "sparkle". To capture natural carbonation, vintners tinker with the standard winemaking process, conducting the final stage of fermentation in a closed container that can trap wine's bubbles.

Traditional method

The laborious "traditional method" pioneered in Champagne is still used worldwide for premium wines because of its delicious results: wines with fine creamy bubbles, combining the refreshment of lighter wines with the opulence of richer wines. But cheaper wines are often made by less time-consuming methods – modifying the traditional method or skipping the second fermentation.

1 Make the base wine
A dry, low-alcohol still white wine is made, often from a mix of underripe red and white grapes.

2 Bottle and sweeten
Bottles of base wine are dosed with measured amounts of sugar and yeast, then tightly sealed.

3 Second fermentation
Yeasts consume the sugar, generating alcohol and carbon dioxide, which gets trapped as carbonation.

4 Age on the lees
A spent yeast sediment forms after fermentation. Aging wine with these "lees" adds a doughy flavour and enriches the wine's texture.

5 Clarify the wine
After aging for between 6 months and 10 years, the clear wine is separated from its sediment by inverting bottles and controlled freezing.

6 Top up and sweeten
Lost volume is replaced with wine. Cane sugar is added to offset the wine's hyper-dry edge. For pink styles, red wine is used to add colour.

SPARKLING WINE PRODUCTION AND CHARACTERISTICS

	CHAMPAGNE STYLE	**PROSECCO STYLE**	**ASTI STYLE**
PRODUCTION METHOD	Fermented twice, second time in sealed bottles	Fermented twice, second time in sealed tanks	Fermented once, in sealed tanks
KEY FACTOR	Flavour and texture enriched by long-term lees aging	Bottled young to preserve freshness	Fermentation interrupted to retain sweetness
CARBONATION	Fine bubbles; long-lasting creamy mousse	Medium bubbles; persistent frothy mousse	Larger bubbles; short-lived foamy mousse
SWEETNESS	Most often dry to very dry	Most often dry to lightly sweet	Always sweet

Terms of sweetness

One of the most confusing aspects of sparkling wines is the label terms that indicate sweetness, which can sound contradictory, thanks to an accident of history. When French Champagne first became popular, it was sweetened with as much sugar as modern soft drinks. But over time, customers wanted drier styles, so vintners added less sugar and labelled these bottlings as *demi-sec* or *sec*, meaning half-dry or dry. When export markets demanded even drier wines, they had to come up with a new word to mean "drier than dry". The term *brut* was coined, meaning savage and unrefined, to convey their near-total absence of sweetening.

A real *brut*

Brut wines fall below the level of perceptible sweetness and dominate the realm of premium modern sparkling wines. Confusingly, "extra-dry" wines are not drier, as their name suggests, but are sweeter than the *brut* norm.

DEMI-SEC
Fully sweet

EXTRA-DRY
Faintly sweet

BRUT
Very dry

BRUT NATURE
Extremely dry, with no added sugar

Chapter Checklist

Here is a recap of some of the most important points you've learned in this chapter.

✓ Wine is made through **fermentation**, a process in which living yeasts consume grape sugar and convert it into **alcohol and carbon dioxide**.

✓ Most wines are dry, especially those over 13% alcohol, because fermentation naturally **depletes grape sugar**.

✓ Vintners can make **sweet wine** by interrupting fermentation, by concentrating grapes before fermentation, or by sweetening a dry wine.

✓ White wines can be made from **grapes of any colour**, because the grape skins are removed before fermentation; but reds and rosés can only be made from **dark-skinned grapes**.

✓ White wines taste more like grape juice and are fermented cold to preserve their **fresh taste**. Red wines taste more like grape peels and are fermented warm to extract colour, flavour, and tannin compounds.

✓ Rosés start fermentation with their **skins**, as for reds, but these are soon removed, and the wines finish fermenting as if they were whites.

✓ Fermenting or aging wine in oak barrels will concentrate and enrich its **mouthfeel**. If some of the barrels are new, the wine will also pick up **oaky flavours**.

✓ Oak aging is more necessary for red wines than whites, because it **softens and mellows** the harshness of grape-skin compounds.

✓ Some wines are **fortified** with added distilled spirit, raising their alcohol content to 15–20%. Most, but not all, are sweet dessert wines.

✓ **Carbonation** is a natural by-product of fermentation. Most **sparkling wines** are made by refermenting a still wine in a sealed container to trap the bubbles.

GRAPE-GROWING CHOICES

Quality, Intensity, and *Terroir*

Any winemaker will tell you that what happens in the vineyard is more important than what happens at the winery. Since wine is made from only grapes, every factor that affects their flavour and quality will be reflected in the glass. The land's geography – from the larger region's macroclimate, to the intimate folds of its terrain – significantly shapes the flavour potential of its fruit. Farming decisions at every level have a direct impact as well: not simply when to pick the grapes or what to plant where, but the critical question of how to manage the life cycle of the land.

Location, Location, Location

Wine's flavour is more deeply affected by the place where it is grown than most agricultural products. Everything about the vineyard informs how its wine will taste – from macro-level geographic factors like latitude, to micro-level nuances like soil composition; from unchangeable features like terrain, to variable conditions like the weather at harvest.

Making sense of wine

Many of the most confusing aspects of wine start to make more sense once you understand a few central concepts about the importance of the land.

KNOWN NAMES
The largest wine regions, like California or Tuscany, make the cheapest everyday wines but benefit from name recognition. Premier appellations are typically tiny places that no one's ever heard of, like Rutherford or Barolo.

A wine's appellation, or formal region of origin, is the most important quality factor listed on any wine's label.

Exceptional wine can only come from great vineyards. Cabernet Sauvignon may be a noble grape, but it needs very specific growing conditions: its wine wouldn't taste good if it was grown in the Sahara or Siberia. This is why so many European wines are named after their region, like Côtes du Rhône, and not after their grapes, like Grenache.

The smallest appellations are, by definition, the most prestigious and almost always make superior wine.

Specificity about where the grapes were grown is associated with greater quality potential and therefore higher prices. There is no economic incentive to recognize a small appellation inside a larger one unless the land can make better, more distinctive wines. In Europe, the most rigorous quality standards are applied to the smallest appellations.

Smaller and smaller

Within any larger wine region – California, for example – the best vineyard zones establish their own smaller appellations to distinguish their wines from the pack and increase their value. Over time, these subzones – like Napa Valley – are judged by their wines' quality, and those with the best track record command higher prices. If an appellation gets famous enough, its top vintners will start the process again, carving out an even smaller subzone, as has been the case with Napa's Rutherford or Howell Mountain appellations.

**Regional appellation:
Burgundy**
£ £ £ £

**District appellation:
Côte de Beaune-Villages**
£ £ £
£ £ £

**Village appellation:
Puligny-Montrachet**
£ £
£ £
£ £

**Vineyard appellation:
Le Montrachet**
£
£
£
£

This 8-hectare (20-acre) vineyard makes fewer than 50,000 bottles per year.

Small wonders
Like an exclusive Mayfair address in London, the smallest of Burgundy's appellations – such as Le Montrachet – are the most prestigious, and they make tiny amounts of exceptional, expensive wine.

APPELLATIONS AND ORANGES

Appellations are formal regions of wine origin that signal the value of a vineyard's real estate. Just as oranges from Florida command premium prices, so do wines from places like Bordeaux. But wine appellations go much further to recognize superior land, such as the legendary village of Margaux within the respected Médoc peninsula of Bordeaux. The most historic wine regions typically have the most complicated appellation structure. Burgundy's largest appellation, Bourgogne, encompasses 100 others, for example – from regions, to districts, to villages and beyond. The smallest are a few dozen *grand crus* – or single-vineyard appellations – that denote the very best Burgundy wines.

Geography and Climate

Grapevines need certain conditions to grow, so all wine regions have some things in common. They are in temperate latitudes with enough warm summer days to ripen grapes, but they get cold enough in winter for their vines to have a dormant season. Within these boundaries, however, there is a lot of regional variation that affects how wine will taste.

Relative ripening

Vineyard geography is reflected in wine flavour in many ways, most significantly through its impact on ripening (see Chapter 4). Grapes ripen faster and more thoroughly in South Australia, for example, than they do in New Zealand, because they are planted closer to the equator and are not cooled on all sides by frigid waters. Coastal Tuscan vines see some clouds and rain in the growing season, while Argentina's vines grow in near-desert conditions at the base of the Andes.

Ground control

A wine region's topography sometimes needs a boost from its geology – for example, Chardonnay grapes struggle to ripen in Chablis and need as much sun as possible in this chilly zone of northern France. Prime vineyards here require southern exposure, and even these sites need good weather to make sound wines. But the finest wines of Chablis come from its six best vineyards, known as its *grands crus*. They occupy a single south-facing slope and feature unusually pale chalky soil that reflects the sun's warmth back up to the grapes from below. The combination of terrain and soil boosts ripeness dramatically, making wines from these vineyards taste unlike Chardonnays made anywhere else in the world.

Matching grape to region

Vintners juggle lots of information when deciding which grapes to plant where. Burgundy's native Pinot Noir and Chardonnay grapes, for example, are well adapted to cool growing conditions, while thicker-skinned Cabernet Sauvignon from Bordeaux requires much more warmth to ripen.

Too high: too dry and windy

PRIDE OF PLACE
Where grapes are grown is of great importance in wine – not just in broad terms of country or climate, but down to which side of a hill they're planted on.

SOUTHERN EXPOSURE

Pinot Noir bakes when it gets too hot, but it still needs sunlight to develop intense flavour. In Burgundy, this grape's finest wines are all grown on an escarpment called the Côte d'Or ("Golden Slope"), which faces the rising sun. For centuries, it has been recognized that the vineyards in the centre of the slope make the finest wine, and many of these have been granted prestige *grand cru* status. However, grapes grown just above or just below on the hillside don't perform as well, so their vineyards are classified as either next-best *premier cru* sites or are lumped in with the more generic wines that are bottled under the name of their village. Internationally, Pinot Noir follows this model, too: vintners in cool regions – from Canada, to New Zealand – plant this grape on sunward slopes to achieve the same effect.

GOOD

BETTER

BEST

BETTER

GOOD

Good, better, best
In Burgundy's Côte d'Or, the "best" *grand cru* sites for Pinot Noir are located mid-slope, as shown above, flanked by "good" village-level land and "better" *premier cru* sites.

Too low: too wet and humid

The Effects of *Terroir*

Variations in geography and climate can make wines made from the same grape variety taste remarkably different from one region to the next. But smaller variations in terrain and soil composition within the same region can also affect ripening potential, thereby altering a wine's flavour.

What is *terroir*?

Terroir means earth or soil in French, but the term has been adopted in wine-speak to mean location-specific flavour, roughly the "taste of the place". *Terroir* is often described as an "earthy" or "mineral" scent but can manifest itself in wine's ripeness, texture, and finish, too. Some professionals can identify a wine's vineyard by taste alone, but *terroir* is not obvious to the average wine drinker. If wine were music, *terroir* wouldn't be a song's melody or arrangement as much as the distinctive acoustics of a specific venue or recording studio – you'd have to be an enthusiast to recognize it in tracks by different artists.

Reading about *terroir*, it's natural to wonder if there's actual dirt in your wine. There's not, but it's been known for centuries that vineyard soil plays a strong role in wine flavour, and it has become clear more recently that farming choices can amplify or suppress wine's *terroir*. The mechanisms aren't fully understood, but the interplay of life cycles in the vine's environment appear to hold the answer, particularly microbiological activity such as soil renewal and fermentation. Certainly, systemic chemical treatments like herbicides obscure *terroir* traits in wine, suggesting a tasteable connection with the web of life below ground that leads many premium vintners to practise organic or natural farming.

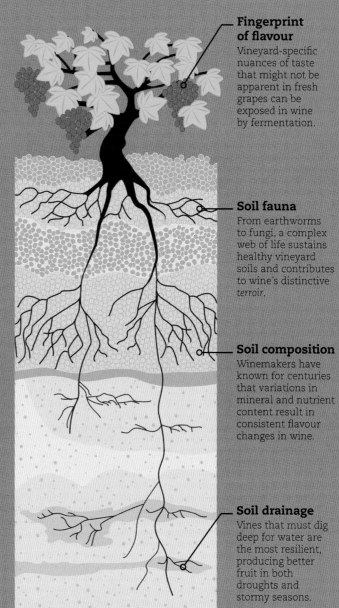

Fingerprint of flavour
Vineyard-specific nuances of taste that might not be apparent in fresh grapes can be exposed in wine by fermentation.

Soil fauna
From earthworms to fungi, a complex web of life sustains healthy vineyard soils and contributes to wine's distinctive *terroir*.

Soil composition
Winemakers have known for centuries that variations in mineral and nutrient content result in consistent flavour changes in wine.

Soil drainage
Vines that must dig deep for water are the most resilient, producing better fruit in both droughts and stormy seasons.

Tasteable environment
Vineyard soils and ecosystems are major quality factors in grape growing, and their effects can be tasted in the wine glass.

TIME TO GET FUNKY

We know microbiology can create great flavour complexity, as with raw-milk cheeses like Roquefort or Gruyère. Wine- and cheese-making traditions have led the Old World to embrace a little funky individuality, and earthy *terroir* traits are often celebrated in European wines. New Worlders tend to view microbes of all kinds as threats to be eradicated, so their wines more often emphasize squeaky-clean fruit flavours, especially for bargain wines.

The importance of soil

The concept of *terroir* – that we can taste the effects of vineyard environment – is a powerful tool for understanding how the fine-wine world works. Complex appellation systems and vineyard-ranking hierarchies are all attempts to organize wines around their *terroir*.

One clear example of the importance of soil is found in Bordeaux. Cabernet Sauvignon makes the region's top wines, but its thick skins need ample heat to ripen fully, so this variety performs much better in the well-drained gravels that line the river's "Left Bank" than in the moist clay found everywhere else. It's not a coincidence that in a ranking of top red wine estates for the 1855 World's Fair, later adopted as Bordeaux's *grand cru* classification, 90 per cent were clustered in four adjacent gravelly villages on the Médoc peninsula.

Early-ripening Merlot makes more reliable wines on clay. However, because the land is more marginal and the wine less prized, most is sold as everyday regional Bordeaux wines.

MANY MEANINGS
Narrowly applied, a wine's *terroir* is the individuality of taste and smell that its vineyard imparts. More broadly, a region's *terroir* is its unique combination of flavour-influencing factors, including climate, landscape, and soils.

Left Bank Médoc
Warm, dry gravel boosts ripening potential: ideal for Cabernet Sauvignon.

Right Bank Bordeaux
Cool, damp clay restricts ripening potential: better suited to Merlot.

Farming for Quantity or Quality?

Even if they were grown in the same appellation, grapes for easy-drinking bargain wines would be cultivated very differently from those destined for super-premium luxury wine. Artisanal wines taste different from mass-produced wines for the same reasons that heirloom tomatoes from your garden taste different from supermarket tomatoes.

WHERE TO PLANT VINES

Flat and fertile land is tractor-friendly and productive, making it ideal for high-volume operations. Steeper, hard-scrabble sites are more difficult to cultivate and yield less fruit, but their grapes make better, more age-worthy wines.

Bulk and premium wines

Vineyards for bulk wine and premium wines are managed with opposing priorities in terms of productivity and agricultural philosophy. Value-oriented vintners purchase their grapes from growers who operate at maximum efficiency to stay competitive. Farming for the mass market may require fertilizing, irrigating, and mechanized spraying to boost crop volume and keep prices low. Ambitious vintners, however, farm by hand, often growing grapes on their own land. Since bumper crops dilute flavour, yields per vine are deliberately suppressed and the land is cultivated with little or no chemical intervention.

ESTATE, OR NOT ESTATE?

Vintners have more control over quality factors when they grow their own grapes. New World wine labels may indicate vineyard ownership with phrases like "estate bottled". In Europe, each region has different terms for a wine estate – *domaine* in Burgundy, *château* in Bordeaux, *tenuta* in Tuscany – but you'll find the vintner's role defined in the small print. If it doesn't reference land ownership or growing grapes, the wine was made from purchased fruit.

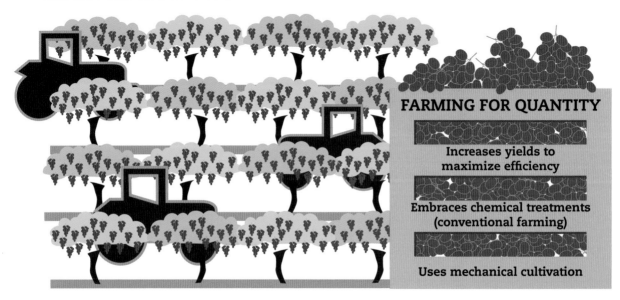

FARMING FOR QUANTITY

Increases yields to maximize efficiency

Embraces chemical treatments (conventional farming)

Uses mechanical cultivation

Types of farming

Prior to the Industrial Revolution, all farming was organic by today's standard. But the agricultural norm now involves boosting productivity with fertilizers and fungicides, herbicides and pesticides, all of which are routine for grape growing, too. However, vintners have long known that reducing or eliminating chemicals in the vineyard increases wine's quality potential.

Not all premium wines are made from organic grapes. But the finer the wine, the more likely it is to have been cultivated as naturally as possible. Some vintners make the effort to certify their grapes as organic to convey this commitment to their customers. A few go further, adopting even more exacting standards of natural farming to qualify their fruit as

biodynamic. Some scoff that biodynamic practices seem more like superstition than science, but it's hard to argue with results. Wines produced this way consistently display more individuality, more *terroir*, and a longer finish – all qualities prized by collectors of fine wine. However, natural farming is rather expensive, so these practices are most common in luxury-priced wines than in the bargain bin.

Managing vineyard yields

Grapevines do a more thorough job of ripening grapes when they bear fewer of them. Overburdened vines may produce grapes with adequate sugar for winemaking, but they are often weak in flavour or unbalanced in components like acidity. Vintners must sacrifice crop volume if they want to improve wine quality, which helps explain why prices of premium wines can climb so high.

USING ORGANIC GRAPES

For a wine to be certified organic, winemakers may not use any additives, but introducing a tiny amount of sulphur before fermentation has been an essential step of winemaking for centuries. Omitting this step does not change the wine's sulphur content when bottled, but it does destabilize wine and significantly shorten its shelf life. As a result, you'll typically see labels refer to wine "made from organic grapes" more often than saying it is "organic wine".

FARMING FOR QUALITY

Reduces yields to improve flavour

Avoids chemical treatments (natural farming)

Uses hand-cultivation

THE TASTING
Identifying Vineyard Factors

Compare wines from different appellations and quality levels at home

Sample these four wines side by side to get a sense of how vineyard location and winemaking techniques affect wine style.

1 Bear in mind that both pairs of wines are made with the same grape variety and hail from the same wine region. However, in each case the first wine is a more generic, affordable style from a bigger appellation, while the second is a more ambitious premium wine from a smaller sub-appellation.

2 Notice how, although the pairs share a basic resemblance, wines 2 and 4 are riper and more intense. You should also be able to detect a more distinctive aromatic profile. Affordable wines from large "generic" appellations tend to be milder in flavour, shorter in finish, and less distinctive than premium wines from smaller, more prestigious appellations.

> Differences in geography and farming practices can produce wines that taste different even when the same grape is used.

1

MODEST
WHITE
BURGUNDY

2

PREMIUM
WHITE
BURGUNDY

For example...

French Mâcon Blanc or a similar modest white Burgundy, like Mâcon-Villages or Bourgogne Blanc

Can you detect...?

Low sugar/dry; High acidity/tart; Low fruit intensity; No oak flavour; Medium alcohol/mid-weight; Simple, easygoing, refreshing

Explanation

Wines bottled under large appellations – like this regional Burgundy – can be perfectly delicious and refreshing. However, their vineyards are more serviceable than exceptional, and the wines may be blended from anywhere in the region.

For example...

French Pouilly-Fuissé or a similar premium white Burgundy, like Meursault or Chassagne-Montrachet

Can you detect...?

Low sugar/dry; Medium acidity/tangy; Medium fruit intensity; Mild oak flavour; Higher alcohol/heavier; More rich, intense, flavourful

Explanation

Wines bottled under smaller sub-appellations – like this village-level Burgundy – have more quality potential, and most will be noticeably more intense. This is especially true in Europe, where quality regulations are stricter in smaller appellations.

3   **4**

MODEST AMERICAN PINOT NOIR   PREMIUM AMERICAN PINOT NOIR

For example...

California Pinot Noir; or alternatively a bargain Shiraz from Southeast Australia

Can you detect...?

Paler colour; Low sugar/dry; Moderate acidity/tangy; Medium fruit intensity; Mild oak flavour; Medium alcohol/mid-weight; Young, simple, cheerful

Explanation

Farming may be less regulated in the New World, but wines from huge appellations like California still tend to be blends sourced from regions of little pedigree. The wines can be enjoyable but are usually simple crowd-pleasers, without much depth or complexity.

For example...

Carneros Pinot Noir or one from Russian River or Sonoma Coast; or alternatively a premium Australian Barossa Shiraz

Can you detect...?

Darker colour; Low sugar/dry; Moderate acidity/tangy; Higher fruit intensity; Stronger oak flavour; Higher alcohol/heavier; More dense, aromatic, complex

Explanation

Where conditions are ideal for better wines, sub-appellations are formed. These vineyards produce deeper, more characterful wines, and by commanding higher prices, the vintners can justify lowering yields and improving quality.

Chapter Checklist

Here is a recap of some of the most important points you've learned in this chapter.

✓ The most important **quality factor** on a wine's label is its **appellation**, or formal region of origin.

✓ Smaller appellations almost always make **better wine** than bigger appellations.

✓ In large wine regions, like Burgundy or California, the best vineyard zones establish their own **sub-appellations** to distinguish their wines.

✓ **Vineyard geography**, including a region's climate and terrain, has a marked impact on **ripening**.

✓ It is common sense that grapes are rarely planted where they don't **perform well**.

✓ Geographical and climatic variations mean wines from the same grape variety **taste very different** from one region to the next.

✓ The French term *terroir* is used in wine-speak to mean location-specific flavour, roughly translating as the **"taste of the place"**.

✓ Vineyards growing grapes for **bulk wines** and those growing grapes for **premium wines** are managed with opposing sets of priorities in terms of their **productivity** and **agricultural philosophy**.

✓ The finer the wine, the more likely it is that its grapes were cultivated as **naturally as possible**, with minimal chemical treatment. They also tend to have a longer finish and more **individuality of flavour**.

✓ Large **"generic" appellations** tend to produce wines that are milder in flavour, shorter in finish, and less distinctive than premium wines. They are also more **affordable**.

CULTURAL PRIORITIES

History, Tradition, and Innovation

Wines from different countries taste different, but not simply because of geography. Humankind plays as great a role as nature in determining the outcome of winemaking, steering the process towards desired results that vary from one culture to the next. The history of wine's development in Europe and eventual expansion during the colonial era helps explain many of wine's mysteries. Globalization may be in full swing, but there remains a tasteable distinction between most Old World and New World wines – a reflection of differences in heritage and gastronomic sensibilities.

Old World or New World?

One of the most useful tools that wine professionals rely on is the distinction between wines made in Europe, or the Old World, and those made in the Americas and southern hemisphere, known collectively as the New World.

Differences in style

Terms like "Old World" and "New World" may sound archaic, but they are still used in the wine trade because they are still relevant. Not only are European wines often labelled according to their own unique rules (see pp.52–3), but they typically taste different from other wines in ways that can be anticipated before you pull a cork. Even when the same grape variety and same winemaking methods are used, Old World and New World wines generally follow a tasteable pattern, as described below.

Old World flavour profile
- More "traditional" – designed to taste best with food;
- Lighter in weight/alcohol;
- Lower in sweetness (among dry styles);
- Higher in acidity;
- More subtle and earthier in fruit character;
- Milder in oak flavour (where oak is used);
- Harsher in tannins (reds only).

New World flavour profile
- More "modern" – designed to taste best alone;
- Heavier in weight/alcohol;
- Higher in sweetness (among dry styles);
- Lower in acidity;
- Bolder and jammier in fruit character;
- Stronger in oak flavour (where oak is used);
- Softer in tannins (reds only).

WINE NATIONS
Dozens of countries make wine, but the global wine market is dominated by France, Italy, Spain, Germany, Portugal, and Austria in the Old World, plus the USA, Australia, Argentina, Chile, South Africa, New Zealand, and Canada in the New World.

THE WORLD OF WINE

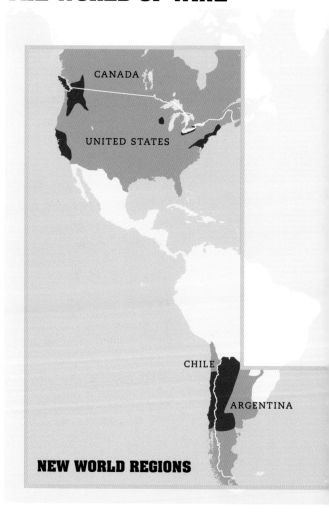

NEW WORLD REGIONS

Non-grape variables

Such observable differences as those listed opposite do not derive from the type of grapes used in winemaking, since all fine-wine varieties are of European origin. Instead, they result from differences in two other variables that affect how wine tastes: the vineyard environment and human winemaking decisions.

The geography and climate of the place

Old World wine regions are almost always cooler and cloudier than the New World wine regions that grow the same grape varieties. As a result, European grapes tend to achieve lower degrees of overall ripeness. Most New World regions are considerably sunnier, warmer, and drier in climate, which makes it easier to achieve higher degrees of grape ripeness.

The history and culture of the people

Influenced by centuries of winemaking heritage, Old World wines are often geared towards time-honoured goals like aging well and flattering local cuisine. New World wines tend to be shaped by a spirit of innovation and more reliant on technology. They are typically designed around very different priorities, such as pleasing a global audience on first sip and impressing wine critics.

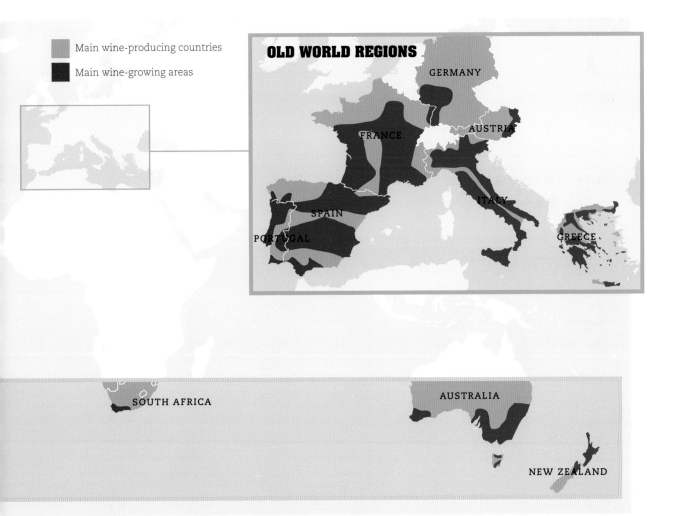

Main wine-producing countries

Main wine-growing areas

OLD WORLD REGIONS

GERMANY

FRANCE

AUSTRIA

ITALY

SPAIN

PORTUGAL

GREECE

SOUTH AFRICA

AUSTRALIA

NEW ZEALAND

Wine History in Europe

Wine as we know it developed in Europe, as did all of the grape varieties used around the world today. Many puzzling aspects of today's European wine make more sense when we consider their historical context.

Factors for refining wine

Southern regions on the Mediterranean, such as Italy and Spain, have the longest winemaking history, the greatest proliferation of native grape varieties, and still make the most wine in terms of volume. However, Europe's best wines, in quality terms, historically came from cooler regions further north, such as France and Germany, where a few specific grapes made smaller amounts of finer wine. This pattern was shaped by the confluence of two factors in the Middle Ages – one environmental and one socioeconomic:
• Wine quality improves when challenging vineyard conditions, such as cold climates or stony slopes, reduce total fruit production per vine (see pp.160–61).
• Investing time, land, and effort into improving wine quality might not have been worthwhile for the average medieval farmer but made sense for the powerful monastic orders of central France.

BEFORE TECHNOLOGY

European winemaking traditions were well established long before the industrial and technological revolutions. Farming was always organic by definition, and winemaking was based on generations of trial and error, not on an understanding of fermentation's complex chemistry. Before wines could be refrigerated or stabilized, they needed to be as dry and age-worthy as possible. And since wine was rarely served without food, vintners naturally favoured styles that flattered their local cuisine, even if they seemed a little sour or bitter on first sip.

VINEYARD TIMELINE

c.8000 BC

Grapes were first made into wine in the Caucasus region of modern-day Georgia. The practice migrated from the Black Sea into the Mediterranean basin in the Stone Age, and ancient civilizations – from the Phoenicians, to the Greeks – spread winemaking around its shores, planting mostly in places where olives thrived. Vines were easiest to cultivate and most productive in these regions – zones with mild winters and dry, sunny summers. Wine soon became a staple of the Mediterranean diet alongside olive oil.

c.100 BC to c.AD 200

Vines were first planted in cooler zones when the Romans pushed northwards in the mid-1st century BC. Where olive trees give way to oak forests, cultivating wine grapes becomes more challenging: with less summer warmth, fruit does not ripen as easily. Only select varieties could adapt to chilly conditions and made the best wine when planted in the sunniest sites. Cooler northern vineyards often produced less fruit per vine than those in warmer zones further south, but over time their wines proved to be more concentrated and more resistant to spoilage.

History of quantity vs quality

Prior to the Roman era, wine was only made in southern Europe, where vines thrive easily and are prolific. Fine wines later emerged from colder regions, nearer the vine's northern limits, since grapes that struggle to survive yield less fruit and make better wine.

Pre-Roman vineyard area

Limits of grapevine range

Important wine region

5th to 11th centuries AD

Most of those making wine had little incentive to work harder to produce smaller amounts of wine in riskier weather conditions. Choosing quality over quantity might never have caught on outside a few enclaves of the ruling class if Europe had not been Christianized in the Middle Ages. With wine symbolizing the blood of Christ in the rite of communion, it had an exalted status. Some of the most influential monastic orders of the medieval era were based in France's Burgundy region. These ascetic monks helped transform wine from a rustic dietary staple to an elegant luxury product.

12th to 15th centuries

Modern grape-growing and winemaking methods largely derive from those practised by Cistercian and Benedictine monasteries in the medieval kingdom of Burgundy. Their expertise endured in part because they recorded their successes and failures. When these influential groups expanded, they brought with them wine traditions that valued quality over quantity. These flourished most in places where vines could survive but were less prone to Mediterranean-style bumper crops. By the end of the Middle Ages, regions like Burgundy and Bordeaux were famed for their exceptional wine.

France and Fine-Wine Icons

The French may not have been the first to make wine, but they were the first to pursue quality systematically on a grand scale. France had a head start on fine wine by a few hundred years and, outside of German rivalry in white wines, faced little competition before the 1800s. As a result, for more than five centuries, anyone anywhere who wanted to improve the quality of their wine would naturally look to France.

Global standard-bearers

Outside of Europe, almost all fine wines are made with grapes that are native to France in the image of famous French wines like white Burgundy, red Bordeaux, and sparkling Champagne. Even in countries that have their own wealth of native grape varieties, such as Italy, Spain, Portugal, and Greece, the best wines are generally made using French techniques, and many are aged in French oak barrels. Some are even "improved" by adding famous French grapes, like Cabernet Sauvignon, to blends based on local grapes like Tuscan Sangiovese or Castillian Tempranillo. And when winemaking rules were standardized throughout the European Union, the quality-oriented French system was adopted for all: naming wines after their place of origin, regulating permitted grapes and maximum yields, and establishing formal hierarchies based on wine quality.

Six of France's wine zones are far more influential than the rest, and three of these have a dominant presence in the fine-wine world. Burgundy, Bordeaux, and Champagne are well worth learning a little about because of their global significance as the archetypes for the majority of fine wines. All Chardonnay and Pinot Noir is made in the image of French Burgundy. Every Cabernet Sauvignon and Merlot wine is modelled on French Bordeaux. Every wine with bubbles is, in some way, paying homage to French Champagne.

The wines of three more regions – the Rhône Valley, the Loire Valley, and Alsace – may be less well known to wine drinkers, but they loom large for international vintners as the archetypes for wines like Shiraz, Sauvignon Blanc, and Pinot Grigio.

SIX FRENCH WINE REGIONS AND THEIR ICONIC STYLES

A significant proportion of the world's finest wines are inspired by a short list of French wines, the regions and grapes of which are named below.

BURGUNDY: Chardonnay, Pinot Noir

BORDEAUX: Cabernet Sauvignon, Merlot, Malbec, Sauvignon Blanc

CHAMPAGNE: sparkling Chardonnay/Pinot Noir blends

RHÔNE VALLEY: Syrah (aka Shiraz), Viognier, Grenache (aka Garnacha) blends

ALSACE: Pinot Gris (aka Pinot Grigio), Riesling, Pinot Blanc

LOIRE VALLEY: Sauvignon Blanc, Chenin Blanc, Cabernet Franc

THE BIG SIX FRENCH WINE REGIONS

While many regions of France make wine, six are of disproportionate importance in the global wine marketplace: Burgundy, Bordeaux, Champagne, the Rhône Valley, the Loire Valley, and Alsace.

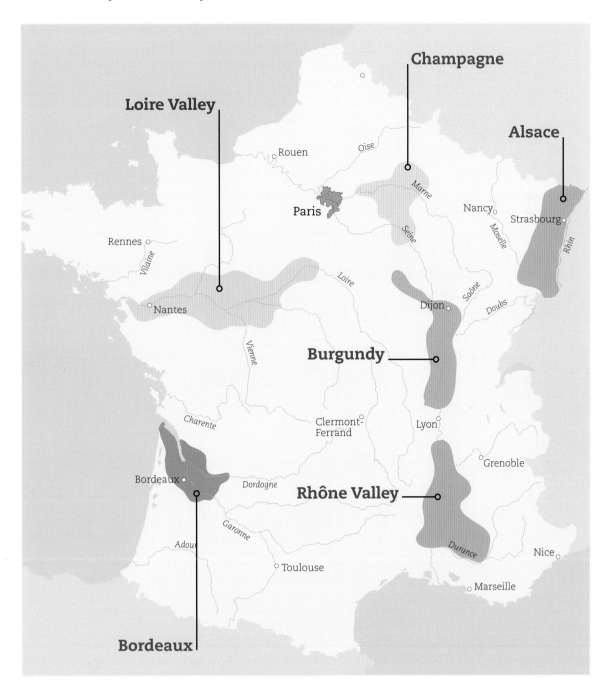

Winemaking in the Colonies

Winemaking arrived in the Americas and southern hemisphere during their colonization by Europeans, and these regions remain relative newcomers, especially with regard to fine wines. Only since the 1960s or 70s have New World wines been able to rival Old World wines in quality – but in doing so they sparked a global wine boom and revolutionary changes in how wine is made and sold worldwide.

Necessity and invention

Early New World vintners were pioneers in new lands. With no local winemaking heritage, the natural choice was to follow European "recipes". However, because their circumstances were so radically different – in terms of climate, technology, and markets for their products – their wines tasted radically different, too. Where the Old World classics tend to be lighter and milder, leaner and more earthy, New World wines tend to be bolder and heavier, more ripe and fruity in scent. This happens because most New World wines are grown in warmer regions and designed for instant gratification, while wines from cooler Old World regions are customarily more food-oriented and built to last.

MORE MODERN, LESS TRADITIONAL

As a general rule, wines from New World regions share "modern" sensibilities that distinguish them from the more "traditional" wines of Europe.

VINEYARD TIMELINE

16th to 18th centuries

Productive workhorse grape varieties were introduced to most New World colonies from Europe early on. In some regions, initial experiments were unsuccessful, as in North America, where vinifera vines lacked resistance to a local insect pest. Where vines did thrive, most wines remained rudimentary for quite some time. But with growing prosperity, ambitious vintners tried their hands at more famous grapes from French regions like Bordeaux and Burgundy to improve their wines. Some early experiments were recognized quickly for their quality potential, as with the sweet wines of South Africa's Constantia region.

19th to mid-20th centuries

Most New World vineyards were planted in warm, sunny regions like California and South Australia, where overripeness and drought were greater dangers than underripeness and rain. Winemakers had to improvise and, without local traditions to lean on, turned to science and technology for guidance. Most wines were simple everyday styles, and the most urgent commercial needs were to improve efficiency and increase production. Innovations in irrigation, mechanization, and chemical farming were pioneered and widely embraced. However, fine wines from quality-oriented estates also improved by leaps and bounds in this period.

New World exploration

European *Vitis vinifera* vines were planted far and wide in the colonial era. However, they did not always thrive immediately in new territories, and competitive fine wines would not emerge for centuries in most places.

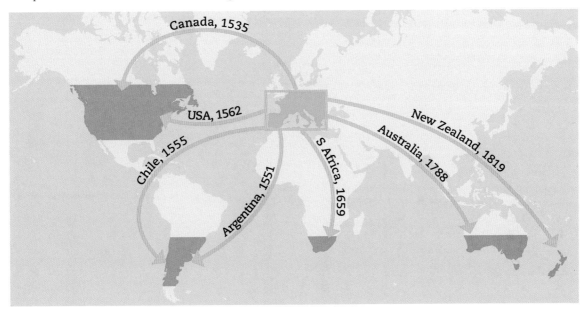

Canada, 1535
USA, 1562
Chile, 1555
Argentina, 1551
S Africa, 1659
Australia, 1788
New Zealand, 1819

Late 20th century

New World wines improved rapidly in the postwar period, and by the 1980s the best could rival their French archetypes in quality. However, they didn't taste identical to Old World wines; they had their own fruitier flavour profile that was often stronger and bolder due to greater ripeness. This resulted from differences in geography, of course, but also from the differences between traditional winemaking practices in Europe and more modern techniques used in the colonies. Also, lacking traditional pedigrees, New World wines needed to wow on first sip to compete, not just work well with food.

Early 21st century

Today's competitive global market is still changing how wines taste. The once stark stylistic divide between Old World and New World wines is becoming less clear-cut over time. European vintners are making wines that are riper and more ready to drink to compete with the upstarts from the colonies. Winemakers in the Americas and southern hemisphere are producing wines that are more refreshing and flattering to food as they hit their stride. Ultimately, though, you can still expect more emphasis on instant gratification from the New World and more restrained food-oriented sensibility from the Old World.

THE TASTING

Identifying Old World and New World Styles

Compare European and international wines at home

Sample these wines side by side to get a sense of how variations in geography and culture combine to produce wines that taste very different even when the same grape is used.

KEY DIFFERENCES
New World wines tend to be more modern: riper and fruitier, designed for a strong first impression. European Old World wines tend to be more traditional: leaner and drier, designed to be flattering food partners.

OLD WORLD WHITE WINE

NEW WORLD WHITE WINE

OLD WORLD RED WINE

For example...

French Loire Valley Sauvignon Blanc, such as Sancerre, Pouilly-Fumé, Touraine, Quincy; or substitute with unoaked white Bordeaux

Can you detect...?

Very low sugar/very dry; Very high acidity/very tart; Medium-low fruit intensity; No oak flavour; Low alcohol/light; Noticeable "earthy" scent, like wet leaves and stones

The French way

Sauvignon Blanc barely ripens in northern France, so these wines are austere and food-oriented.

For example...

New Zealand Sauvignon Blanc; or substitute with Chilean Sauvignon Blanc or an American version from California or Washington

Can you detect...?

Low sugar/dry; High acidity/tart; Medium-high fruit intensity; No oak flavour; Medium alcohol/mid-weight; Very "fruity" scent, like fresh tropical fruit

The New Zealand way

New Zealand also makes cool-climate, unoaked Sauvignon Blanc but in a much more modern style that is riper and easier to enjoy without food.

For example...

Italian Primitivo (aka Zinfandel) from southern Italy's Puglia region; or alternatively, a French Bourgogne/Pinot Noir

Can you detect...?

Very low sugar/very dry; Very high acidity/very tart; Medium fruit intensity; Mild oak flavour; Medium alcohol/mid-weight; Noticeable "earthy" scent, like dried leaves or root vegetables

The southern Italian way

Southern Italian vintners prioritize seafood-friendliness in their wines, so grapes are harvested early enough to retain vibrant acidity.

Lean vs lush

Both pairs of wines are made with the same grape variety and in a similar way. But in each case, the European one will taste more "traditional" in style: lighter and leaner, lower in sugar and higher in acidity, and with aromas that seem more earthy and less fruity. The New World wine will be heavier and riper, slightly higher in sugar, and lower in acidity. It will feature more dessert-like smells, even if it is dry, and is more likely to have noticeable oak flavour.

**NEW WORLD
RED WINE**

For example...
Red Zinfandel (aka Primitivo) from any region of California; or alternatively, a California Pinot Noir

Can you detect...?
Lowish sugar/dry or faintly sweet; Moderate acidity/tangy; High fruit intensity; Stronger oak flavour; High alcohol/heavy; Very "fruity" scent, like jam or prunes

The American way
Known as Zinfandel in California, the same grape gets different treatment in the USA, where wines are judged on first sip and more often served with red meats and sweet sauces.

Chapter Checklist

Here is a recap of some of the most important points you've learned in this chapter.

✓ Even when using the same **grape variety** and same **winemaking methods**, Old World and New World wines often taste different.

✓ In Europe (the Old World), grapes are generally grown in **cooler regions**, so they tend to achieve lower degrees of **overall ripeness**.

✓ New World regions are often considerably **sunnier, warmer, and drier**, making it easier to achieve higher degrees of grape ripeness.

✓ Wines made in the Old World are often geared towards time-honoured ideals such as **aging well** and **pairing with local food**.

✓ Shaped by **innovation** and more reliant on **technology**, New World wines are typically built around pleasing a **global audience** and impressing **wine critics** on first sip.

✓ Southern regions on the Mediterranean have the longest **winemaking history**. They also have the greatest number of **native grape varieties** and make the most wine.

✓ The French were the first **to pursue wine quality systematically** on a grand scale and, for more than 500 years, provided the model for anyone anywhere who wanted to **improve the quality** of their own wine.

✓ Six of **France's wine zones** are far more **influential** than the rest: Burgundy, Bordeaux, Champagne, the Rhône Valley, the Loire Valley, and Alsace.

✓ Winemaking arrived in the **Americas and southern hemisphere** when those areas were **colonized by Europeans**. These regions are relative **newcomers** to the wine world, especially in terms of fine wine.

DISCOVERING WINE GRAPES AND REGIONS

Once we are comfortable with the big picture, it's time to get down to business, to get acquainted with the major players in the wine world. The grape varieties used to make wine and the regions where wine is made are the most important variables in how a wine will taste. Now that we understand more about how grape flavours shift with ripeness and how geography and culture can affect winemaking outcomes, studying grapes and regions will be much more productive.

There are dozens of wine grapes and hundreds of wine appellations of relevance to wine drinkers. It isn't necessary or even useful to study them all unless wine is your career. But there is a short list of top grapes worth remembering because they are so popular and so influential. And all wine lovers should familiarize themselves with the world's main wine regions, even if only in the broadest sense. After all, just a few dozen very special places on earth are blessed with the right conditions to make great wine. Now that you're a wine expert, you'll want to explore them all.

Check out the
wine grapes
and regions
that best suit
your tastes.

MUST-KNOW WINE GRAPES

The Top 10 Vine Varieties

There are thousands of grape varieties, but the vast majority of modern wines are made with only a few dozen. Of these, a handful have earned celebrity status for their quality and popularity with wine drinkers, such as Chardonnay and Riesling, Cabernet Sauvignon and Pinot Noir. Fine wine as we know it was pioneered in France, so most of these "rock star" grapes are of French heritage, but they are now truly international, cultivated far and wide. Since so many modern wines are labelled by grape variety, it's well worth getting to know the members of the global Top 10.

Grape Varieties

There are many species of grapevine grown around the world, but wine is made with a single species called *Vitis vinifera*, native to Eurasia. The grape names we see on wine labels – like Chardonnay and Shiraz – are the names of grape varieties within this vinifera species. Grape varieties are like breeds of dog: all are members of one species, but they have been bred for specific characteristics. In grapes, varieties may be bred for eating fresh or winemaking, for red wine or white wine, to survive a region's harsh winters or another's summer droughts.

Workhorse grapes

There are thousands of grape varieties, but only a few dozen are of commercial significance in winemaking. Of these, a short list of ten represents the vast majority that wine drinkers are likely to encounter on labels. These are not the ten most widely planted grapes on earth; those are often workhorse grapes, like Airén and Cinsaut, used for making bulk wine or brandy. And the list excludes many grapes that make truly exceptional wine and are popular in their home region but haven't caught on elsewhere, such as Tempranillo and Chenin Blanc.

TOP 10 GRAPE VARIETIES

This Top 10, in no particular order, includes just the most famous grapes – the wine world's jet-set celebrities. They are the grapes we see most often on labels because they are wildly popular and planted all over the world, not just on their home turf but abroad, too.

White wine grapes

- Chardonnay
- Sauvignon Blanc
- Riesling
- Pinot Grigio/Pinot Gris
- Moscato

Red wine grapes

- Cabernet Sauvignon
- Merlot
- Pinot Noir
- Syrah/Shiraz
- Grenache/Garnacha

MORE FAMOUS OVERSEAS

Why do European grapes earn more name recognition when they're grown in the New World than they do at home? The traditional convention for naming wines in Europe is to use the place name. The type of grape used is not always mentioned. In the Americas and southern hemisphere, printing the grape name on the label is the norm. Sangiovese may be the number-one grape in Italy, but its name isn't as familiar as the names of its most famous wines, like Chianti or Brunello di Montalcino. Meanwhile, Malbec is a household name simply because vintners in Argentina, where most is grown, place it on the label.

Why grapes?

Wine can be made from all sorts of fruit, but grapes are the fruit of choice because they have the sweetest juice. Wine grapes contain at least 20 per cent fermentable sugar when ripe and over 70 per cent water, which makes them ideal for making into an alcoholic drink.

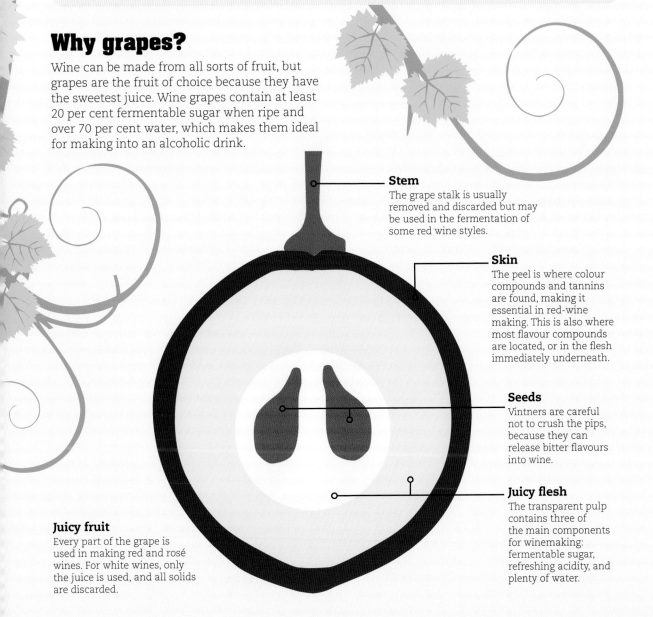

Stem
The grape stalk is usually removed and discarded but may be used in the fermentation of some red wine styles.

Skin
The peel is where colour compounds and tannins are found, making it essential in red-wine making. This is also where most flavour compounds are located, or in the flesh immediately underneath.

Seeds
Vintners are careful not to crush the pips, because they can release bitter flavours into wine.

Juicy flesh
The transparent pulp contains three of the main components for winemaking: fermentable sugar, refreshing acidity, and plenty of water.

Juicy fruit
Every part of the grape is used in making red and rosé wines. For white wines, only the juice is used, and all solids are discarded.

Chardonnay

WHITE WINE GRAPE

No other grape can match the popularity of Chardonnay, which can make some of the richest, strongest white wines on earth without losing finesse. Chardonnays are almost always dry in style, and only mass-market brands flirt with a hint of sweetness. The vine adapts well to varying climates, so every country that produces wine grows at least a little Chardonnay.

APPLEY FLAVOUR FAMILY

— THE FLAVOUR RANGE —

CRAB APPLE   GREEN APPLE   PINEAPPLE   APPLE PIE

LOW RIPENESS/
COOL CLIMATE

HIGH RIPENESS/
WARM CLIMATE

Seasoned with oak

Chardonnay is very subtle in flavour, so vintners often amplify its aromatics by fermenting in new barrels. Grapes must be fully ripe for oak to be a pleasing accent, however, so its presence tends to be strongest in the heaviest wines from the warmest regions. New World Chardonnays are so often oaky, for example, that many wine drinkers think their toasty cognac-like flavours are inherent to the grape, but this is not so. Unoaked Chardonnays, sometimes called "unwooded" or "naked", can taste as crisp and mild as Pinot Grigio.

THE CHARDONNAY STYLE RANGE

Even when made in different styles and regions, wines from this grape fall within the sensory categories highlighted below.

	LOW	MEDIUM	HIGH
Colour	White	N/A	N/A
Colour Depth	Pale	Moderate	Dark
Sweetness	Dry	Lightly sweet	N/A
Acidity	Soft acidity	Tangy	Tart
Fruit Intensity	Mild	Flavourful	N/A
Oak Presence	None	Mild oak	Strong oak
Weight/Body	Light	Mid-weight	Heavy

RED-LIKE WHITE

Red wines are typically heavier and oakier than whites, but Chardonnays can compete on both counts. Not only are they often oaked (unlike most white wines), but they feel richer for another reason, too. Chardonnay can produce more sugar than other green grapes without losing refreshing acidity, and this boosts the alcohol content of its wines.

Where's it from?

Chardonnay originated in France's Burgundy region, where quality viticulture developed in medieval times. Even today, all white wines from Burgundy are 100 per cent Chardonnay. Classy, understated "white Burgundy" remains the benchmark Chardonnay style, emulated by vintners worldwide. Warmer New World regions like California and Australia grow riper Chardonnay, making bold, fruity, opulent wines. These are tremendously popular and conveniently labelled with the grape name. Cooler regions, like New Zealand and Canada, make lighter, brighter, more Burgundian styles.

OTHER TOP CHARDONNAY REGIONS

①	USA	California: Sonoma, Santa Barbara, Monterey; Other states: Washington, Oregon, New York
②	AUSTRALIA	South Australia: Adelaide, Padthaway; Other states: Victoria, New South Wales, Western Australia
③	CHILE	Casablanca Valley, Maipo Valley, Aconcagua
④	SOUTH AFRICA	Coastal Region, Stellenbosch, Cape South Coast
⑤	NEW ZEALAND	Hawkes Bay, Gisborne, Marlborough
⑥	CANADA	Niagara Peninsula, Okanagan Valley

☆ ARCHETYPE: FRENCH WHITE BURGUNDY

Typically unoaked in coolest regions and modest appellations: Bourgogne Blanc, Mâcon-Villages, Chablis, St-Véran, Viré-Clessé

Typically barrel-fermented in warmer premium appellations: Meursault, Puligny-Montrachet, Pouilly-Fuissé, Chassagne-Montrachet

Chardonnay is also one of three grapes grown in neighbouring Champagne: *Blanc de blancs* is 100 per cent Chardonnay.

The golden child of wine
Winemakers love Chardonnay for many reasons. The vines adapt well to diverse climate conditions, the golden-tinged grapes make excellent wine in a variety of different styles, and the Chardonnay name is trusted by wine drinkers worldwide.

Sauvignon Blanc

Wines made from Sauvignon Blanc are more recognizable than most whites, thanks to their sharp acidity and distinctive pungent scent, typically of green foods such as herbs, vegetables, or even green fruit – from lime, to honeydew melon. These wines are tremendously popular, largely because they deliver reliably good value at reasonable prices.

WHITE WINE GRAPE

HERBAL FLAVOUR
FAMILY

— THE FLAVOUR RANGE —

| CRAB APPLE | GRAPEFRUIT | PASSION FRUIT | KIWI FRUIT |

LOW RIPENESS/
COOL CLIMATE

HIGH RIPENESS/
WARM CLIMATE

Twin styles

Most Sauvignon Blanc wines are medium-bodied and dry, but they can be made in one of two distinct styles. The most common is the cool-climate Loire model, popularized in New Zealand: sharp and citrusy unoaked wines, with mouthwatering acidity. Where greater ripeness is possible, such as in California, the white Bordeaux model is sometimes followed for premium wines. Using oak and blending with Semillon enriches and softens this "savage" grape to give wines that are plumper, less "green" in flavour, and less aggressive in their acidity.

THE SAUVIGNON BLANC STYLE RANGE

Even when made in different styles and regions, wines from this grape fall within the sensory categories highlighted below.

	LOW	MEDIUM	HIGH
Colour	White	N/A	N/A
Colour Depth	Pale	N/A	N/A
Sweetness	Dry	N/A	N/A
Acidity	N/A	Tangy	Tart
Fruit Intensity	N/A	Flavourful	Bold
Oak Presence	None	Mild oak	N/A
Weight/Body	Light	Mid-weight	N/A

WILD VINE

The name Sauvignon may derive from the French word *sauvage* (meaning untamed or savage) and might refer to this grape's resemblance to wild vines or possibly to the ferocity of its scent. Either way, the name was passed on to its offspring, the famed red Cabernet Sauvignon grape.

Where's it from?

Sauvignon Blanc is indigenous to Bordeaux on the Atlantic coast of France, where it is the primary white grape in dry Bordeaux Blanc and Graves wines. However, Sauvignon Blanc has also been grown for centuries in the upper reaches of the Loire Valley further north. It is the sharp, tart white wines made there, in appellations like Sancerre and Pouilly-Fumé, that serve as the grape's main international benchmark. Around the world, Sauvignon Blanc is grown to some degree in most wine regions, but it has been most enthusiastically embraced in New Zealand and the USA.

Paris · Loire Valley

FRANCE

Bordeaux

Bordeaux and Loire Valley
(5)
(2)
(4)
(3)
(1)

OTHER TOP SAUVIGNON BLANC REGIONS

(1) **NEW ZEALAND** South Island: Marlborough, Canterbury; North Island: Hawkes Bay, Gisborne

(2) **USA** California: Sonoma, Napa, Central Coast; Washington: Columbia Valley

(3) **SOUTH AFRICA** Coastal Region, Cape South Coast

(4) **CHILE** Casablanca Valley, Maipo Valley

(5) **ITALY** Trentino, Alto Adige, Friuli

☆ ARCHETYPES: FRENCH WHITE BORDEAUX AND LOIRE WHITES

Bordeaux: Sauvignon Blanc-based blends with Semillon
Typically unoaked and bottled young in modest appellations: Bordeaux, Entre-Deux-Mers

Typically barrel-fermented and aged in premium appellations: Graves, Pessac-Léognan

Loire Valley: 100 per cent Sauvignon Blanc
Typically unoaked and bottled young in all appellations: Sancerre, Pouilly-Fumé, Touraine

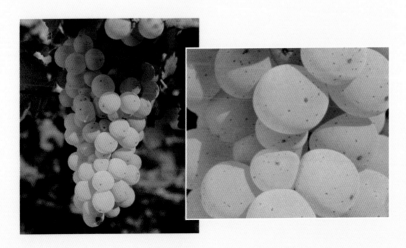

Prolific and flavourful

Sauvignon Blanc is an uncommonly vigorous vine that can yield bumper crops without losing much flavour intensity. However, its aromatics can tilt towards the vegetable realm when too much of its energy is spent producing shoots and leaves.

Riesling

If Riesling has a superpower, it is the ability to make flavourful balanced wines at freakishly low alcoholic strength. Vintners often make pleasing sweet wines from Riesling as a result, since it is less essential to convert grape sugar into alcohol than for other varieties. These wines have become Riesling's claim to fame because they succeed at something other grapes fail to do well.

WHITE WINE GRAPE

APPLEY FLAVOUR FAMILY

← LIME ←— **THE FLAVOUR RANGE** —→ GREEN APPLE   PEACH   APRICOT →

LOW RIPENESS/ COOL CLIMATE

HIGH RIPENESS/ WARM CLIMATE

How sweet is it?

The most popular and most widely known style of Riesling takes its inspiration from the lightly sweet wines of Germany's Mosel and Rheingau regions – wines that feature the sweet/tart balance of green apples. However, Riesling can be found at every degree of sweetness – from bone-dry, to candy sweet dessert wines – both inside Germany and in other parts of the world. Dry interpretations model themselves on the French Alsace style, where Riesling makes graceful wines that are fuller-bodied and much less sweet.

THE RIESLING STYLE RANGE

Even when made in different styles and regions, wines from this grape fall within the sensory categories highlighted below.

	LOW	MEDIUM	HIGH
Colour	White	N/A	N/A
Colour Depth	Pale	Moderate	N/A
Sweetness	Dry	Lightly sweet	Fully sweet
Acidity	N/A	Tangy	Tart
Fruit Intensity	Mild	Flavourful	Bold
Oak Presence	None	N/A	N/A
Weight/Body	Light	Mid-weight	Heavy

BUILT FOR AGING

Wines made from Riesling have exceptional aging potential and can improve in the cellar for decades longer than most white wines. People often assume that lighter whites need to be drunk young, but Riesling has a strong natural resistance to oxidation, thanks in part to its high levels of acidity.

Where's it from?

Riesling is native to the southwestern German valleys of the Rhine and its tributaries between Frankfurt and Trier, where it makes delicate wines that often feature a touch of natural grape sugar. Across the border in France, Riesling also has a long history in Alsace, where it traditionally makes a stronger, drier wine. This vine makes its best international wines in colder climates, too. Vintners making Riesling in North America and New Zealand most often follow the sweeter German style, while those in Austria and Australia tend to favour the drier French approach.

Rhine Valley and Alsace

OTHER TOP RIESLING REGIONS

1. **USA**
   Washington: Columbia Valley;
   New York: Finger Lakes;
   Other states: California, Oregon

2. **AUSTRIA**
   Lower Austria, Vienna, Burgenland

3. **AUSTRALIA**
   South Australia: Clare Valley, Eden Valley;
   Other states: Victoria, Western Australia,
   Tasmania

4. **CANADA**
   Niagara Peninsula, Okanagan Valley

5. **NEW ZEALAND**
   South Island: Marlborough, Otago, Nelson

☆ ARCHETYPES: GERMAN RIESLING AND FRENCH ALSACE RIESLING

Germany: 100 per cent Riesling
Traditionally light, tart, and lightly sweet – often below 11% alcohol – in top appellations: Mosel, Rheingau, Pfalz, Rheinhessen

France: 100 per cent Riesling
Traditionally mid-weight, tart, and dry – usually over 12.5% alcohol – in Alsace

Small and intense
Riesling grapes are very small, which increases the flavour intensity of their wines, since the flesh closest to the berry's skin is highest in aromatic compounds. Compared to other fine-wine grapes, it ripens very early and produces healthy yields.

Pinot Grigio/Pinot Gris

This is an odd grape in many ways. Not only is it a red grape that makes white wine under two different names, but its wines have a split personality. Under its French identity, Pinot Gris makes wines that are opulent and flavour-rich; while as Pinot Grigio from northern Italy, it makes one of the most popular wines in the world in a much lighter, much milder style.

WHITE WINE GRAPE

APPLEY FLAVOUR
FAMILY

GREEN PEAR — **THE FLAVOUR RANGE** — RED APPLE — PEACH — CANTALOUPE

LOW RIPENESS/
COOL CLIMATE

HIGH RIPENESS/
WARM CLIMATE

The grey Pinot

As its name suggests, this grape is related to Burgundy's red Pinot Noir. It is a paler-skinned mutation that looks pinkish red rather than deep purple – hence its original name Pinot Gris: grey Pinot. Nowadays, though, we more often see it labelled in Italian: Pinot Grigio.

In the New World, the name used often reflects the wine's style. Vintners using the lighter Italian model and name harvest early to retain freshness. Those labelling their wine Pinot Gris are more likely to let the grapes ripen more fully, French-style, making stronger and more fragrant wine.

THE PINOT GRIGIO/PINOT GRIS STYLE RANGE

Even when made in different styles and regions, wines from this grape fall within the sensory categories highlighted below.

	LOW	MEDIUM	HIGH
Colour	White	Pink	N/A
Colour Depth	Pale	Moderate	Dark
Sweetness	Dry	Lightly sweet	N/A
Acidity	Soft acidity	Tangy	Tart
Fruit Intensity	Mild	Flavourful	N/A
Oak Presence	None	Mild oak	N/A
Weight/Body	Light	Mid-weight	Heavy

BRASSY ROSÉ

Pinot Grigio grapes are technically red, but they lack the colour saturation needed to make satisfying red wines so are typically made into white wine instead. However, if the grapes are fermented with full skin contact, they can make a coppery pink rosé.

Where's it from?

Originally from Burgundy in France, Pinot Gris migrated east and settled comfortably in Alsace, where it still makes rich, plump wines. From there, it travelled across Germany and into the Dolomites in what is now northern Italy. It was common practice to harvest grapes early in these valleys, at lower ripeness than in sun-drenched Alsace, and the resulting wines were much lower in alcohol and milder in flavour. When the vine spread to the plains around Venice, this early-harvest approach remained the norm for Italian Pinot Grigio because it was easy-drinking and inexpensive to produce.

OTHER TOP PINOT GRIGIO/PINOT GRIS REGIONS

1 USA   California: Sonoma, Central Coast; Oregon: Willamette Valley

2 GERMANY   Pfalz, Baden

3 CANADA   Niagara Peninsula, Okanagan Valley

4 AUSTRIA   Styria, Burgenland

5 NEW ZEALAND Hawkes Bay, Gisborne, Marlborough

6 AUSTRALIA   South Australia, Victoria

☆ ARCHETYPES: ITALIAN PINOT GRIGIO AND FRENCH ALSACE PINOT GRIS

Italy: 100 per cent Pinot Grigio
Light, mild, and crisp "low ripeness" style – usually below 13% alcohol – in top appellations: Venezie, Trentino, Friuli

France: 100 per cent Pinot Gris
Rich, aromatic, and plump "high ripeness" style – usually over 13% alcohol – in Alsace

A faded grape

Two genes in grapes produce the colour compounds that result in purple skins. Pinot Gris is a mutation of Pinot Noir in which one of these has been deactivated, resulting in its odd faded purple coloration.

Moscato

A diverse range of wine styles is made from Moscato, but whether they're fresh and fruity or dark and raisiny, almost all are sweet and smell of flowers. The perfumed scent derives from terpenes – aroma compounds that cause Moscato to be markedly more pungent than other wine styles (though similarly terpene-rich Gewurztraminer comes close).

WHITE WINE GRAPE

FLORAL FLAVOUR FAMILY

← GREEN GRAPE   LYCHEE   — **THE FLAVOUR RANGE** —   ROSEWATER   DRIED APRICOT →

LOW RIPENESS/ COOL CLIMATE

HIGH RIPENESS/ WARM CLIMATE

From juicy to raisiny

The aromatic intensity of Moscato can seem unbalanced in dry wines, so it tends to be used to make fully sweet styles. The most famous Moscatos are made by using either temperature control or additional distilled spirit to interrupt fermentation, as with the low-alcohol, bubbly Moscatos of Asti and the high-alcohol, liqueur-like Muscats of the south of France. However, in many sunny regions – such as Spain, Portugal, and Australia – the grapes are dried before winemaking begins, to make a dark, thick, and sticky fortified dessert wine.

THE MOSCATO STYLE RANGE

Even when made in different styles and regions, wines from this grape fall within the sensory categories highlighted below.

	LOW	MEDIUM	HIGH
Colour	White	Pink	Red
Colour Depth	Pale	Moderate	Dark
Sweetness	Dry	Lightly sweet	Fully sweet
Acidity	Soft acidity	Tangy	Tart
Fruit Intensity	N/A	N/A	Bold
Oak Presence	None	N/A	N/A
Weight/Body	Light	Mid-weight	Heavy

MUSKY NAMES

Moscato is known as Muscat in French and Moscatel in Spanish, and its name can even be an adjective when variants of other grapes display a floral scent, as with Chardonnay Musqué. But the similar-sounding Muscadet, a white from northern France, is confusingly of no relation and bears no aromatic resemblance whatsoever.

Where's it from?

Moscato's fine-wine potential was already well known in ancient Greece, and it may be a common ancestor of many top grapes. It is not a single variety but, rather, a family of grapes with more than 100 distinct variants, many cultivated for table grapes or raisins throughout the Mediterranean. While most Moscato varieties are white, some are purple and can be used to make red wine. Wines made from these fragrant grapes are common in much of southern Europe but are also found in the New World.

OTHER TOP MOSCATO REGIONS

① FRANCE   Rhône, Languedoc-Roussillon (sweet), Alsace (dry)

② PORTUGAL   Setúbal, Douro

③ AUSTRALIA   Victoria: Rutherglen;
              Other states: New South Wales,
              South Australia

④ USA   California

⑤ GREECE   Samos, Patras, Rhodes

☆ ARCHETYPES: ITALIAN MOSCATO AND SPANISH MOSCATEL

Piedmont, Italy: 100 per cent Moscato Bianco
Low alcohol, sweet, sparkling, and fresh tasting – under 10% alcohol – in Asti

Andalusia, Spain: 100 per cent Muscat of Alexandria
High alcohol, sweet, fortified, and from dried grapes – over 15% alcohol – in Sherry and Malaga

Going green

Moscato can be found in all three common grape colours – green, purple, and pinkish red – but the green variant known as Moscato Bianco or Muscat Blanc à Petits Grains is the most prized for fine wines.

Cabernet Sauvignon

RED WINE GRAPE

Cabernet Sauvignon is the king of red wine grapes. Compared to its rivals, it has unusually small berries and thick skins, resulting in more purple solids and less clear juice. In red wines, more dark grape skins result in more colour, flavour, and tannins, so these traits are very intense in Cabernet Sauvignon wines, especially in those from low-yielding premium vineyards.

BLACK-FRUIT
FLAVOUR FAMILY

| ROASTED PEPPER | BLACKCURRANT | | BLACKBERRY | BRANDIED CHERRY |

LOW RIPENESS/
COOL CLIMATE

HIGH RIPENESS/
WARM CLIMATE

Perfect blending grape

Rich in natural preservatives, Cabernet Sauvignon can seem harsh when young, but its resistance to oxidation is a blessing for age-worthy premium wines. Pure Cabernet Sauvignon's intensity in colour, flavour, and tannin can yield lean, aggressive wines, but it is perfect for blending with milder grapes. When it takes a dominant role, Cabernet is often softened by adding fruitier wine from fleshier grapes like Merlot or Shiraz. In smaller proportions, it can add density and aging potential to wines made with thinner-skinned grapes, such as Merlot, Sangiovese, or Malbec.

THE CABERNET SAUVIGNON STYLE RANGE

Even when made in different styles and regions, wines from this grape fall within the sensory categories highlighted below.

	LOW	MEDIUM	HIGH
Colour	N/A	N/A	Red
Colour Depth	N/A	Moderate	Dark
Sweetness	Dry	N/A	N/A
Acidity	N/A	Tangy	Tart
Fruit Intensity	N/A	N/A	Bold
Oak Presence	None	Mild oak	Strong oak
Weight/Body	N/A	Mid-weight	Heavy

MYSTERY BLENDS

Some of Cabernet Sauvignon's top wines don't list its name on the front label. Not only do European classics like Bordeaux and Bolgheri rarely mention their grapes, but international blends are not permitted to name a grape unless the wine contains at least 75 per cent of that variety.

Where's it from?

Cabernet Sauvignon is indigenous to Bordeaux, where it has historically dominated the blend in the most prestigious wines of France's premier red wine region. Cabernet Sauvignon's flavour density and capacity to age gracefully have earned it a role in the top red wines of many nations. In the New World, it produces the most expensive and collectible red wines made in the USA, Chile, and South Africa, which are often Bordeaux-inspired blends.

OTHER TOP CABERNET SAUVIGNON REGIONS

① **USA** — California: Napa Valley, Sonoma, Paso Robles; Washington: Columbia Valley

② **ITALY** — Tuscany, Trentino

③ **CHILE** — Maipo Valley, Rapel Valley, Aconcagua

④ **AUSTRALIA** — South Australia: Coonawarra

⑤ **SOUTH AFRICA** — Coastal Region, Stellenbosch, Paarl

☆ ARCHETYPE: FRENCH RED BORDEAUX

Dark, intense blends, with strong oak and high tannin

Typically dominates blends in the warmest premium appellations: Haut-Médoc, Margaux, Pauillac, St-Estèphe, St-Julien, Moulis

Typically has a supporting role in cooler modest appellations: Bordeaux, Graves, St-Emilion

Sun-loving variety

Cabernet Sauvignon vines bud later in the spring than most Bordeaux varieties, and their fruit takes longer to ripen in the autumn. Their small thick-skinned berries need ample sun to develop to their full potential in colour and flavour.

Merlot

If Bordeaux's Cabernet Sauvignon is a muscular superhero, its close relation Merlot is its lithe sidekick with a sexier name. Wines made from this variety are not as dark, tannic, or intense as those of Cabernet Sauvignon as a rule. They are softer and milder, with more voluptuous fruit flavours – characteristics that make Merlot more appealing for drinking young.

RED WINE GRAPE

BLACK-FRUIT
FLAVOUR FAMILY

| TOMATO | BLACK PLUM | BLACKBERRY | CHERRY PIE |

LOW RIPENESS/
COOL CLIMATE

HIGH RIPENESS/
WARM CLIMATE

The price of popularity

Merlot is so crowd-pleasing that it is often exploited for volume in everyday wines, and its reputation has been devalued a little by cheap and cheerful bottlings. However, when planted in top vineyard sites and made to rigorous standards, Merlot makes wines of incredible power and grace. In Bordeaux, this grape is typically relegated to marginal land; however, cult wines made with 100 per cent Merlot, like the legendary Château Pétrus, command higher prices than their Cabernet-based rivals, proving that this variety is one of the world's finest red grapes.

THE MERLOT STYLE RANGE

Even when made in different styles and regions, wines from this grape fall within the sensory categories highlighted below.

	LOW	MEDIUM	HIGH
Colour	N/A	N/A	Red
Colour Depth	N/A	Moderate	Dark
Sweetness	Dry	N/A	N/A
Acidity	Soft acidity	Tangy	Tart
Fruit Intensity	N/A	Flavourful	Bold
Oak Presence	None	Mild oak	Strong oak
Weight/Body	N/A	Mid-weight	Heavy

DRINK ME NOW

Merlot often gets overshadowed by Cabernet Sauvignon, because its wines are lighter, softer, and do not age as gracefully. But in a world where instant gratification is the name of the game, Merlot's supposed weaknesses are really its strengths.

Where's it from?

Merlot and Cabernet Sauvignon are closely related grapes from Bordeaux that share a family resemblance in aromatics but differ in their power, colour, and tannic grip. In Bordeaux, Merlot is by far the most widely planted of the two because it ripens much earlier and is therefore a more economically viable variety. However, this grape truly comes into its own in the Americas, making luscious, friendly red wines labelled under its own name, from Chile in the south, to California and Washington in the north.

OTHER TOP MERLOT REGIONS

(1) **USA** — California: Napa Valley, Sonoma; Washington: Columbia Valley

(2) **CHILE** — Maipo Valley, Rapel Valley, Aconcagua

(3) **ITALY** — Northern Italy, Tuscany

(4) **NEW ZEALAND** — Hawkes Bay, Marlborough

(5) **CANADA** — Okanagan Valley, Niagara Peninsula

☆ ARCHETYPE: FRENCH RED BORDEAUX

Mid-weight, flavourful blends with soft tannin and mild oak

Typically dominates blends in cooler modest appellations: Bordeaux, Graves, St-Emilion, Pomerol

Typically plays a supporting role in the warmest premium appellations: Haut-Médoc, Margaux, Pauillac, St-Estèphe, St-Julien, Moulis

Fragile but generous

Merlot's thinner skins and looser clusters make it more fragile in the vineyard than other Bordeaux varieties like Cabernet Sauvignon, but this disadvantage is more than offset by its early ripening and generous yields per vine.

Pinot Noir

In many ways, Pinot Noir is the polar opposite of Cabernet Sauvignon. Pinot Noir has thin skins, not thick, and makes much lighter, paler wines that are not as well suited to blending or long-term aging. Cabernet Sauvignon needs extra heat to ripen fully, while Pinot Noir needs cooler conditions to retain its seductive earthy charm and falls flat in places where it gets too ripe and fruity.

RED WINE GRAPE

RED-BERRY
FLAVOUR FAMILY

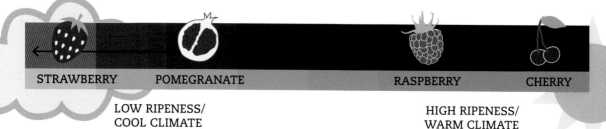

| STRAWBERRY | POMEGRANATE | RASPBERRY | CHERRY |

LOW RIPENESS/
COOL CLIMATE

HIGH RIPENESS/
WARM CLIMATE

Seductive finesse

Pinot Noir is Cabernet Sauvignon's closest rival for the red wine crown – indeed, many feel it makes superior wines. While Cabernet can perform reliably in many wine regions and sets itself apart with sheer power, Pinot Noir is much more fickle and seduces with its finesse.

This seemingly weaker red wine only truly shines in a handful of regions, and it can disappoint when conditions aren't just right. But when Pinot Noir excels, it makes wines that are hauntingly beautiful and speak directly to the soul in a way that Cabernet cannot.

THE PINOT NOIR STYLE RANGE

Even when made in different styles and regions, wines from this grape fall within the sensory categories highlighted below.

	LOW	MEDIUM	HIGH
Colour	N/A	N/A	Red
Colour Depth	Pale	Moderate	N/A
Sweetness	Dry	N/A	N/A
Acidity	Soft acidity	Tangy	Tart
Fruit Intensity	N/A	Flavourful	Bold
Oak Presence	None	Mild oak	Strong oak
Weight/Body	N/A	Mid-weight	Heavy

FINGERPRINTING

The term *terroir* was coined in Burgundy to capture Pinot Noir's uncanny knack of tasting slightly different in every place it's grown. Centuries ago, it was noted that each aspect of a vineyard – from soil type, to orientation of its slope – could create a recognizable flavour, a unique fingerprint of the land, captured in its wine.

Where's it from?

Pinot Noir is, in one sense, the original wine grape; it is the red grape of Burgundy, where fine wine as we know it was born in medieval France. Pinot Noir prefers cooler growing conditions than most red grapes and is too fragile for large-scale farming. Outside of Burgundy, it makes exceptional wine in only a few small regions like Oregon and California in the USA, New Zealand and southeastern Australia, and Germany and northern Italy.

OTHER TOP PINOT NOIR REGIONS

① USA   California: Sonoma, Santa Barbara, Monterey; Oregon: Willamette Valley

② GERMANY   Pfalz, Baden, Rheingau

③ NEW ZEALAND   Central Otago, Martinborough, Marlborough

④ ITALY   Trentino-Alto Adige

⑤ AUSTRALIA   Yarra Valley, Adelaide Hills, Tasmania

⑥ SOUTH AFRICA Franschoek, Walker Bay, Cape South Coast

⑦ CANADA   Niagara Peninsula, Okanagan Valley

☆ ARCHETYPE: FRENCH RED BURGUNDY

All Burgundy red wines except Beaujolais are 100 per cent Pinot Noir

Typically light, pale, and tart in modest appellations: Bourgogne, Mercurey, and Côte de Beaune villages like Santenay and Chorey-lès-Beaune

Richer, darker, and more fragrant in premium appellations: most Côte de Nuits villages like Gevrey-Chambertin, Nuits-St-Georges, and select Côte de Beaune villages like Volnay and Pommard

Pinot Noir is also one of three grapes grown in neighbouring Champagne.

Hard work pays off

Pinot Noir is an early-ripening variety that performs best in cooler regions, where its final rush to ripeness is slowed. The finest variants of this cultivar are low-yielding and demanding to farm, but the results are well worth the effort.

Syrah/Shiraz

RED WINE GRAPE

SPICED-FRUIT FLAVOUR FAMILY

Whether it's called by its original French name Syrah or its southern hemisphere alias Shiraz, this Rhône grape is a true powerhouse. Its wines can rival Cabernet Sauvignon for intensity, depth, and aging capacity because the variety has similarly small berries with thick, dark skins. Like Cabernet, it needs ample sun to reach full ripeness but has more juicy fruit character to help it stand alone more easily.

RASPBERRY   BLACK PLUM   BLACKBERRY JAM   BLUEBERRY PIE

LOW RIPENESS/ COOL CLIMATE   HIGH RIPENESS/ WARM CLIMATE

Flavour and colour booster

Syrah's distinctive spicy scent, blue-tinged colour, and preservative tannins make it a marvellous blending partner for intensifying milder or paler grapes. While it can taste delicious and balanced on its own, many vintners soften its impact with small amounts of other grapes. This pattern is inspired by Syrah's traditional role in the Rhône, where most is used to bolster paler Grenache, as with Côtes du Rhône. In smaller appellations, it is often mellowed with a smidgen of local green grapes. Syrah is more generally seen unblended in the New World, often as Shiraz.

THE SYRAH/SHIRAZ STYLE RANGE

Even when made in different styles and regions, wines from this grape fall within the sensory categories highlighted below.

	LOW	MEDIUM	HIGH
Colour	N/A	N/A	Red
Colour Depth	N/A	Moderate	Dark
Sweetness	Dry	Lightly sweet	N/A
Acidity	Soft acidity	Tangy	Tart
Fruit Intensity	N/A	Flavourful	Bold
Oak Presence	None	Mild oak	Strong oak
Weight/Body	N/A	Mid-weight	Heavy

PEPPER POT

Many Syrah wines have an uncanny smell reminiscent of pepper. In chilly regions and at low ripeness, it can come across as a pickled green-peppercorn scent, but with more sunshine it develops into a cracked black-pepper smell that can make you want to sneeze. However, at the very highest ripeness levels, this aroma becomes less prominent.

Where's it from?

Syrah hails from the south of France, where its primary use is as a *vin médecin*, strengthening blends in the southern Rhône Valley. Syrah does make its own wine in a few tiny appellations further north, along the Rhône's steep banks, like tart Crozes-Hermitage and spicy Côte-Rôtie, but these are rare, and many are quite expensive. As a result, it is in jammier New World wines that Syrah takes centre stage, most notably as Australia's signature grape Shiraz.

Paris○

FRANCE

Northern Rhône Valley

☆ ARCHETYPE: FRENCH NORTHERN RHÔNE REDS

Northern Rhône Valley Syrah-based wines – 80–100 per cent; dark, tannic red wines with intense peppery aromatics

Modest appellations: Crozes-Hermitage, St-Joseph

Premium appellations: Hermitage, Côte-Rôtie, Cornas

Rhône Valley

OTHER TOP SYRAH/SHIRAZ REGIONS

① AUSTRALIA — South Australia: Barossa, McLaren Vale; Other states: Victoria, New South Wales, Western Australia

② USA — California: Napa Valley, Sonoma, Santa Barbara; Washington: Columbia Valley

③ SOUTH AFRICA — Coastal Region, Paarl, Stellenbosch

④ CHILE — Maipo Valley, Rapel Valley, Aconcagua

⑤ SPAIN — Castilla-La Mancha, Catalonia

⑥ CANADA — Okanagan Valley

Thick-skinned and intense
Syrah grapes look blue-black on the vine, and the berries can be as small and thick-skinned as Cabernet Sauvignon. However, despite their intense colour and flavour compounds, Syrah skins generally contain lower levels of preservative tannins.

Grenache/Garnacha

RED WINE GRAPE

The Rhône Valley's workhorse grape can make affordable easy-drinking red wines, as well as sappy, quaffable rosés. But it can also produce rich, concentrated premium reds with savoury spiced aromatics and quite high alcohol levels. Since Grenache oxidizes easily, quickly turning rusty orange, vintners often dose it with dashes of darker Rhône grapes like Syrah or Mourvèdre as a natural preservative.

SPICED-FRUIT
FLAVOUR FAMILY

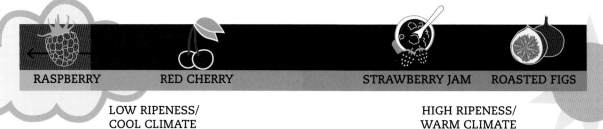

| RASPBERRY | RED CHERRY | STRAWBERRY JAM | ROASTED FIGS |

LOW RIPENESS/
COOL CLIMATE

HIGH RIPENESS/
WARM CLIMATE

Widely planted but rarely named

Grenache wines feature ripe red-fruit flavours, like strawberry jam, often with accents of white pepper and cured ham. Outside its native Spain, where it is called Garnacha, this grape is rarely named on labels despite being the world's most planted wine grape. Many of Grenache's most famous French wines don't mention grapes by tradition, and its least ambitious wines go by generic brand names. Most Grenache wines are blends, often with Rhône partners Syrah and Mourvèdre, so they often fall short of the 75 per cent requirement for labelling by grape.

THE GRENACHE/GARNACHA STYLE RANGE

Even when made in different styles and regions, wines from this grape fall within the sensory categories highlighted below.

	LOW	MEDIUM	HIGH
Colour	N/A	Pink	Red
Colour Depth	Pale	Moderate	N/A
Sweetness	Dry	Lightly sweet	N/A
Acidity	Soft acidity	Tangy	N/A
Fruit Intensity	N/A	Flavourful	Bold
Oak Presence	None	Mild oak	Strong oak
Weight/Body	Light	Mid-weight	Heavy

THINK PINK

In addition to its rock-star red status, Grenache is the world's premier grape for making dry pink wines, thanks to its snappy, fresh strawberry flavours. It is no coincidence that dry rosé wines are specialities of the grape's home turf in southern France, in zones like the Rhône and Provence, as well as northeastern Spain.

Where's it from?

This grape traces its roots to Spain's arid Aragón, where it is called Garnacha, but its most influential role is as Grenache in France's southern Rhône Valley. The majority of French Grenache wines are blends, most often with Syrah and Mourvèdre in Rhône wines like Châteauneuf-du-Pape and Côtes du Rhône, but also with other Spanish grapes like Carignan in Languedoc and Roussillon. Outside Europe, Grenache grows in California and South Africa but is most important in Australia, often in Rhône-style blends labelled GSM, for Grenache, Shiraz, and Mourvèdre.

Paris○

FRANCE

Southern Rhône Valley ○

② ☆ **Rhône Valley**

④

①

⑤   ③

OTHER TOP GRENACHE/GARNACHA REGIONS

① **SPAIN**   Catalonia, Aragón, Navarra

② **OTHER FRANCE** Languedoc, Roussillon, Provence

③ **AUSTRALIA**   South Australia: McLaren Vale, Barossa; Other states: New South Wales, Victoria

④ **USA**   California

⑤ **SOUTH AFRICA** Coastal Region

☆ ARCHETYPE: FRENCH RHÔNE BLENDS

Southern Rhône Valley Grenache-based blends – 70 per cent plus; rich-textured red wines with meaty, peppery flavours

Modest regional-level appellation: Côtes du Rhône

Premium village-level appellations: Châteauneuf-du-Pape, Gigondas, Vacqueyras

Dry mid-weight rosé wines with fresh berry flavours

Modest regional-level appellation: Côtes du Rhône

Premium village-level appellation: Tavel (rosé only)

A many-clustered thing

Grenache is known for its natural tendency to produce many clusters that can be very large in size. Reversing the pattern of most red grapes, its wines often look paler when grown in warmer regions and darker in cooler zones.

The Best of the Rest

Beyond the Top 10, there are many more fascinating grape varieties for wine lovers to explore, such as those in the chart below. The countries with the greatest proliferation of native wine grapes are those where grapes have been grown the longest and where climate conditions are vine-friendly. For example, Italy is the single largest producer of wine on earth, and every one of its 20 regions makes wine. But very little Italian wine is made from the Top 10; the vast majority use local varieties, and even the most widely planted, Sangiovese, makes up less than 15 per cent of Italy's total vineyard area.

	GRAPE	NATIVE REGION	FAMOUS APPELLATIONS
WHITE GRAPES	Pinot Blanc	Burgundy, France	Alsace; Germany; Italy
	Semillon	Bordeaux, France	Sauternes; Australia
	Chenin Blanc	Loire Valley, France	Vouvray; South Africa
	Viognier	Rhône Valley, France	Condrieu; California
	Gewurztraminer	Pfalz, Germany	Alsace; California
	Grüner Veltliner	Lower Austria	Wachau; Kamtal
	Albariño	Galicia, Spain	Rías Baixas; Vinho Verde
RED GRAPES	Gamay	Burgundy, France	Beaujolais; Niagara Peninsula
	Cabernet Franc	Bordeaux, France	Bordeaux; Chinon; Canada
	Carmenère	Bordeaux, France	Chile
	Malbec	Southwest France	Argentina; Cahors
	Sangiovese	Tuscany, Italy	Chianti; Montalcino
	Barbera	Piedmont, Italy	Alba; Asti; Langhe
	Nebbiolo	Piedmont, Italy	Barolo; Barbaresco
	Montepulciano	Abruzzi, Italy	Abruzzo
	Aglianico	Campania, Italy	Taurasi; Vulture
	Zinfandel	Croatia; Italy	California; Apulia
	Monastrell	Valencia, Spain	Bandol; Jumilla
	Tempranillo	Castilla y León, Spain	Rioja; Ribera del Duero
	Pinotage	South Africa	Stellenbosch; Paarl

YET MORE UNIQUE GRAPES

Spain, Portugal, and Greece, like Italy, have dozens of their own unique wine grapes, but these are rarely cultivated outside their native zones. For historical reasons, French grapes have the edge in New World vineyards.

TYPICAL WINE STYLE	ALSO KNOWN AS
Light, tangy whites	Pinot Bianco
Can be dry or fully sweet	
Lightly sweet whites	Steen
Rich, floral whites	
Pungent, floral whites	Traminer
Light, tangy whites	
Light, tangy whites	Alvarinho
Light, fruity reds	
Herbal, mid-weight reds	
Strong, herbal reds	
Strong, earthy reds	
Tart, mid-weight reds	
Tart, mid-weight reds	
Intense, earthy reds	
Tangy, mid-weight reds	
Strong, spicy reds	
Strong, jammy reds	Primitivo
Dark, strong reds	Mourvèdre; Mataro
Tangy, mid-weight reds	
Strong, meaty reds	

Chapter Checklist

Here is a recap of some of the most important points you've learned in this chapter.

✓ The grape names on wine labels are all **varieties** within the **Vitis vinifera** species.

✓ Grapes are well suited to winemaking due to their **high sugar and water** levels.

✓ **Chardonnay** adapts well to varying climates, so every wine-producing country grows at least a little of this popular variety.

✓ Because of its sharp acidity and distinctive pungent scent, **Sauvignon Blanc** is more recognizable than most white wines.

✓ Germany's **Riesling** is considered by many experts to be the world's finest wine grape, but it can range confusingly from dry to sweet.

✓ **Pinot Gris** is capable of making ripe, rich wines but is much more popular in a lighter, brighter form as **Pinot Grigio**.

✓ Despite the many styles of **Moscato**, almost all are sweet and smell strongly of flowers.

✓ **Cabernet Sauvignon** is the most famous of Bordeaux's red varieties. The world's most expensive and age-worthy reds tend to be made with this variety.

✓ Although **Merlot** is better known for bargain wines, it can make powerful and elegant examples when it is not exploited for volume.

✓ **Pinot Noir** is Cabernet Sauvignon's closest rival for the red wine crown – indeed, many feel it makes superior wines.

✓ **Syrah**, also known as **Shiraz**, makes intensely flavoured wines that have the **tannic structure** necessary for long-term aging.

✓ **Grenache** can make hefty, fleshy, bold reds that belie their pale colour. They often feature **savoury scents** such as white pepper or even cured ham.

MUST-KNOW WINE REGIONS

The World's Top Vineyard Zones

Wine is made anywhere grapes grow, but most
world-class wine is produced in a short list
of regions. The classic European wine zones
share certain grape-friendly qualities – dry,
sun-drenched summers and mild winters –
that offer great winemaking potential.
There, local native grapes abound, and not
all wines are made from famous varieties.
In the Americas and the southern hemisphere,
vines thrive in diverse landscapes – from sunny
South Africa, to chilly Canada. Wine can be
like vicarious travel, transporting drinkers to
exotic locales with the pull of a cork.

The Wine Regions of Europe

The complex overlapping geography of the world's wine appellations can only be truly captured in atlas form, but familiarity with the world's most significant sources is all most wine drinkers need. Europe leads global wine production, and its appellation maps are particularly intricate due to both its long wine history and each nation's complicated wine regulations.

Old World domination

For centuries, Western Europe made the world's best wines, and it still makes the most in volume. France, Italy, and Spain are the world's top three producers, despite their small size compared to many New World nations. Four more European countries make and export enough wine to be of importance in the global wine market: Germany, Portugal, Austria, and – to a lesser extent – Greece. The proliferation of native grape varieties in these European nations can confound wine drinkers, as can labelling regulations that are organized differently than they are elsewhere, with the appellation playing a much more important role. Since many European wines are named after their region of origin – like Champagne and Chianti – as opposed to their grape, it's very helpful to get acquainted with the geography of the Old World.

EUROPEAN LEADERS

The majority of the world's wine is made on its original home turf in Europe. Seven nations here rank among the top 15 wine-producing countries in the world: France, Italy, Spain, Germany, Portugal, Greece, and Austria. Per capita wine consumption remains highest here as well, but it is on the decline. Since global demand for wine is growing, emphasis is shifting to international export markets.

FRANCE p.210

Wine-growing regions

Leader of the pack
France leads global wine production in both volume and value, with its most famous wines, such as Champagne, Bordeaux, and Burgundy, commanding uncommonly high prices.

SPAIN p.220

Most land under vine
Spain comes a close third in total production but leads in vineyard area. Many vintners are just beginning to send wine outside Europe, and exports have doubled since the turn of the 21st century.

GERMANY p.222

AUSTRIA p.223

Eastern block

Austria's mountains in the west are not suitable for grapes, so wine is made only in its easternmost third. It ranks 15th among the world's winemaking nations.

Double take

Germany is the world's tenth-largest wine producer, making mostly white wines. However, as a nation, it consumes more than twice as much wine as it makes.

ITALY p.216

Close second

Italy was once the global leader in wine production but is now second to its closest rival, France. Although it is smaller in area than the state of California, every one of its 20 regions makes wine.

PORTUGAL p.224

More than Port

Portugal is the world's 12th-largest wine producer, despite its tiny size. It is best known for its fortified wines, but the world is now also discovering its other offerings.

Grape potential

Most arable terrain in Greece is vine-friendly, and grapes are grown here for wine, raisins, and currants. This nation is 14th in global wine production.

GREECE p.225

France: Burgundy

The Burgundy region of central France, known as Bourgogne in French, is famous for its sensual, expressive wines and world-class native grapes. Burgundy wines are made from single varieties without blending: Chardonnay for whites, and Pinot Noir for all reds except those of the Beaujolais district. Top Burgundies are matured in new oak barrels and are renowned for their food-friendly qualities and cool-climate characteristics.

Background

Modern fine wine traces its roots to medieval Burgundy, and the region remains notoriously difficult for wine drinkers to master. Intricacies of geology, history, and law have resulted in 100 sub-appellations, mystifying labels, and vineyards co-owned by dozens of growers. Yet huge demand for top Burgundy drives prices sky-high, and these are some of the world's most expensive wines. Burgundy's appellation hierarchy, where wines from the smallest defined regions have the highest quality potential, serves as the model for all European wine law. Most regions stop carving out smaller appellations at the village level to avoid confusion, but individual vineyards are recognized in Burgundy. Superior vineyards may be ranked as either *premier cru* or *grand cru*, which mean roughly first class and top class respectively.

Burgundy's wine districts

• **Bourgogne** Entry-level Burgundy wines under this name can be grown anywhere in the region. They may be described as *blanc* for crisp, dry Chardonnay whites or *rouge* for pale, earthy Pinot Noir reds.

• **Chablis** The coolest of Burgundy's districts grows only Chardonnay and is known for its tart, dry white wines that are generally unoaked.

• **Côte d'Or** The finest Burgundies come from famous villages like Chassagne-Montrachet and Chambolle-Musigny on this sunny escarpment south of Dijon.

• **Côte Chalonnaise** This smaller region makes well-crafted, reasonably priced white and red wines under village appellations like Rully and Mercurey.

• **Mâconnais** This large and productive region grows mostly Chardonnay – from affordable, refreshing Mâcon, to more opulent Pouilly-Fuissé.

• **Beaujolais** Only Gamay grapes are grown here – no Pinot Noir – to make light Beaujolais reds that are fruity, affordable, and often unoaked.

BURGUNDY AT A GLANCE

Cool-climate region of northern France

Most popular wines
Bourgogne: basic regional whites and reds
Mâcon, Chablis: crisp, clean whites
Mercurey, Santenay: tart, earthy reds
Beaujolais: light, fruity reds

Most prestigious wines
Meursault, Puligny-Montrachet: toasty, rich whites
Vosne-Romanée, Gevrey-Chambertin: silky, earthy reds

France: Champagne

The Champagne region produces the finest sparkling wines in the world, deftly balancing opulence and austerity. Most are very dry wines carrying the label term *brut* to indicate their lack of sweetness, and all feature refreshingly low alcohol and high acidity. The Chardonnay and Pinot Noir grapes of neighbouring Burgundy are grown here, along with Pinot Meunier, a local Champenois grape in the same family that ripens much earlier.

Background

Located near Paris, Champagne has a very cold climate compared to other wine regions, and its bubbly wines are a creative adaptation to adverse weather conditions. Grapes are picked well below standard ripeness and used to make a still, white base wine that is very light, dry, and sour. Sugar is added to spark a second fermentation, and the resulting natural carbonation is trapped in each bottle. The wines are carefully aged on their yeasty sediment for months or years to acquire toasty flavour. Most Champagnes are blends of red and white grapes, but the grape skins are discarded early so as to make white wines. Since grape flavour varies widely from year to year, most wines are blended from multiple vintages to maintain consistency.

Champagne's sparkling wine styles

● **Non-Vintage Champagne** Entry-level Champagnes are blended from multiple vintages and multiple grapes and age at least 18 months before release.
● **Vintage Champagne** Naming a year on the label indicates a superior "luxury *cuvée*" made with the fruit of a single harvest. Such wines must be aged longer on the lees – at least 3 years – before release.
● **Rosé Champagne** Pink Champagnes are usually dry and delicious, typically tinted with a splash of red Pinot Noir at the final stage of winemaking to deepen their colour and flavour.

Regulated Champagne label terms

● *Brut*, *Extra-Dry*, and *Demi-Sec* These are regulated sweetness terms that mean, respectively, very dry, faintly sweet, and very sweet.
● *Blanc de Blancs* Meaning "white wine from white grapes", this Chardonnay-only category is a premium wine with exceptional aging potential.

CHAMPAGNE AT A GLANCE

Cold-climate region of northern France
Most popular wines
Non-Vintage: dry sparkling white wines
Speciality variations
Rosé: dry sparkling pink wines
Vintage: intense premium sparkling wines
Blanc de blancs: age-worthy sparkling white wines

France: Bordeaux

Bordeaux is the largest wine region of France and makes the world's most influential fine wine. The appellation takes its name from the port of Bordeaux, capital of Aquitaine. Most Bordeaux wines are red, and the region's tradition of aging the finest in new oak barrels has been adopted worldwide. Many other quality-oriented practices debuted here, too, such as estate-bottling and awarding special *grand cru* status to the finest wines.

Background

Blending multiple grapes is the norm in Bordeaux, where regulations permit up to eight local varieties. In practice, dry wines are based on one of three indigenous grapes that have international celebrity status: Cabernet Sauvignon, Merlot, or Sauvignon Blanc. Prime sites are dedicated to Cabernet Sauvignon, which performs best along the Gironde estuary's Left Bank. Merlot, being easier to ripen, is Bordeaux's workhorse grape, and it takes the lead in value-oriented wines. However, it can also produce exceptional wines on the river's Right Bank. White Bordeaux wines are less common. Most are dry Sauvignon Blanc-based blends, but the golden Semillon-based dessert wines of Sauternes are lusciously sweet exceptions. The finest examples of all styles spend time in new oak barrels.

Bordeaux's wine districts

• **Bordeaux** This entry-level regional appellation covers dry red, white, and rosé wines grown anywhere in the region – typically Merlot-based reds and Sauvignon Blanc-based whites. Entre-Deux-Mers whites and reds from Bourg and Blaye are of similar style.

• **Médoc** This district on the river's Left Bank is the only region where Cabernet Sauvignon thrives and dominates the blend in reds, especially in villages such as Margaux and St-Estèphe.

• **Graves** This Left Bank region makes both red and white wines. Reds typically feature nearly equal parts Merlot and Cabernet Sauvignon.

• **Right Bank** Several small appellations on the other side of the river are known for making exceptional Merlot-based red wines, like Pomerol and St-Emilion.

• **Sauternes and Barsac** These sweet wines from the Graves made with shrivelled Semillon grapes set the world standard for luscious, oaky dessert wines.

BORDEAUX AT A GLANCE

Médoc
Paris
Right Bank
Blaye
Bourg
Libourne
Left Bank
Bordeaux
GIRONDE
Graves
Bordeaux region boundary
Entre-Deux-Mers

Moderate-climate region of western France

Most popular wines
Bordeaux, Graves: dry mid-weight reds and whites
Médoc: superior dry reds

Most prestigious wines
Pauillac, Margaux: intense, tannic reds
Pomerol, St-Emilion: softer, fleshier reds
Sauternes: heavy, sweet oaky whites

France: Loire Valley

The longest river in France is the Loire, the banks of which are lined with cool-climate wine regions along its path westwards to the sea. Ripening grapes can be a challenge in this northern region, so light white and sparkling wines are its claim to fame. The Loire's vineyards fall into three distinct climate zones, each favouring different grape varieties.

Background

The Loire's top appellations are Sancerre and Pouilly-Fumé, upriver from Orléans. These dry white wines are produced with 100 per cent Sauvignon Blanc, but this Bordeaux grape is made differently in this colder zone, entirely unoaked and unblended. Downstream, the river's warmer mid-section is perfect for the Loire's most important indigenous grape Chenin Blanc, whose white wines like Vouvray can range from bone-dry to dessert-sweet. Red and pink wines are grown here, the best using another Bordeaux grape: Cabernet Franc. Finally, nearest the sea, Melon grapes make brisk, dry white Muscadet.

Loire Valley's top white wine styles

- **Sancerre and Pouilly-Fumé** Tart, dry white wines that scour the palate clean, these are the archetypes for most modern Sauvignon Blanc.
- **Vouvray and Montlouis** These Chenin Blanc whites can be dry or sweet, still or sparkling, but the most popular are lightly sweet *demi-sec* wines.
- **Chinon and Bourgueil** These pale, herbal-scented reds made with Cabernet Franc are very light, very tart, and very dry.
- **Rosé d'Anjou** Light pink wines, these are lightly sweet from a blend of local grapes.
- **Coteaux de Layon and Bonnezeaux** These decadent late-harvest dessert wines are made with shrivelled Chenin Blanc grapes.

LOIRE VALLEY AT A GLANCE

Cool-climate region of northern France

Most popular wines
Muscadet: light, subtle dry whites
Vouvray: lightly sweet whites
Rosé d'Anjou: lightly sweet pink wines

Most prestigious wines
Sancerre, Pouilly-Fumé: tart, herbal whites
Chinon, Bourgueil: light, tangy reds

France: Rhône Valley

The Rhône Valley is a southern French region known for hearty reds and dry rosés. Rhône wines aren't as high-profile as those from Bordeaux or Burgundy, but New World vintners have embraced and popularized Rhône grapes like Syrah and Grenache (aka Shiraz and Garnacha) because they thrive in hot, dry climates. Rhône wines share a spiced flavour profile, but there are significant differences between those of the north and the south.

Background

Below Lyon, northern Rhône vineyards cling to stony slopes as the river carves a path down from the Alps; but when it nears the Mediterranean, the valley's terrain flattens and grows wide. The vast majority of vineyards are on the southern Rhône's warm, stony flats where it's possible to make affordable wines in volume. High-yielding Grenache is the primary grape here, but many others – like Syrah and Mourvèdre – are blended in to boost colour and flavour. The northern Rhône makes only tiny amounts of wine, because its steep vineyards are only worth cultivating where stellar wine can be made. Syrah is the only red grape planted in northern Rhône appellations.

Southern Rhône Valley appellations

- **Côtes du Rhône** This basic appellation is known for its affordable, flavourful Grenache-based red blends but also includes dry whites and rosés from anywhere in the Rhône region. Wines from superior communes are labelled Côtes du Rhône-Villages.
- **Châteauneuf-du-Pape and Gigondas** These prestige village appellations include the region's finest Grenache-based blends: heavy reds with intense, spicy aromatics.
- **Tavel** This appellation makes only dry Grenache-based rosés, some of the world's top pink wines.
- **Muscat de Beaumes-de-Venise** These are very sweet, very fragrant Vin Doux Naturel dessert wines.

Northern Rhône Valley appellations

- **Hermitage, Côte-Rôtie, and Cornas** These prestige wines are the world's original Syrah wines – intense inky wines, with fiercely peppery flavour.
- **Crozes-Hermitage and St-Joseph** These lesser appellations make lighter, more affordable Syrah-based wines, often more tart and earthy.
- **Condrieu** This white wine appellation makes tiny amounts of fleshy, floral, oaky Viognier wine.

RHÔNE VALLEY AT A GLANCE

Côte-Rôtie
Condrieu
Vienne
LOIRE
ISÈRE
Hermitage
Bourg-de-Péage
Cornas
Valence
Côtes du Rhône
ARDÈCHE
DRÔME
Montélimar
Paris°
Orange
GARD
VAUCLUSE
Avignon
Arles
Châteauneuf-du-Pape

Warm-climate region of southern France

Most popular wines
Côtes du Rhône Rouge: flavourful spicy reds
Côtes du Rhône Rosé: dry pink wines

Most prestigious wines
Châteauneuf-du-Pape: powerful spicy reds
Hermitage, Côte-Rôtie: intense peppery reds

France: Alsace

Alsace is a picturesque region on France's northeastern border with Germany. Its territory has long been contested, and Alsace wines reflect both French and German cultural influences quite clearly. This virtual Garden of Eden for white-wine makers combines exceptional amounts of daytime sun to develop aromatic flavour with bracingly cool nights to retain refreshing acidity, but it is too far north to make satisfying reds.

ALSACE AT A GLANCE

Cool-climate region of northern France

Most popular wines:
Pinot Blanc: soft, unoaked whites
White blends: fragrant, lightly sweet whites

Most prestigious wines:
Riesling: sharp, dry whites
Pinot Gris: opulent, peachy whites

Background

A strong German influence is immediately apparent in Alsace wines thanks to their tall, Rhine-style "fluted" bottles and labels that specify grape varieties. Fragrant German grapes such as Riesling and Gewurztraminer are among the region's distinctive specialities. However, French grapes – such as Pinot Gris, Pinot Blanc, and Pinot Noir – make up the majority of vineyard plantings. Both cultures shape the wine styles. Alsace wines are drier and stronger than their German counterparts, in a food-flattering style inspired by French whites like Chablis and Sancerre. While the Alsace tradition has been to make drier whites, many modern wines feature a little more overt sweetness.

Alsace's top wine styles

● **Pinot Blanc and Pinot Auxerrois** Either grape can be called Pinot Blanc in Alsace, and they are often blended. These easygoing mid-weight whites are dry and reminiscent of unoaked Chardonnay.
● **Riesling** Germany's noble Riesling is made as a stronger, drier style in France, producing fragrant food-oriented whites that age brilliantly.
● **Pinot Gris** This pale variant of Pinot Noir makes opulent, peachy wines in Alsace that are heavier, more fragrant, and often sweeter than those made the Italian way under the name Pinot Grigio.
● **Gewurztraminer** This grape of Austrian heritage is famous for its Moscato-like floral perfume. It makes unusually dense and flavourful white wines that may be fully dry or lightly sweet.
● **Pinot Noir** Very few Alsace wines are red, and only Burgundy's elegant, earthy Pinot Noir grape may be used.

Italy: Tuscany

Toscana, or Tuscany, is a region of rolling hills on Italy's Mediterranean coast. A broad swathe of arable land in a mountainous nation, it is the top wine-producing region in Italy, which is itself one of the world's top two wine producers. Most Tuscan wine is red, and almost all Tuscan reds are made primarily with the region's native Sangiovese grape, typically as the main ingredient in a blend with other varieties.

Background

Tuscany's most well-known wine is Chianti, from its largest appellation. This central zone has many subdistricts, of which Chianti Classico – in the heartland of Chianti, between Florence and Siena – is most renowned. Further south, the hilltop town of Montalcino is famed for its unique thick-skinned variant of Sangiovese, the Brunello clone that makes deeper, darker, more age-worthy wines. The past half-century has brought fine-wine sensibilities to a region previously more focused on volume.

Tuscany's red wine appellations
• **Chianti and Chianti Classico** These medium-bodied dry red wines are made primarily with Sangiovese grapes. Pale, tart, and tannic, these food-friendly offerings are Italy's best-known red wines.
• **Brunello di Montalcino and Rosso di Montalcino** Made entirely with a special clone of Sangiovese, these Montalcino reds have more colour, flavour, and body. Brunellos are aged premium wines; Rossos are younger.
• **Toscana Rosso** This is a broad, loosely regulated category that can range from simple everyday reds to luxurious prestige wines. They are usually, but not always, Sangiovese-based.

Tuscany's white wine appellations
• **Vernaccia di San Gimignano** These brisk unoaked white wines are dry, tart, and lightweight.

Tuscan terms
• *Riserva* This is a legal term for wines that have been given more aging before release.
• **Super-Tuscan** This informal term was originally coined for non-traditional prestige wines, often using French grapes, but has become a catch-all description for Tuscan blends.

TUSCANY AT A GLANCE

Chianti Classico
Chianti
Rome
Florence
Pisa
Livorno
TUSCANY
Siena
Perugia
UMBRIA
Montalcino
Bolgheri
Toscana
LAZIO

Moderate-climate region of central Italy
Most popular wines:
Chianti: tart, dry Sangiovese-based red blends
Toscana Rosso: Chianti-like, but more modern – often riper and fruitier
Most prestigious wines:
Brunello di Montalcino: intense aged reds made with a superior type of Sangiovese grapes (Brunello clone)
Bolgheri: strong reds, often blends of Cabernet Sauvignon and Merlot with Sangiovese; this is the home of the original Super-Tuscans

Italy: Piedmont

Piedmont has Italy's longest history of fine winemaking, thanks in part to its proximity to France, Europe's pioneer in valuing quality over quantity. The region is framed by mountains to the north, west, and south, and its name means "foothills". Frequent fogs and cloudy days can make it difficult to ripen grapes here, so hillside vineyards with extra sun exposure are essential in this challenging environment.

Background

Chilly Piedmont's most popular wine is sweet, frothy Asti. Along with its semi-sparkling cousin Moscato d'Asti, it is the international benchmark for fragrant, lip-smacking Moscato wines. However, Piedmont's claim to fame in the fine-wine world is a matched pair of epic red wines: Barolo and Barbaresco. They are named after adjacent towns and made entirely with Nebbiolo grapes. Only prime sunward slopes allow this stubborn grape to ripen properly, so two other local red grapes, Barbera and Dolcetto, occupy lesser sites. Both formerly made only simple young wines of everyday quality, but top Barberas have come to rival the great Nebbiolos. Less well known but well worth seeking out are Piedmont's dry whites: lean, sharp Gavi and soft, fragrant Arneis.

Piedmont's red wine styles
- **Barolo and Barbaresco** These premium age-worthy, tannic red wines are made with Nebbiolo grapes. Austere, earthy, and very powerful, they rank among Italy's most respected.
- **Barbera d'Alba and Barbera d'Asti** Medium-bodied red wines made with Barbera grapes, these range from seafood-friendly refreshers to denser, oaky prestige wines. All have high levels of acidity.
- **Dolcetto** These medium-bodied red wines made with Dolcetto grapes are often fruity and fresh tasting, with mild acidity and a vivid purple colour.

Piedmont's white wine styles
- **Asti and Moscato d'Asti** These are sparkling and semi-sparkling sweet wines from Moscato Bianco grapes. Fermentation is interrupted to make a style that is essentially half sparkling wine, half white grape juice.
- **Gavi** Subtle dry whites made with Cortese grapes.
- **Arneis** Fragrant dry whites made with Arneis grapes.

PIEDMONT AT A GLANCE

Moderate-climate region of northwestern Italy

Most popular wines:
Asti: sweet, sparkling Moscato
Barbera: tart mid-weight reds
Dolcetto: soft, fruity young reds

Most prestigious wines:
Barolo: tannic, full-bodied Nebbiolo reds that require aging
Barbaresco: Barolo-like but a touch lighter and brighter

Italy: Triveneto

Known collectively to locals as the Triveneto, the northeastern Italian regions of the Veneto, Friuli-Venezia Giulia, and Trentino-Alto Adige have a distinct cultural heritage that is reflected in their wines. This trio surrounds Venice, stretching from fertile coastal plains in the south, to alpine valleys in the north. Most of Italy's vines of French heritage are planted in the Triveneto, many for centuries, and wine labels usually name their grape alongside their appellation in the manner of Germany and the New World.

Background

The Triveneto's climate favours white wines, and the region's most visible exports – Pinot Grigio and Prosecco – are both light and fresh tasting. Low-lying areas make quirky whites, like floral Friulano and nutty Soave from Garganega grapes; however, French varieties such as Pinot Grigio, Chardonnay, and Pinot Bianco dominate in the mountains of Alto Adige and Trentino. The Triveneto's most popular reds are the fruity Valpolicellas of Verona, but the region also makes excellent mid-weight reds from native grapes like Lagrein and Refosco, as well as from French imports like Merlot and Pinot Noir.

Northeastern Italy's top white styles

- **Pinot Grigio** The Venezie and cooler regions of Trentino and Alto Adige are famous for their light, mild Pinot Grigios, but warmer vineyards in Friuli often make stronger, oakier variations on the style.
- **Prosecco** This light, fresh sparkling wine is made in the sub-alpine hills of the Veneto and often features a faint touch of sweetness.
- **Friulano** This fragrant grape's lively dry wines were long known as Tocai but were forced to change names to respect the legacy of Hungary's Tokaj region.

Northeastern Italy's top red styles

- **Valpolicella** Verona's environs produce delightful wines based on the Corvina grape, ranging from easy-drinking bargain wines to denser premium bottlings.
- **Amarone della Valpolicella** This luxury variant of Valpolicella is made by drying grapes for a month or more before winemaking – one of Italy's strongest wines.
- **Merlot and Pinot Noir** Northern Italy is better known for whites but also makes many light, refreshing cool-climate reds that are typically labelled by grape.

THE TRIVENETO AT A GLANCE

Cool-climate region of Mediterranean Europe

Most popular wines
Pinot Grigio delle Venezie: light unoaked whites
Prosecco: light sparkling wines
Valpolicella: light, fruity reds

Most prestigious wines
Amarone: intense, raisiny reds

Italy: The South

Southern Italy has historically been a source of cheap anonymous reds, but radical changes have seen it emerge as a quality wine zone with great potential. Centuries of poverty shaped this region's wine culture, favouring quantity over quality as a rule. For most of the 20th century, roughly 90 per cent of the region's wine was sold off in bulk, and when a regulatory structure was imposed, its requirements were initially manipulated to prop up the mediocre status quo.

Background

Southern Italy is dominated by craggy mountains and coastlines. Naples provides the area with a metropolitan anchor, but the culture and economy remain rooted in farming and fishing. Most southern Italian wines are red and share a flavour profile that suits the local cuisine, regardless of their grape: tart, dry reds, with fiery spiced-fruit flavours. However, the region's rare white wines are turning heads, too, for their uncommon aromatic character.

Southern Italy's top red grapes

● **Aglianico** This ancient grape produces pungent wines that combine power and grace in appellations like Campania's Taurasi and Aglianico delle Vulture in Basilicata.

● **Montepulciano** This productive grape from Abruzzi is best known for easy-drinking mid-weight reds, but premium bottlings show great potential.

● **Negro Amaro** The "black and bitter" grape of Puglia is known for its dark colour and high tannins, which provide the Salento region's premium wines with great aging potential.

● **Nero d'Avola** Sicily's most aromatic red variety is often sold under its own name, delivering Syrah-like reds of uncommon intensity.

● **Primitivo** Known as Zinfandel in California, this Croatian grape is widely planted in Puglia, making lighter, tangier, and more seafood-friendly wines.

Southern Italy's top white grapes

● **Fiano** This grape from Campania offers dry white wines that feature Rhône-like weight and floral aromatics.

● **Insolia** This Sicilian native makes snappy, tart wines in cool mountain vineyards that will please fans of Sauvignon Blanc.

SOUTHERN ITALY AT A GLANCE

Warm-climate region of Mediterranean Europe

Most popular wines
Montepulciano: soft, fruity reds
Nero d'Avola: tart, aromatic reds
Primitivo: tangy, earthy reds

Most prestigious wines
Taurasi: intense spicy reds
Fiano: rich, fragrant whites

Spain

Spain has a longer history of growing grapes and making wine than most of France, but the region was slower to modernize and focus on quality. In a remarkably swift turnaround sparked by joining what is now the European Union, Spain is making world-class wines, many of which blend Old World traditions with New World techniques to broaden their international appeal. Modest Spanish wines deliver exceptional value in both reds and whites, while ritzier appellations like Priorat and Ribera del Duero rival France's Burgundy and Italy's Barolo for critical acclaim.

Background

From hot, sunny Andalusia to cool, breezy Galicia, Spain is blessed with varied vine-friendly terrain and noble native grapes. Red Tempranillo and white Albariño earn rave reviews for wines like Rioja and Ribera del Duero, Toro and Rías Baixas, in the north. Further east, indigenous reds like Garnacha and Monastrell carpet Mediterranean shores from Valencia to Barcelona. In challenging climates, Spain makes quirky wines that are wholly unique, like fizzy underripe Basque

Txakoli and nutty sun-dried Sherries from Jerez. Elsewhere, Spanish vintners follow international inspiration – applying the methods of French Champagne to local Catalan grapes to make sparkling Cava, for example.

Spain's top red wine styles

- **Rioja** Spain's best-known red wines are mid-weight Tempranillo blends from this Atlantic-cooled zone south of Bilbao, often given long barrel aging.
- **Ribera del Duero and Toro** Tempranillo is also the main grape in warmer Castilla y León, making denser, stronger wines in these appellations along the banks of the Duero river.
- **Priorat and Montsant** These zones near Barcelona make blended reds with old-vine Garnacha and Cariñena. Priorats have more power and prestige, while Montsants are more affordable.
- **Tempranillo, Garnacha, and Monastrell** These three Spanish grapes are often encountered in value-oriented wines that are labelled by grape, particularly those from central Spain.

Spain's top white wine styles

- **Cava** The world's most popular sparkling wine from Catalonia's Penedés region, Cava is typically made with Spanish white grapes but bottle-fermented and lees-aged in the style of French Champagne.
- **Albariño** This bracing seafood-friendly white from the Galician coastal zone of Rías Baixas combines the attributes of refreshing Pinot Grigio and aristocratic Chablis.
- **Jerez-Xérès-Sherry** The world's most diverse range of fortified wines are made from white Andalusian grapes and range from crisp, bone-dry Manzanilla to dark, raisiny Moscatel.

QUALITY AND MATURITY

Spanish vintners have traditionally judged wines by their intensity and aged the best wines longer in casks before they are sold. This is common practice in the red wine regions of Europe, but it has been regulated in Spain. Vintners making ambitious wines can earn the right to use three honorific label terms of ascending rank – *crianza*, *reserva*, and *gran reserva* – to help their customers recognize wines of superior quality that have spent extra time maturing in oak barrels and bottles. Many of these wines are aged beyond their legal mandates and released when they near their peak, often 5–10 years after their harvest for the top wines.

SPAIN AT A GLANCE

Mixed-climate region of Western Europe

Spanish red wines
Rioja: tangy, oaky reds
Ribera del Duero: dense, oaky reds
Garnacha: strong young reds

Spanish white wines
Cava: toasty sparkling whites
Albariño: light, fragrant whites
Sherry/Jerez: nutty fortified whites

Green Spain
Spain's coldest, cloudiest wine region is its northern Atlantic coast. Red grapes don't ripen well here, and the best wines are dry, tart low-alcohol whites that are rarely aged or oaked. The most renowned are Galicia's Albariños from Rías Baixas bordering Portugal – wines of exceptional finesse and fragrance. Less common but with a cult following are the fizzy, cidery Txakoli wines of the Basque Country, near the French frontier.

North Central Spain
Spain's finest reds are almost all Tempranillo-based wines from regions north of Madrid. Rioja is the source of Spain's most iconic reds and the first Spanish region to embrace barrel aging. Nearby Navarra makes Spain's top dry rosés. South and west across the mountains, the Castillian plateau ripens Tempranillo more fully in Ribera del Duero and Toro to make denser, darker reds, while Rueda makes snappy Verdejo-based whites.

Southern Spain
Most premium wines here are fortified whites from coastal Andalusia. The most successful are the Sherries of Jerez – from pale, bone-dry Manzanilla, to dark, sticky-sweet Moscatel. Castilla-La Mancha, south of Madrid, makes most of Spain's value-oriented wines.

Mediterranean Spain
The milder Mediterranean coast's best-known wines come from Catalonia in the north. Cava, the world's number-one sparkling wine, is made in the Penedés, also known for its whites and reds labelled by grape. Nearby Priorat and Montsant make some of Spain's strongest reds, blends based on ancient bush-planted Garnacha. Garnacha and Monastrell are grown in drier zones further south and inland.

Germany

Fine-wine traditions reach back to the Middle Ages in Germany, and until a century ago, German white wines were considered the world's finest. A harsh climate led generations of vintners to focus single-mindedly on perfecting wines from the cold-hardy Riesling grape. Germans like their Rieslings dry these days, but export markets prefer the lightly sweet, low-alcohol style traditionally associated with German wines.

Background

Germany's original quality wine regions, the Mosel and Rheingau, are now joined by the up-and-coming Pfalz, Nahe, and Rheinhessen. The country's cold climate yields tart, low-sugar grapes that don't always ripen fully enough to make balanced dry wines. Since sun-derived grape sweetness and flavour are prized, Germany developed its unique *Prädikat* labelling system around these properties. Top wines are ranked according to the ripeness achieved by their grapes, measured in terms of sugar content at harvest (see below). Degrees of ripeness can vary widely – not only by vineyard location but from one vintage to the next.

Germany's top white wine regions

• **Mosel** The coldest of Germany's wine regions makes some of its most ethereal wines. Most are sweet-tart, and many fall below 10% alcohol.
• **Rheingau** This warmer zone allows the possibility of greater ripeness. Many wines are classically light and sweet-tart or fully dessert-sweet, but some modern styles are heavier in weight and bone-dry.

German label terms

• *Kabinett, Spätlese,* and *Auslese* Indicating *Prädikat* wines, or regulated quality wines, of modest, superior, and exceptional ripeness respectively, these terms are usually found on wines that range from lightly sweet to fully sweet. They may also appear on dry wines, since they technically assess grape sweetness, or potential alcohol, not wine sweetness after fermentation.
• *Beerenauslese* and *Eiswein* These are sweet *Prädikat* wines made from late-harvest grapes of higher and higher sugar content, the final stage being freeze-concentrated icewine from grapes picked in midwinter.
• *Trocken* and *halbtrocken* Meaning dry and half-dry respectively, these terms indicate wine sweetness and are used for wines with very little perceptible sugar.

GERMANY AT A GLANCE

Cold-climate region of Northern Europe

Most prestigious wines
Mosel Riesling: lightly sweet, appley whites
Rheingau Riesling: denser, peachier whites

Other German styles
Spätburgunder: light Pinot Noir reds
Müller-Thurgau: sappy young whites

Austria

Austria is a German-speaking country, but its wines have their own distinctive identity, driven by unique geography and reliance on native grape varieties. Most Austrian wine is grown in Lower Austria (Niederösterreich) along its eastern borders with Hungary and Slovakia. More white than red is made in Austria's cool, continental climate, but all grapes ripen more easily than in Germany, yielding wines that are stronger and more often fermented dry.

Background

Austria's number-one grape is Grüner Veltliner, or the "green grape from Veltlin". Its wines appeal most to fans of Sauvignon Blanc and dry Riesling, since it has similar leafy scents and tangy acidity, but in top sites it can produce wines with the richness of great Chardonnay. Austria's top dark grapes, Zweigelt and Blaufränkisch, make quirky mid-weight reds. But the most decadent of Austria's offerings are its luxurious dessert wines. These opulent, honeyed wines follow a German-style ripeness-based *Prädikat* system that indicates increasing degrees of sweetness and concentrations, from lightly sweet *Spätlese* on up.

Austria's top white wine styles

• **Grüner Veltliner** This grape is rarely seen outside Austria. Its unoaked white wines have a herbal scent and can range from fruity quaffers to complex age-worthy beauties that can rival white Burgundy's complexity.

• **Riesling** While Riesling is not Austria's most planted grape, it makes some of the country's most interesting fine wines, often dry and mid-weight in a style similar to that of Alsace.

• **Weissburgunder and Grauburgunder** These are German aliases for two French grapes better known by their Italian names – Pinot Bianco and Pinot Grigio – that make mild, dry white wines in Austria.

Austria's other wine styles

• **Zweigelt and Blaufränkisch** These cold-hardy reds are close relations that make surprisingly robust and flavourful wines with moderate alcohol.

• **Eiswein and Ausbruch** With milder weather than Germany, Austria uses similar grapes and techniques to make hyper-sweet dessert wines and specializes in winter-harvested icewines.

AUSTRIA AT A GLANCE

Niederösterreich

Vienna

Wien

Vienna

Bratislava

Burgenland

Graz

Steiermark

Cool-climate region of Northern Europe

Top white wines
Grüner Veltliner: light, herbal whites
Riesling: tangy dry whites

Other wine styles
Zweigelt: vibrant, tangy reds
Eiswein: sticky-sweet dessert wines

Portugal

Portugal is very small but has a remarkable array of indigenous grapes. When varietal wines from well-known grapes were all the rage in the 1980s and 90s, Portugal was at a disadvantage: its grapes were unfamiliar to the wider world and were often interplanted in the vineyard rather than blended at the winery. Luckily, Portugal's isolation helped preserve what is now seen as a treasure trove of grapevine diversity.

Background

Historically, fortified wines were considered Portugal's only world-class offerings, and until recently, other Portuguese wines were rarely seen outside the country. Sweet Port, made in northern Portugal's Douro Valley, had pride of place as the world's favourite dessert wine. Less well known but of similar heritage and quality, Madeira hailed from a tropical island that flies the Portuguese flag. The only other Portuguese wines with a global presence were the cheap and cheerful lightly sweet rosés from the Minho, exemplified by mass-market brands like Mateus and Lancers. Nowadays, there is growing interest in this coastal nation's other quirky wines – from spritzy white Vinho Verde, to denser reds from Dão and Alentejo.

Portugal's classic fortified wine styles
- **Port** The strong, sweet Port wines from the Douro Valley are fortified mid-fermentation with distilled spirit. The vast majority are red blends, often of six or more native Portuguese and Spanish grapes.
- **Madeira** Portugal's other great fortified wine is named after the tropical island where it's made. These Sherry-like wines taste nutty, range from dry to fully sweet, and are made from both white and red grapes.

Portugal's other wine styles
- **Vinho Verde** These light, tart wines are affordable, fizzy, and refreshing. They may be white, pink, or red, but they are called *verde* ("green") because their grapes are picked underripe.
- **Alentejo/Tejo** These warmer inland regions in the south make riper, stronger wines – typically dry reds labelled by grape variety.
- **Douro** These dry red wines from Port country are made with the same grapes as Port, yielding vibrant flavour and deep colour.

PORTUGAL AT A GLANCE

Porto/Douro

Vinho Verde

Porto

Dão

Lisbon

Madeira

Lisbon

Funchal

Madeira

Alentejo/Tejo

Mixed-climate region of Western Europe

Top standard wines
Vinho Verde: light fizzy whites
Alentejo: deep, tangy reds

Top fortified wines
Port: sweet liqueur-like reds
Madeira: sweet-tart, nutty whites

Greece

Ancient Greece played an important role in the spread of vines and the refinement of winemaking across the Mediterranean, but the region's wine culture stagnated under centuries of rule by the Ottoman Turks. It wasn't until the country joined the European Economic Community in 1981 that significant changes took place and premium Greek wine became a modern reality.

Background

Most of the coastal terrain of Greece shares a sunny Mediterranean climate and, like Italy, is home to hundreds of indigenous grape varieties. While most of these are cultivated as table grapes or for drying into raisins or currants, a few dozen have earned a reputation for making excellent wine, such as white Assyrtiko from the southern islands or red Agiorgitiko from the mainland north. In numerical terms, a few large-scale producers dominate Greek production, and export markets still see mostly traditional styles like piney *retsina* or sweet Muscat and Mavrodaphne. But increasingly, small vintners are introducing the wine world to new flavours from Greece, most of which are dry, tangy wines well suited to the region's traditional Mediterranean cuisine.

Greece's top dry wine styles

• **Assyrtiko** The tart, dry whites of Santorini are based on this hard-scrabble vine and tend to please fans of French Sauvignon Blanc.
• **Moschofilero** This fragrant pink grape is cultivated on the Peloponnese peninsula, where it makes plump whites that feature exotic floral aromas.
• **Xynomavro** Found planted throughout central and northern Greece, this tannic grape has a name meaning "sour red". It performs best in Naoussa and Amyndeo.
• **Agiorgitiko** This grape makes the tangy mid-weight reds of Nemea and is sometimes compared to Italian Sangiovese for its versatility and food-friendliness.

Greece's top sweet wine styles

• **Muscat and Mavrodaphne** Sweet white Muscat and red Mavrodaphne abound in Greece. They are typically fortified wines made using the Port method.

GREECE AT A GLANCE

Warm-climate region of Mediterranean Europe

Up-and-coming white wines
Santorini: bracing, tart whites
Moschofilero: aromatic, floral whites

Up-and-coming red wines
Xynomavro: tannic dry reds
Nemea: tangy mid-weight reds

The Wine Regions Outside Europe

New World wine areas occupy vine-friendly zones across the western and southern hemispheres. Learning the wine geography of these regions is less essential than it is for Europe, since their appellations are generally fewer in number, larger in area, and far less complicated in regulatory terms. Wines are also typically labelled by grape variety in the New World, and fewer different grapes are grown, which makes label navigation easier for wine drinkers. However, this can make it harder to differentiate between individual wines and can limit the diversity of flavours available.

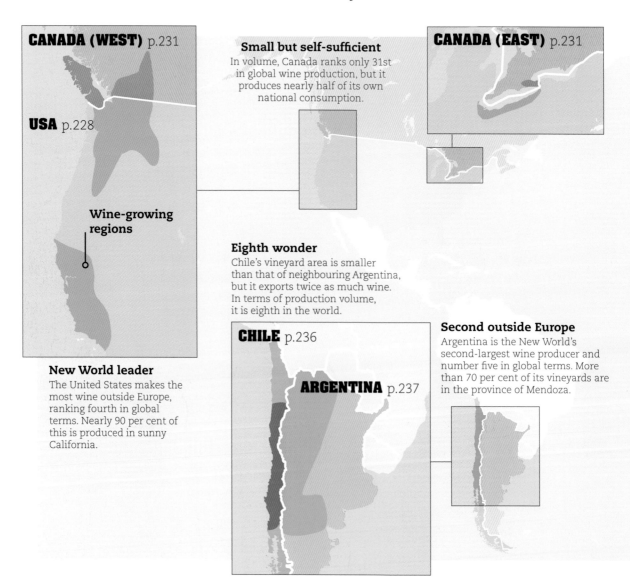

CANADA (WEST) p.231

USA p.228

Wine-growing regions

Small but self-sufficient
In volume, Canada ranks only 31st in global wine production, but it produces nearly half of its own national consumption.

CANADA (EAST) p.231

Eighth wonder
Chile's vineyard area is smaller than that of neighbouring Argentina, but it exports twice as much wine. In terms of production volume, it is eighth in the world.

CHILE p.236

ARGENTINA p.237

Second outside Europe
Argentina is the New World's second-largest wine producer and number five in global terms. More than 70 per cent of its vineyards are in the province of Mendoza.

New World leader
The United States makes the most wine outside Europe, ranking fourth in global terms. Nearly 90 per cent of this is produced in sunny California.

Brave new world

While the former colonies are often larger in territory than European nations, they tend to make less wine. The United States leads the pack as the world's fourth-largest producer, but over 85 per cent of its output never leaves its shores. Argentina, Australia, Chile, and South Africa are also among the global top ten, and all have a growing presence in export markets. New Zealand generates far less volume but looms larger in international importance than many bigger rivals. Canada's total is even smaller, and little is exported, but it gains in visibility by being a part of the lucrative North American market for fine wine.

TOP NEWCOMERS

These seven New World nations rank among the world's top wine regions due to their importance in the global market. By volume, China, Russia, and Brazil make more wine, but their international visibility is very low in comparison with these countries.

AUSTRALIA p.232

Pioneers down under
Australia is the seventh-largest wine producer on earth and a leading centre of research and innovation in the New World. Its vineyard regions hug its cool southern coast.

A true newcomer
New Zealand was barely a blip on the global wine radar until its Marlborough Sauvignon Blancs rose to prominence in the 1990s. Today, it ranks 17th in world wine production.

NEW ZEALAND p.234

SOUTH AFRICA p.235

Grapes of the Cape
Very little wine is made on the African continent, but South Africa's Western Cape region has an ideal climate for growing grapes. The nation is the world's ninth-biggest source of wine.

USA: California

California makes considerably more wine than any New World wine nation. Only France, Italy, and Spain produce a greater volume than the United States, and nearly 90 per cent of US wine comes from California. Ample sunshine and scarce rainfall result in exceptionally ripe grapes with bold flavour and rich texture – the hallmarks of California wine.

Background

Wines from California have shown promise since the mid-1800s, but major setbacks derailed their progress for a hundred years. An insect plague at the turn of the 20th century ravaged vineyards, and then came Prohibition, which outlawed winemaking from 1920 to 1933. Bulk wines were the first to recover in the postwar period, and it wasn't until the 1970s that fine wine re-emerged in earnest. California vintners and American wine drinkers are now leading forces in the global wine boom that has revolutionized the wine world. Today, the state makes some of the finest wines on earth.

California's broad Central Valley produces most of its everyday wine but is too hot for fine wines. Premium wine zones hug Northern California's coastline in two groups, above and below the Bay Area, where fruit's rush to ripeness is slowed by the cool Pacific air. The North Coast is known as California's wine country, encompassing the most famous and historic wine appellations, such as Napa Valley and Sonoma's Russian River Valley. The Central Coast stretches south from San Francisco to Santa Barbara, incorporating up-and-coming wine zones like Paso Robles and Monterey.

NEW WORLD NAMES

All wine labels list their appellation, but in the USA and most New World nations the grape variety is shown as the primary style indicator. Pioneering vintners in new territories studied the European classics to decide which vines to plant and how to make wine, but the Old World system of naming wines by place could not be adopted. Since this practice is based on historical precedent, it is simply not workable in emerging regions. Instead, American wine laws are designed for maximum flexibility for vintners, with basic controls on the accuracy of label statements. Unlike European wine regulations, they do not attempt to impose quality standards for each appellation by mandating specific grape varieties or limiting yields.

California's top red wine styles

- **Cabernet Sauvignon and blends** This grape revels in California's sunshine, making world-class wines in sheltered zones like Napa Valley and Paso Robles.
- **Zinfandel** This uniquely American style is a warm-climate speciality, high in colour and alcohol, with flavours like baked berry desserts, especially in areas with older vineyards, such as Lodi and Dry Creek.
- **Merlot** In places like Napa Valley, this underrated grape excels, making plush reds that are high in flavour but low in harsh tannin.
- **Pinot Noir** This thin-skinned grape thrives in cool coastal regions like Sonoma, Santa Barbara, and Monterey, making seductive mid-weight wines.

California's top white wine styles

- **Chardonnay** California's number-one grape produces plump, fruity wines particularly well in cool zones such as Sonoma and Santa Barbara. They may or may not feature oaky flavour.
- **Sauvignon Blanc** Sometimes labelled Fumé Blanc, this grape's wines are often less acidic and less herbal here than in other countries.

CALIFORNIA AT A GLANCE

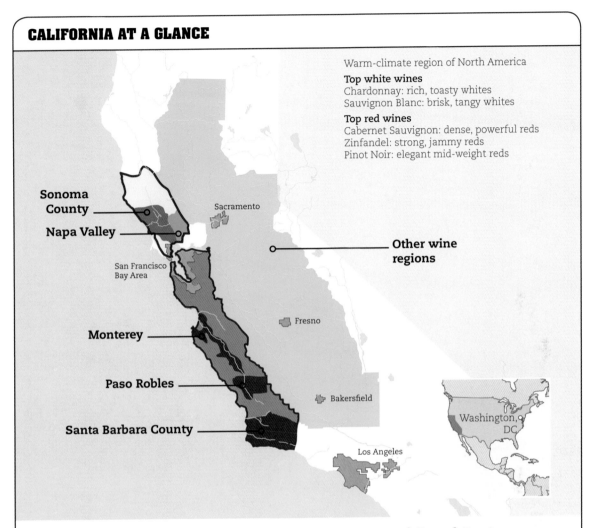

Warm-climate region of North America

Top white wines
Chardonnay: rich, toasty whites
Sauvignon Blanc: brisk, tangy whites

Top red wines
Cabernet Sauvignon: dense, powerful reds
Zinfandel: strong, jammy reds
Pinot Noir: elegant mid-weight reds

Sonoma County
Napa Valley
Sacramento
San Francisco Bay Area
Other wine regions
Monterey
Fresno
Paso Robles
Bakersfield
Santa Barbara County
Los Angeles
Washington, DC

North Coast

This is California's prestige wine zone, encompassing four counties north of the San Francisco Bay: Sonoma and Mendocino on the coast, and Napa and Lake counties one step inland.

Sonoma is the largest North Coast county and features the most variation in climate. Foggy zones near the water, such as Russian River Valley and Carneros, specialize in cool-climate wine styles like Chardonnay, Pinot Noir, and sparkling wines. Inland appellations like Alexander Valley and Dry Creek Valley are warmer and better known for heavier reds such as Cabernet Sauvignon and Zinfandel.

Napa Valley is a fraction of Sonoma's size but is denser in vineyards and more famed for its premium wines. Sheltered by a range of mountains, Napa is warmer, with a climate more uniformly suited to red grapes. The Bordeaux partners Cabernet Sauvignon and Merlot perform exceptionally well and are often blended, both in flat valley-floor appellations like Rutherford and in steeper terrain like Howell Mountain and Stags Leap District.

Mendocino's climate and landscape are similar to Sonoma's, but its vineyards are more sparse.

Lake County's climate resembles that of the northern Napa Valley.

Central Coast

Most often seen as a regional appellation on wine labels, the Central Coast stretches south from the Bay Area to Santa Barbara. Despite being further south than the North Coast, these valleys are typically cooler, because coastal ridges channel the Pacific breezes deeper inland. Santa Barbara, San Luis Obispo, Monterey, and Santa Cruz counties make exceptional Chardonnay, Pinot Noir, and Syrah, while the enclave of Paso Robles is better known for bolder reds such as Cabernet Sauvignon and Zinfandel.

USA: Pacific Northwest

California may dominate American production, but its neighbours in the Pacific Northwest also make exceptional wines. Washington and Oregon share a border and are similar in size but couldn't be more different in their wine styles. Oregon is known for small amounts of ultra-premium Pinot Noir and Pinot Gris, while Washington produces far greater amounts of more affordable Merlot, Cabernet Sauvignon, Chardonnay, and Riesling.

Background

The stylistic divide reflects the region's geography, with east and west separated by the Cascade Mountains. Oregon's primary wine region, the Willamette Valley south of hipster Portland, is wedged between the Cascades and the coast. Being relatively cool, it is perfect for growing Pinot Noir, a fickle grape that's hard to farm but of great value when perfected.

Washington's main wine region is the Columbia Valley near the cow towns of Yakima and Walla Walla, on the eastern "dry side" of the Cascades, where irrigation makes it possible to grow fruit on an arid plateau. Daytime sun and warmth here can easily ripen thick-skinned red grapes, while cold desert nights allow white grapes to retain brisk acidity.

Pacific Northwest's top red styles
• **Oregon Pinot Noir** The Willamette Valley is considered one of the world's best sources of soulful, expressive Pinot Noir outside Burgundy.
• **Washington Merlot** This variety makes uncommonly powerful wines in the Columbia Valley, belying the grape's "soft and fruity" reputation.
• **Washington Syrah** Exceptional full-bodied Syrahs are made in central Washington, with deep colour and strong aromatic character.

Pacific Northwest's top white styles
• **Oregon Pinot Gris** These light-hearted wines are mid-weight, unoaked, and dry. Most are heavier than Italian Pinot Grigio but milder than French Pinot Gris.
• **Washington Riesling** Washington makes lovely Chardonnay and Sauvignon Blanc, but its Riesling is something truly special, usually in the lightly sweet German style.

PACIFIC NORTHWEST AT A GLANCE

Mixed-climate region of North America
Most popular wines
Washington Riesling: lightly sweet whites
Oregon Pinot Gris: dry unoaked whites
Most prestigious wines
Oregon Pinot Noir: silky mid-weight reds
Washington Syrah: intense peppery reds

Canada

Visitors to Canada are often surprised to discover a thriving wine industry: wine country doesn't fit our picture of the great white north. Very little local wine is exported, but Canada supplies about half of its own wine needs. The region's most prestigious style is its luscious icewine, inspired by German and Austrian dessert wines. They are made with overripe grapes, the juice of which is freeze-concentrated by being left on the vine well into winter.

Background

Most vines can't survive more than a day or two below –10°C (14°F), and only a handful of Canadian regions have mild enough winters to support grape growing. Canadian fine-wine making began in earnest in Ontario's Niagara Peninsula, between the Great Lakes. But today there is just as much to be excited about on the west coast in British Columbia, where the Okanagan Valley is making exceptional wines in the foothills of the Canadian Rockies. While both regions are known for cool-climate specialities, such as Riesling and Pinot Noir, the west is more consistently able to ripen grapes that need more sun and warmth, such as Cabernet Sauvignon and Syrah.

Canada's top wine styles

- **Icewine** The most prized Canadian wines are freeze-concentrated dessert wines made by letting grapes hang on the vine into January.
- **Riesling** This cool-climate white grape from Germany adapts well to Canadian vineyards and is typically made in a light, sweet-tart German-inspired style.
- **Cabernet Franc** This thinner-skinned relation of Cabernet Sauvignon thrives in Canada, making snappy, cedary mid-weight red wines.
- **Pinot Gris** Performing brilliantly in these sunny but cool regions, Pinot Gris here is more often modelled on rich Alsace Pinot Gris than lighter Italian Pinot Grigio.
- **Pinot Noir** Lighter reds from this finicky variety can be heartbreakers, and Canadian vintners are showing promise in both Ontario and British Columbia.
- **Syrah** Though this variety is more commonly seen from warmer climates, British Columbia is making great Syrah: intense, fragrant reds.

CANADA AT A GLANCE

BRITISH COLUMBIA

Okanagan Valley

Vancouver

Victoria

Other wine regions

ONTARIO

Toronto

Niagara Peninsula — Hamilton

Detroit

Buffalo

Other wine regions

Ottawa

Washington, DC

Cool-climate region of North America

Most popular wines
Riesling: lightly sweet whites
Chardonnay: mid-weight dry whites
Cabernet Franc: tangy mid-weight reds

Most prestigious wines
Icewine: sticky-sweet dessert wines

Australia

Most of Australia's landmass is too hot for vineyards, but many of its southern regions are blessed with a grape-friendly Mediterranean climate. A lot of 20th-century innovations in grape growing and winemaking were pioneered here. These ideas have been spread by Australian winemakers who consult on northern-hemisphere harvests while their own vines lie dormant in winter.

Background

In global wine production, Australia ranks among the top ten, but because it is sparsely populated, its vintners focus more on exports than those of most New World nations. As a rule, the finest wines are grown in areas that benefit from the cooling influence of either the mountains or the sea, with most falling within 300 km (185 miles) of the coastline between Sydney and Adelaide. Everyday bargain wines are more often grown in warmer, irrigated zones further inland, such as the flats of the Murray River's drainage basin.

Many grapes of European heritage are grown in Australia, including Chardonnay and Cabernet Sauvignon. However, the most widely planted is Australia's signature grape Shiraz. This French variety, known elsewhere as Syrah, adapts well to warm climates. Australian wines are almost always labelled by grape variety, according to the New World norm, with one significant difference: Australian blends must list all of their component grapes in order of importance.

GEOGRAPHICAL INDICATIONS

Many of Australia's most popular wines are labelled under a single generic appellation – South East Australia – that encompasses the vineyards of five states and about 90 per cent of the country's plantings. Premium wines, though, are often bottled under the names of smaller appellations, or geographical indications, following the "smaller is better" model that dominates the wine industry.

AUSTRALIA AT A GLANCE

Warm-climate region of the southern hemisphere

Top white wines
Chardonnay: rich, fruity whites
Riesling: tart dry whites

Top red wines
Shiraz: dark, jammy reds
Grenache: strong, raisiny reds

WESTERN AUSTRALIA

Perth

Margaret River

Other wine regions

Western Australia

Western Australia is a massive state that covers the western third of the continent. Only a small area of coastal land near Perth is suitable for wine growing, and this remote region is home to more small independent vintners than larger winery conglomerates. The finest wines come from the Margaret River region, famed for its outstanding Chardonnay and Shiraz.

South Australia

Many of Australia's most respected appellations lie within a short drive of Adelaide. South Australia's southeastern corner offers prestige wine regions along the coast and volume-oriented vineyards in the drainage of the Murray River. Barossa and McLaren Vale loom large as the country's most famous sources of Shiraz, while the cooler Clare Valley makes stunning dry Riesling. To the south, Coonawarra and the Limestone Coast produce some of Australia's top Cabernet Sauvignon and Chardonnay.

Australia's top red wine styles

- **Shiraz** This is the Australian moniker for the French Syrah grape. It makes strong, dark, flavourful wines here, ranging from fun and fruity to brooding and intense.
- **Grenache blends** Other Rhône varieties also thrive in Australia, like Grenache, often seen in so-called GSM blends with small amounts of Shiraz and Mourvèdre in the model of French Côtes du Rhône.
- **Cabernet Sauvignon and blends** Cabernet Sauvignon is less widely planted here than in other New World zones and makes lighter, tangier wines. It is often blended with Shiraz.

Australia's top white wine styles

- **Chardonnay** Australia's diverse geography provides a wide array of Chardonnays – from tangy cool-climate, to luscious warm-climate styles – many of which are unwooded, or made without new oak flavour.
- **Riesling** Australian Riesling wines are most often dry and tart in the French Alsace style, with exceptional lime and green-apple aromatics.
- **Semillon** Best known for making France's top sweet wine, Sauternes, this lesser-known grape makes all sorts of whites down under – from bone-dry to sticky sweet, from brisk and unoaked to toasty and barrel-fermented.

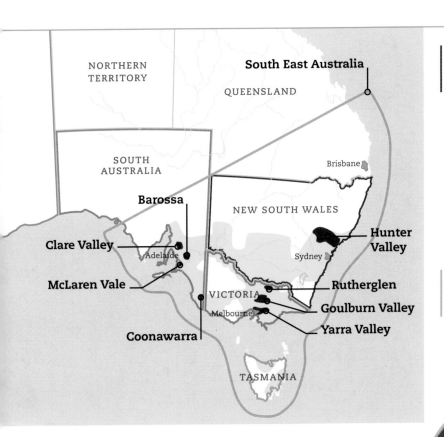

New South Wales

The Hunter Valley, near Sydney, was the first region to show fine-wine potential, so Australia's wine history is deepest in New South Wales. This area makes outstanding Chardonnay and Shiraz and has a unique take on Semillon. Most New South Wales production comes from the interior's irrigated Murray–Darling basin, but ambitious vintners also make exciting wines in the cooler hills of the Great Dividing Range, in smaller appellations like Mudgee and Hilltops.

Tasmania

The smallest and coldest of Australia's states is Tasmania, an island in the frigid Southern Ocean. The region is known for white wines such as Chardonnay and Riesling, but it is earning recognition for great sparkling wine and Pinot Noir as well.

Victoria

The southernmost and coolest of Australia's mainland states, Victoria specializes in cool-climate wine styles, like white and sparkling wines. The coastal zones that surround Melbourne, such as Yarra Valley and the Mornington Peninsula, are ideal for grapes that love cool weather, like Pinot Noir and Chardonnay. The mountain valleys of the Great Dividing Range, like Goulburn, make great dry whites and reds in a variety of styles. Northeastern towns like Rutherglen are famed for their sweet and fortified dessert wines, or "stickies", modelled on Port and Sherry.

LAND OF OZ

The regions of Australia that produce wine all cluster along its southern shores in zones that feature a vine-friendly Mediterranean climate.

New Zealand

While it may seem like a major player in the wine world today, known primarily for its refreshing whites, New Zealand's wine industry is much younger than those of its New World competitors. Significant commercial plantings began in the 1970s as part of a national economic restructuring, and a decade later one style emerged to vault New Zealand to international stardom: Sauvignon Blanc from Marlborough. Tart, dry, and citrusy, these wines follow the Loire Valley model of Sancerre but feature more exuberant herbal and tropical aromatics.

Background

New Zealand is unusual among New World regions in that its vineyard zones are colder in climate – more like cool moist European zones than the hotter, drier areas that make wine in the United States, Australia, and South America. However, this is exactly what makes New Zealand wines stand out, combining the clean, fruity character associated with modern New World winemaking with the bracing acidity and food-friendliness more commonly found in Old World European wines. The dramatic success of New Zealand Sauvignon Blanc has boosted global interest in other cool-climate growing regions and the fortunes of tart, dry white wines fermented in stainless steel everywhere.

New Zealand's top white wine styles

• **Sauvignon Blanc** Unoaked and bracingly tart, these mid-weight, dry whites feature intense citrus and green-herb aromas. The distinctive Marlborough style has become an international benchmark for the grape.

• **Chardonnay** This grape performs brilliantly in New Zealand's coastal zones, especially along the North Island's southeastern coast. Its wines feature a zing of green-apple acidity and may be oaked or unoaked.

New Zealand's top red wine styles

• **Pinot Noir** New Zealand is one of very few international regions where this fickle grape makes world-class wines, particularly in the South Island's Central Otago region.

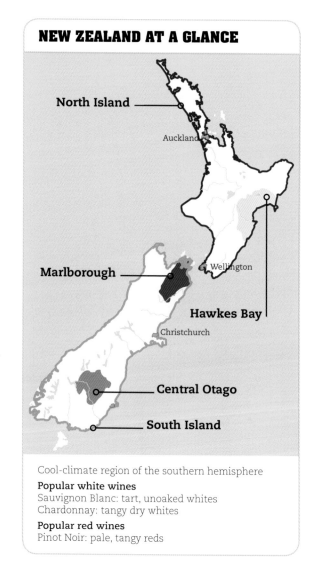

NEW ZEALAND AT A GLANCE

North Island

Auckland

Marlborough

Wellington

Hawkes Bay

Christchurch

Central Otago

South Island

Cool-climate region of the southern hemisphere

Popular white wines
Sauvignon Blanc: tart, unoaked whites
Chardonnay: tangy dry whites

Popular red wines
Pinot Noir: pale, tangy reds

South Africa

Most of the African continent is too hot for making fine wine, but South Africa's Western Cape region has a Mediterranean climate. This region was one of the first in the New World to explore fine-wine making in the late 1600s and was considered a top-notch source by the early 1800s. However, the 20th century proved a major setback for South African wine. After insect pests ravaged vineyards early on, vintners turned to bulk wines, and for decades much of the country's wine was distilled into cheap brandy.

Background

Before Apartheid was lifted in the 1990s, trade embargoes blocked many export markets just as the global wine boom began. Now, however, the world is once again recognizing the distinctive character and quality potential of South African wines, which have an uncommon complexity. Volume-oriented production is based in sun-baked interior valleys, while premium winemaking occurs in cooler coastal zones. Despite the warmth, South Africa's wines are often more food-oriented and less fruit-forward than other New World regions.

South Africa's top red wine styles

- **Pinotage** South Africa's signature grape variety was a result of crossing Pinot Noir with an obscure but productive Rhône grape called Cinsaut. Pinotage makes intense red wines, with a smoky, meaty scent.
- **Cabernet Sauvignon and blends** South African Cabernet-based wines have an earthy character, particularly from Stellenbosch and Paarl.

South Africa's top white wine styles

- **Chenin Blanc** This Loire Valley grape thrives in South Africa, making thrilling styles – from light and sweet, to full-bodied, dry, and barrel-fermented.
- **Chardonnay and Sauvignon Blanc** These grapes do well in cooler zones, often in a crisp, dry style.

SOUTH AFRICA AT A GLANCE

Warm-climate region of the southern hemisphere

Most popular wines
Chenin Blanc: lightly sweet whites
Pinotage: strong, smoky reds

Most prestigious wines
Chardonnay: barrel-fermented whites
Cabernet Sauvignon: intense, earthy reds

Coastal Region

Paarl

WESTERN CAPE

Breede River Valley

Cape Town

Stellenbosch

Johannesburg

Cape South Coast

Chile

This long, thin nation has made wine since the Spaniards arrived, but only recently has it earned a reputation for world-class quality. Chile stretches for thousands of miles, sandwiched between the Pacific Ocean and the peaks of the Andes. Its wine country occupies a series of temperate vine-friendly valleys surrounding the capital city of Santiago, enjoying months of cloud-free skies in summer and mild winters.

Background

French vine varieties were introduced to Chile in the 19th century, and today Cabernet Sauvignon, Merlot, and Sauvignon Blanc dominate Chile's exports, along with Chardonnay. Chile also cultivates one grape found nowhere else: Carmenère. Prized for its intense flavour, this red Bordeaux grape hadn't been seen in France for nearly a century when it was discovered in Chile, interplanted with its close relation Merlot.

With exceptional sun exposure, cool nights, and a long, dry growing season, Chilean vineyards rarely experience the wet weather and insect pests that can plague other regions. Chile's geography, along with low-cost land and labour, attracted international capital and winemaking expertise in the 1990s, largely through joint ventures, and wine quality has since improved by leaps and bounds.

Chile's top wine styles

• **Carmenère** Chile's signature grape makes red wines that resemble its Bordeaux relations Merlot and Cabernet Sauvignon, producing intense dark, herbal-scented wines with great quality potential.

• **Cabernet Sauvignon, Merlot, and Bordeaux-style blends** Chile makes exceptional wines with Bordeaux varieties, and many of the best are blends from regions like the Maipo, Rapel, and Aconcagua valleys. Compared to other New World examples, they are often made with more French-style food-oriented sensibilities.

• **Chardonnay and Sauvignon Blanc** White grapes thrive in regions of Chile that are close to the cool Pacific coast, such as the Casablanca Valley. Chardonnays tend to be crisp and refreshing, with premium examples displaying the most oak character. Sauvignon Blanc is also proving itself here, making snappy, tart wines that echo the unoaked, herbal New Zealand style.

CHILE AT A GLANCE

Other wine regions

Maipo Valley

Santiago

Casablanca Valley

Rapel Valley

Santiago

Mixed-climate region of the southern hemisphere
Most popular wines
Merlot: mid-weight dry reds
Chardonnay: mid-weight dry whites
Most prestigious wines
Carmenère: dark, aromatic reds
Cabernet Sauvignon: intense, age-worthy reds

Argentina

The largest wine region in Latin American is Argentina's Mendoza province. At the edge of the Andes, the high-elevation plains of Cuyo produce dense, lush red wines that have long been prized in South America, but only in the past 20 years has the rest of the world discovered why. Mendoza's high-desert climate provides the daytime warmth and sunlight that are crucial for ripening dark-skinned grapes. At night, temperatures plunge, slowing the process and retaining the acidity necessary for making balanced fine wines.

Background

Compared to its competitors, Argentina was slow to export its wines beyond South America. Since its primary grape varieties were unfamiliar to international wine drinkers – just blips on the global wine radar – they faced an uphill struggle to earn confidence from wine drinkers. Argentina's number-one grape, Malbec, has no significant presence outside Argentina. Since it doesn't ripen well in its native France, it is rarely grown there or elsewhere. White Torrontés is a local cultivar descended from European varieties but with no Old World roots of its own. In Argentina, both grapes perform brilliantly, producing wines with enough personality and complexity to turn heads around the world.

Argentina's top wine styles

- **Malbec** These flavourful red wines are dark and rich, with floral and earthy aromatics. Premium bottlings are dense and oaky, while bargain brands tend to be lighter and fresher.
- **Bonarda** This milder red variety is no relation to the Bonarda grown in northern Italy. It makes soft, fruity wines in an easy-drinking style.
- **Torrontés** The floral-scented white wines from this variety are typically dry and unoaked but have a distinctive scent reminiscent of Moscato.
- **International varieties** Argentina's climate is well suited to grape growing, and recent years have seen more experimentation with famous grapes such as Chardonnay and Cabernet Sauvignon.

ARGENTINA AT A GLANCE

Warm-climate region of the southern hemisphere

Popular white wines
Torrontés: fragrant dry whites

Popular red wines
Malbec: dark, intense reds
Bonarda: lighter, fruity reds

How to Achieve *Vinlightenment*

Many wine lovers find themselves overwhelmed when they try to learn more about wine. The key is to focus on core concepts, not reams of details, and you must also learn to trust your senses.

Trust Your Taste Buds

- **Embrace your personal tastes** Don't feel pressured to adopt "sophisticated" preferences. The only person worth impressing is yourself.

- **Keep an open mind** Wine perceptions change with food context, temperature, and even with your moods, so give wine styles second chances.

- **Bend the rules** Don't let stodgy ideas about wine cramp your style. Wine for breakfast? Wine on the rocks? Mixing two wines? Go for it.

- **Try new things** You'll never know what's out there until you taste it, so don't let past preferences limit your future experiences.

- **Don't sweat the details** It's easy to get wrapped up in wine minutiae on multiple levels, but this can interfere with your enjoyment.

Learn How to Describe Wine

- **Use simple language** Wine's most important traits can be summed up in a few basic terms that have concrete meanings.

- **One sense at a time** Each of our senses except hearing contribute to our perceptions of wine.

- **Assess sensory traits** Rank colour and colour depth, sweetness and acidity, fruit and oak flavours, and weight and carbonation from low to high.

- **Don't worry about naming smells** Identifying flavours and scents takes practice. Stick to judging their overall intensity and broad categories.

- **Notice highs and lows** Most wines fall in the crowded middle ground on most traits, but qualities that fall outside the norm are the most distinctive and most helpful.

Get Comfortable with Wine Shopping

- **Judge books by their cover** Packaging decisions often provide useful insights into a vintner's philosophy and intended audience.
- **Crunch the numbers** When shopping, a few helpful figures – such as a wine's age, price, and alcohol content – can tell you a fair amount about its style.
- **Read the fine print** Getting familiar with two main labelling formats can make wine shopping less confusing.
- **Stick to your budget** Drinking well doesn't require overspending. Consider wines off the beaten track or bargains in 3-litre boxes.
- **Ask for help without ceding control** Sales staff can be a great resource, but there's no need to let them decide what you'll spend.

Explore the Full Range of Wine Styles

- **Sample by the glass when possible** Restaurants offer a great opportunity to expand your experience without committing to a full bottle.
- **Step outside your comfort zone** Most people start out with a favourite wine style, but there may be others you'd like even more if you tried them.
- **Don't judge on first sip alone** Wine's acidity can shock the palate at first. Second and third sips give a better sense of a wine's attributes.
- **Take a moment to savour new wines** Give them a minute or two of your attention, then file them in your mental database for future reference.
- **Use your words** Putting your thoughts into words will make it much easier to remember a wine later, even if they aren't wine terms or spoken aloud.

Taste the Sunshine in Your Glass

- **Work backwards from alcohol content** In dry wines, alcoholic strength is a reasonably accurate indicator of ripeness, with 13.5% being the norm.

- **Look for more oomph in stronger wines** The higher a dry wine's alcohol content, the more likely it is to taste more intense and to be oak-aged.

- **Look for more refreshment in lighter wines** The lower a dry wine's alcohol content, the more likely it is to taste milder and feature bracing acidity.

- **Smell the ripeness spectrum** Herbal, earthy aromas occur most in cool-climate wines, while warm-climate offerings have more dessert-like spiced-fruit aromas.

- **Don't let sweet wines fool you** Alcohol content isn't a sound guide with speciality categories like dessert wines and fortified wines.

Play with Your Food and Wine

- **Put wine in its place** Wines are better suited to supporting roles than being the star of the show, so let food flavours take centre stage.

- **Strike a match** Try choosing wines that echo a dominant feature of the dish, whether it's taste or texture, scent or flavour.

- **Adjust for food chemistry** Pick tangy wines for salty foods and sweet wines for sugary foods.

- **Watch out for spicy heat** Don't forget that alcohol amplifies the "burn" of spicy foods, while lighter wines tame the flames.

- **Defy the rules** It's your wine, so you should drink what you like – even if it doesn't fit the usual guidelines.

Test Your Wine Savvy

- **Guess which wines aren't fully dry** Wines with sweetness are usually low-alcohol whites, and those with the most sugar often come in small bottles.

- **Deduce which wines taste of oak** Older, more expensive wines are more likely to feature the flavour of oak barrels.

- **Predict which wines are most tart** Wines that are younger, lower in alcohol, or that come from colder regions are generally most acidic.

- **Estimate which wines are most food-oriented** Many European wines can seem a little too tart or dry alone and are designed for serving with salty food.

- **Gauge which wines will have the strongest flavour** Wines from warm regions with high alcohol often feature very bold fruit and oak flavours, especially those from the Americas and southern hemisphere.

Relax and Enjoy Yourself

- **Banish snobbery and pretence** It's a grave injustice that something as inherently relaxing and social as wine is seen as uptight and standoffish.

- **Live vicariously through grapes** Wine's scent evokes its region and culture – close your eyes, take a sniff, and be transported.

- **Skip the traditional homework** Don't bother memorizing reams of wine data. If there's something you want to know, you can always look it up.

- **Live in the moment** Wine is perfectly suited for reminding us that any day spent with friends and family is an occasion worth celebrating.

- **Raise a glass to your success** You've taken on a thorny topic and picked up some tricks of the trade. Here's to a long life of eating well and drinking better.

Glossary

Acidic, acidity
Detectable presence of sourness; one of the six true taste sensations detected by the tongue's taste buds.

Age-worthy
A descriptive term for wines that resist oxidation, thanks to high levels of natural preservative components like tannin or acidity.

Alcohol
Ethanol, the psychoactive component in adult beverages such as wine; an organic compound derived from sugar by the metabolism of living yeast cultures.

Antioxidant
A substance that inhibits oxidation or its properties, as with phenolic compounds in grape skins, such as tannin.

Aperitif
Alcoholic drink designed to pique the appetite before a meal. Many light wines are served as aperitifs, but the term "aperitif wines" may also refer to flavoured and fortified wine-based drinks, such as all Vermouths, Lillet, or Dubonnet.

Appellation
A formal region-of-origin statement indicating where a wine's grapes were grown; mandatory on all wine labels.

Archetype
Original specimen or pattern on which subsequent examples are modelled.

Aromatics
Wine components perceived by the nose that convey sensations of both scent and flavour.

Astringency
In wine, the mouth-drying effect of tannins, which are found in grape skins and suppress salivation.

Barrel
Round storage vessels made of oak used in the maturation or fermentation of wine.

Barrel aging
A common practice in the making of red wine, where young, fresh wines are stored in oak barrels after fermentation for anywhere from a few weeks to a few years.

Barrel fermentation
A white-winemaking practice, where grape juice is fermented into wines in oak barrels that are often aged on their yeast sediments for up to a year.

Barrique
Traditional French-style 225-litre wine barrel; associated with styles in which new oak flavour is imparted during aging.

Biodynamic
A form of natural farming that maintains the inter-related ecosystem, including soil, plants, and animals; also a rigorous agricultural certification system that prohibits use of non-native and synthetic vineyard treatments and organizes cultivation around the lunar cycle.

Bitter, bitterness
One of the six sensations detected by the tongue's taste buds (an example might be hops in beer); often confused with the tactile astringency of tannin in wine (as in black tea).

Blend
A wine made from several different grape varieties.

Body
Descriptive term for wine's texture, typically driven by alcohol content. See **Weight**.

Bold
Term for wine that is high in aromatic or flavour intensity.

Brand name
A wine's commercial identity; may be the vintner's name or a proprietary name for a product range.

Browning
In wine, a visible sign of age and oxidation. In food, the colour change associated with caramelization and Maillard reactions in certain cooking methods, like searing, frying, and grilling.

Brut
Regulated label term for sparkling wines that have no perceptible sweetness; one step drier than extra-dry.

Bulk wine
The lowest quality category of wines, often used in cheap blends.

Carbonated
Descriptive term for wine that is bubbly, releasing carbon dioxide when opened.

Cellaring
Bottle-aging; maturing of wine by purchasers after release.

Colour compounds
Phenolic wine components such as tannins that are derived from grape skins and that give colour and flavour to red and rosé wines.

Complex
Wine term for simultaneous sensations in wine; typically refers to the presence of many pleasing scents and flavours, especially those generated during fermentation or aging.

Concentrated
Descriptive term for wines with higher-than-average intensity of olfactory scents and flavours; typically refers to fruit rather than oak.

Condense
In chemistry, to change physical matter from gas to liquid. The opposite of evaporate.

Cork taint, corked
Detectable spoilage of wine caused by contact with natural cork; most commonly the presence of TCA (short for 2,4,6-trichloroanisole), a compound that gives wine an unpleasant mildew smell.

Corks
Wine bottle stoppers punched from the bark of the cork oak tree.

Crianza
A regulated Spanish wine-label term for aged wines of good quality; the lowest tier of a hierarchy that includes *reserva* and *gran reserva*.

Crisp
Descriptive term for wines that have a standard, moderately tangy level of acidity.

Cru
A French wine term used for recognizing sites that produce superior wines, typically qualified as top-level *grand cru* or next-best *premier cru*. Often translated as "growth", its meaning is closer to "rank" and is complicated by different criteria in different regions, enforced with varying rigour.

Cuvée, cuvée name
Wine term for a particular bottling of wine, often needed for clarification when more than one is made from the same appellation and grape variety; from the French word for vat. In some regions, a narrower usage indicates a blended wine.

Decanting
Process used for removing wine from its bottle (usually into a vessel known as a decanter) before it is served, either to separate an older red wine from its sediment or to aerate a younger wine.

Demi-sec
Regulated French label term for wines that have an overt sweetness, typically balanced sweet/tart wines.

Dessert wine
A category of wines that feature overt, intense sweetness.

Distilled spirits
High-alcohol beverages such as brandy and whiskey, made from low-alcohol fermented products like wine and beer by vaporizing their alcohol and condensing it in a separate container.

Dry, dryness
Descriptive term for wine with no noticeable presence of sugar; the opposite of sweet and the norm for the majority of wines. Often confused with the mouth-drying effect of tannin in red wines.

Earthy
Term for wine smells that are reminiscent of the outdoors and the farming environment, such as mulch, stones, and fallen leaves.

Estate
A vineyard owned by the vintner who makes its wine, allowing them to farm their own grapes rather than purchasing from a grower, as is the norm.

Estate-bottled
Regulated label term used primarily for New World wines, indicating that the vintner owns and farms the vineyard from whose grapes the wine was made.

Esters
Volatile aromatic compounds that are a major source of scent and flavour in many fruits, as well as in wine.

Evaporate
In chemistry, to change physical matter from liquid to gas; vaporize. The opposite of condense.

Everyday wine
Simple wines that are fairly priced; a step above bulk wines and the cheapest of the fine wines.

Extra-dry
Regulated label term for sparkling wines that have faint perceptible sweetness; one step sweeter than *brut*.

Fermentation
Main stage of winemaking that converts juice into wine; the process by which all alcoholic drinks are made, where living yeast organisms consume and metabolize sugar, breaking it down into alcohol and carbon dioxide.

Fine wine
Premium wines, in which quality is a consideration.

Finish, length
Term for a wine's aftertaste; the duration of this desirable trait is useful for assessing wine quality.

Flabby
Descriptive term for wine that has lower-than-average levels of acidity.

Flavour
In common usage, taste sensations derived from eating and drinking; for purposes of wine analysis, smells that reach the olfactory nerves from the mouth internally via the retro-nasal passage.

Food-friendly, food-oriented
Term for wines that are designed to taste best with food, especially the acid-blocking, fruit-enhancing effects of salt in food.

Fortified wine
Category of wines ranging from 15% to 20% alcohol that contain added distilled spirits, such as Port and Sherry.

Freeze-concentrate
To reduce the water content of a liquid by freezing it and removing its solid ice crystals, as for icewine.

Fruit, fruity
In common usage, sweet edible produce, typically containing seeds of a flowering plant; in wine tasting, a descriptive term for wine smells deriving from grapes or winemaking. When it is prominent, a wine may be described as fruity, fruit-driven, or fruit-forward.

Full-bodied
Term for wines of richer-than-average texture. See **Heavy**.

Generic
Common or non-exclusive. In New World, refers to wines that do not specify a grape variety on their label. In Old World, refers to the most basic wines of a region – for example, generic Chianti as opposed to Chianti Classico from a superior subdistrict.

Grand cru
A French wine quality classification. See **Cru**.

Gran reserva
A regulated label term for top-quality aged wines in Spain and South America.

Grape variety
Cultivar of the grape species *Vitis vinifera*; includes the many grape types used in winemaking.

Green
In fruit, underripe; in wine, displaying characteristics associated with low ripeness, such as high acidity and leafy, herbal aromatics.

Grip
Descriptive term for the astringent, mouth-drying, tactile sensation of tannin found in many red wines.

Harsh
Term for a strong presence of either astringent mouth-drying tannin in red wine or unusually high alcohol in any wine.

Headspace
The upper section of a wine-glass bowl that remains empty in order to allow swirling and to concentrate wine aromas.

Heavy
Descriptive term for wines with a rich, mouth-coating texture; associated with wines that have an alcohol level of more than 14%.

Herbal
Descriptive term for wines with aromas and flavours that resemble herbs, leaves, or vegetables.

Icewine
A dessert wine style made by freeze-concentrating juice, often by harvesting frozen grapes in midwinter.

Indigenous
Originating from a particular region.

Jammy
Descriptive term for wines with aromas and flavours suggestive of fruit that has been cooked or sweetened.

Kabinett
Regulated German label term indicating a quality wine made from grapes of standard ripeness; the lowest of the *Prädikat* levels, *Kabinett* wines are often lightly sweet and low in alcohol, but some are heavier and drier.

Lactone
Aromatic ester found in oak barrels that contributes to oaky flavour in wine.

Late harvest
Label term used for sweet wines, indicating that the fruit was left on the vine longer to become sweeter and riper.

Legs
The drips that form when wine is swirled in a glass – a visible indicator of wine's weight.

Length
See **Finish**.

Light
Term for wines with a sheer, delicate texture, associated with wines of below 13% alcohol.

Maderization
Flavour changes in wine caused by exposure to heat; named after the wines of Madeira.

Maturation
Winemaking stage where wine rests in barrels, tanks, or bottles after fermentation.

Mature
Term for wine at its peak and requiring no further aging.

Mid-weight
Descriptive term for wines with moderate texture, neither light nor heavy, associated with wines of 13–14% alcohol.

Mild
Descriptive term for wine that is low in aromatic or flavour intensity.

Mousse
Descriptive term for the carbonation of wine.

Mouth-drying
See **Tannin**.

Mouthfeel
Tactile sensations of food and drink perceived in the mouth.

Naked
See **Unoaked**.

Neutral barrel
An oak barrel that has been used to store wine for at least 3 years, reducing its ability to impart new oak flavours.

New oak
Oak barrels or products that have not previously come into contact with wine; the flavours and scents that these impart.

New World
Collective term for the wine regions of the Americas and southern hemisphere.

Oak, oaked, oaky
In common usage, a type of tree or its wood; in wine tasting, a descriptive term for wine smells that derive from its contact with new oak barrels or oak flavouring agents during winemaking. Wines exhibiting such smells are said to be oaked.

Off-dry
Lightly sweet; not fully dry.

Old World
Wine term for traditional wine regions of Europe.

Olfactory
Of or relating to the sense of smell.

Organic
Type of natural farming and agricultural certification of its products that prohibits the use of synthetic chemical treatments.

Oxidation, oxidized
The primary source of wine spoilage resulting from prolonged exposure to air, typically avoided during winemaking; a descriptive term for its effects in wine, such as reduced freshness, browned colour, and nutty, cooked-fruit smells.

Pairing
Choosing a wine for its suitability as a flattering partner for a particular food item or dish.

Palate
Technically, the soft flesh of the mouth; also used informally to refer to a person's sensitivity to tastes and smells or their wine preferences.

Phenolic compounds
Colour and flavour compounds found in grape skins, such as tannin and anthocyanin; many are antioxidants with natural preservative properties.

Point scores
Numerical rankings of wines bestowed by magazines and critics; typically assessments of abstract quality on a 100-point scale.

Potential alcohol
Sugar content of grapes prior to fermentation, defining the upper limit of possible alcohol content in wines made from them.

Premier cru
A French wine quality classification. See **Cru**.

Preservative
A substance that slows spoilage and oxidation; may be naturally present in wine, as with tannin, or an additive, such as sulphur dioxide.

Proprietary name
A wine name that is particular to a specific vintner, as with a *cuvée* name or brand name.

Racy
Descriptive term for wine that has high levels of acidity.

Refreshing
Term used for wines with acidity that provides a bracing, restorative sensation.

Reserve, *reserva, riserva*
Wine-label terms that suggest superior quality; regulated in Spain, Italy, and South America, but with no legal standards elsewhere.

Rich
Descriptive term for wines that feel more thick or viscous in the mouth than average; see also **Heavy**.

Ripeness
The final stage of fruit development in the last weeks before harvest, where exposure to sunlight and warmth causes grapes to become sweet, juicy, and ready to pick.

Rosé
Category of wines that are pink in colour, made by giving clear grape juice brief contact with dark grape skins during winemaking.

Saccharomyces
The genus of "sugar-eating" yeasts that produce beverage alcohol; the yeast category used for making wine, beer, and bread.

Salt, saltiness
A common food component that reduces the perceived acidity of wine when served alongside; one of the six true taste sensations detected by the tongue's taste buds.

Sediment
A solid precipitate that settles from a liquid.

Sensory
Of or relating to perceptions of sight, smell, taste, touch, and hearing.

Sharp
Descriptive term for wines that have a high "tart" level of acidity.

Single-vineyard
Wine made from grapes grown on one plot of land.

Soft
Descriptive term for wines that are low in astringent tannin; also sometimes applied to low-acid wines.

Sommelier
Wine steward or wine-specific server in a restaurant; typically also the person in charge of wine purchasing.

Sour
See **Acidic**.

Sparkling
Descriptive term for carbonated wine with bubbles.

Spätlese
Regulated German label term indicating a quality wine made from late-harvest grapes of higher-than-average ripeness; the second lowest of the *Prädikat* levels, *Spätlese* wines are often lightly sweet and modest in alcohol, but some are heavier and drier.

Spritzy
Descriptive term for faintly carbonated wine.

Stainless steel
Material used in most modern fermentation vessels; in white wines, a descriptive term for an unoaked style.

Still
Term used for wine that has no carbonation or bubbles.

Strength
Descriptive term for wine's alcohol content. See **Weight**.

Subtle
Descriptive term for wines with lower-than-average intensity of olfactory scents and flavours.

Sweet, sweetness
Noticeable presence of sugar; one of the six true taste sensations detected by the tongue's taste buds.

Table grapes
Grapes grown for use as fresh produce, often seedless, juicy, and thin-skinned.

Tactile
Of or relating to the sense of touch.

Tannin
Phenolic compound with astringent properties found in grape skins; it acts as a natural preservative. The

term "tannic" describes the dry feeling in the mouth after tasting red wines.

Taste, tasting
In common usage, all sensations derived from eating or drinking or the activity of sampling food or drink; for purposes of wine analysis, only the six sensations detectable with the tongue's taste buds.

Taste buds
The mechanism for perceiving taste sensations: clusters of nerves scattered across the tongue.

Tears
Better known as legs, these are the drips that form when wine is swirled in a glass.

Temperate
Climate category suitable for grape growing – neither too cold in winter nor too hot and tropical.

Terpene
Type of aromatic compound responsible for intense floral scents in grapes like Moscato, Gewurztraminer, and Riesling.

Terroir
Wine term for location-specific sensory characteristics in wine, often distinctive earthy aromas associated with a particular region or vineyard; may also refer to the unique aspects of a region or vineyard's geography that create these traits.

Texture
Descriptive term for wine's body or viscosity, typically driven by alcohol content. See **Weight**.

Toasted, toasty
Descriptive terms for wine with oak smells; nutty, caramelized scents and flavours derived from the flame "toasting" of wood during barrel-making.

Umami
One of the six sensations detected by the tongue's taste buds – an overall "yummy" taste caused by glutamates and amino acids.

Unoaked, unwooded, naked
Descriptive terms for wines that do not come into contact with oak or barrels during winemaking, or that feature no detectable presence of new oak in flavour and scent.

Unwooded
See **Unoaked**.

Vanillin
Principal flavour compound of vanilla beans, also strongly present in oak and a contributor of "oaky" flavours in wine.

Vin Doux Naturel
Type of French dessert wine made by *mutage*, or "Port method" fortification.

Vintage
The year in which a wine's grapes were harvested, often included on wine labels.

Vintner
Producer of wine.

Viscosity
Texture or thickness in a liquid; see **Weight**.

Vitis vinifera
Primary species of grapevine used for winemaking, of Eurasian origin.

Volatile
Evaporates readily at normal temperatures – a characteristic of many wine components, particularly alcohol and flavour compounds such as esters.

Weight
Descriptive term for wine's texture, perceived as thickness or viscosity in the mouth. Wines with more alcohol or lots of sugar feel heavier than those that are lower in alcohol and/or drier.

Winemaking
The process of transforming fresh grapes into wine through fermentation.

Workhorse grape
A grape variety capable of making pleasant wines even at very high yields; often used for bulk wines and bargain wines.

Yeast
Agent of fermentation essential for winemaking: single-celled microscopic organisms that convert sugar into alcohol.

Yield
Measure of vineyard productivity, typically in tons of grapes per acre or hectolitres of juice per hectare.

Young
Descriptive term for wine that is not barrel-aged before release or bottle-aged thereafter; typically applied to wines that are less than two years old.

Index

LONDON, NEW YORK,
MELBOURNE, MUNICH, DELHI

Managing Editor Dawn Henderson
Managing Art Editor Christine Keilty
Senior Jackets Creative Nicola Powling
Production Editor Raymond Williams
Production Controller Oliver Jeffreys
Creative Technical Support Sonia Charbonnier
Publisher Peggy Vance
Design Director Peter Luff

Produced for Dorling Kindersley by
Sands Publishing Solutions
Project Editor David Tombesi-Walton
Project Art Editor Simon Murrell

First published in Great Britain 2014 by
Dorling Kindersley Limited
80 Strand
London WC2R 0RL

2 4 6 8 10 9 7 5 3 1

001–186250–January 2014

A CIP catalogue record for this book is available from the
British Library.

ISBN: 978 1 4093 3868 0

Colour reproduction by Alta Image
Printed and bound in China by South China

Discover more at
www.dk.com

About the author

Sommelier **Marnie Old** is a breath of fresh air in the wine
world, known for her engaging and intuitive explanations of
complex wine topics. She writes a humorous wine column
for the *Philadelphia Daily News* and is a featured speaker at the
annual Food & Wine Classic in Aspen. Formerly the director
of wine studies for Manhattan's esteemed French Culinary
Institute, Marnie also served as the founding education
chairperson for the American Sommelier Association. Her
first book, also published by DK was the popular *He Said Beer,
She Said Wine*, an entertaining debate on food pairing co-
authored with beer legend Sam Calagione, founder of Dogfish
Head Craft Brewery. Marnie has also written the popular *Wine
Secrets* and the award-winning *Wine Simplified*, an interactive
crash-course ebook.

Author's acknowledgments

A number of people helped bring this book to life.
I would like to extend my thanks and deepest appreciation to:
Michael Mondavi, for his enduring support;
Jamie Goode, for the vote of confidence;
Tim Kilcullen, for his frank feedback;
Karyn Gallagher, for her words of encouragement;
Peggy Vance, for her intuitive grasp of the need for this book;
Simon Murrell, for his brilliant visualizations;
David Tombesi-Walton, for his patient attention to detail;
David Ramey, for his last-minute fact-checking;
Eric Miller, for his useful winemaking insights;
Josh Rosenblat and Kaleigh Smith, for volunteering as guinea pigs;
Kevin Zraly, for setting my feet on this path.

**I would also like to thank the wine companies that have
generously provided assistance and permission to reproduce
images of their products:**
Pierre Gimonnet & Fils, Terry Theise, and Michael Skurnik Wines;
Yellow Tail, Casella Wines, and Deutsch Family Wine & Spirits;
Bodegas Muga, Jorge Ordóñez, and Fine Estates from Spain;
SeaGlass Wines and Trinchero Family Estates;
Pacific Rim Wines;
Ramey Wine Cellars;
Concha y Toro USA and Banfi Vintners;
Beaulieu Vineyard and Diageo Chateau & Estate Wines;
Château La Lagune;
Maison Louis Jadot, Tenuta di Nozzole, and Kobrand Corporation;
Dr Loosen and Loosen Bros USA.

Publisher's acknowledgments

Dorling Kindersley would like to thank the following people for
their assistance with this project:
Mandy Earey, Kathryn Wilding, and Kate Fenton for design;
Elizabeth Clinton for editorial.

Packager's acknowledgments

Sands Publishing Solutions would like to thank the following
people for their input on this project:
Natalie Godwin for design assistance; Hilary Bird for the index.